Designs and Applied Principles of Artificial Neural Networks

Designs and Applied Principles of Artificial Neural Networks

Edited by **Jeremy Rogerson**

New Jersey

Published by Clanrye International,
55 Van Reypen Street,
Jersey City, NJ 07306, USA
www.clanryeinternational.com

Designs and Applied Principles of Artificial Neural Networks
Edited by Jeremy Rogerson

International Standard Book Number: 978-1-63240-138-0 (Hardback)

Contents

Preface

The main aim of this book is to educate learners and enhance their research focus by presenting diverse topics covering this vast field. This is an advanced book which compiles significant studies by distinguished experts in the area of analysis. This book addresses successive solutions to the challenges arising in the area of application, along with it; the book provides scope for future developments.

This book presents a broad overview on the current various design modules and applications of artificial neural systems. Artificial neural networks are often dubbed as one of the most acknowledged technologies in the past twenty years. It has been broadly applied in a wide diversity of applications. The aim of this book is to present current developments of architectures, methodologies, and usage of artificial neural networks. The topics in this book majorly deal with two important aspects: the architecture aspect involving dealing with architectures, design, optimization, and the analysis of artificial neural networks; and application aspect dealing with applications of artificial neural networks in a broad spectrum of areas comprising of biomedical, industrial, physics, and financial applications. This book will be an important source of reference for graduate students, and engineers in various organizations.

It was a great honour to edit this book, though there were challenges, as it involved a lot of communication and networking between me and the editorial team. However, the end result was this all-inclusive book covering diverse themes in the field.

Finally, it is important to acknowledge the efforts of the contributors for their excellent chapters, through which a wide variety of issues have been addressed. I would also like to thank my colleagues for their valuable feedback during the making of this book.

Editor

Architecture and Design

Biologically Plausible Artificial Neural Networks

João Luís Garcia Rosa

Additional information is available at the end of the chapter

1. Introduction

Artificial Neural Networks (ANNs) are based on an abstract and simplified view of the neuron. Artificial neurons are connected and arranged in layers to form large networks, where learning and connections determine the network function. Connections can be formed through learning and do not need to be 'programmed.' Recent ANN models lack many physiological properties of the neuron, because they are more oriented to computational performance than to biological credibility [41].

According to the fifth edition of Gordon Shepherd book, *The Synaptic Organization of the Brain*, "information processing depends not only on anatomical substrates of synaptic circuits, but also on the electrophysiological properties of neurons" [51]. In the literature of dynamical systems, it is widely believed that knowing the electrical currents of nerve cells is sufficient to determine what the cell is doing and why. Indeed, this somewhat contradicts the observation that cells that have similar currents may exhibit different behaviors. But in the neuroscience community, this fact was ignored until recently when the difference in behavior was showed to be due to different mechanisms of excitability bifurcation [35]. A bifurcation of a dynamical system is a qualitative change in its dynamics produced by varying parameters [19].

The type of bifurcation determines the most fundamental computational properties of neurons, such as the class of excitability, the existence or nonexistence of the activation threshold, all-or-none action potentials (spikes), sub-threshold oscillations, bi-stability of rest and spiking states, whether the neuron is an integrator or resonator etc. [25].

A biologically inspired connectionist approach should present a neurophysiologically motivated training algorithm, a bi-directional connectionist architecture, and several other features, e. g., distributed representations.

1.1. McCulloch-Pitts neuron

McCulloch-Pitts neuron (1943) was the first mathematical model [32]. Its properties:

- neuron activity is an "all-or-none" process;
- a certain fixed number of synapses are excited within a latent addition period in order to excite a neuron: independent of previous activity and of neuron position;
- synaptic delay is the only significant delay in nervous system;
- activity of any inhibitory synapse prevents neuron from firing;
- network structure does not change along time.

The McCulloch-Pitts neuron represents a simplified mathematical model for the neuron, where x_i is the i-th binary input and w_i is the synaptic (connection) weight associated with the input x_i. The computation occurs in soma (cell body). For a neuron with p inputs:

$$a = \sum_{i=1}^{p} x_i w_i \tag{1}$$

with $x_0 = 1$ and $w_0 = \beta = -\theta$. β is the bias and θ is the activation threshold. See figures 1 and 2. The are p binary inputs in the schema of figure 2. X_i is the i-th input, W_i is the connection (synaptic) weight associated with input i. The synaptic weights are real numbers, because the synapses can inhibit (negative signal) or excite (positive signal) and have different intensities. The weighted inputs ($X_i \times W_i$) are summed in the cell body, providing a signal a. After that, the signal a is input to an activation function (f), giving the neuron output.

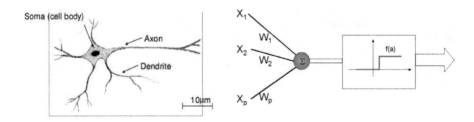

Figure 1. The typical neuron.   **Figure 2.** The neuron model.

The activation function can be: (1) hard limiter, (2) threshold logic, and (3) sigmoid, which is considered the biologically more plausible activation function.

1.2. The perceptron

Rosenblatt's perceptron [47] takes a weighted sum of neuron inputs, and sends output 1 (spike) if this sum is greater than the activation threshold. It is a linear discriminator: given 2 points, a straight line is able to discriminate them. For some configurations of m points, a straight line is able to separate them in two classes (figures 3 and 4).

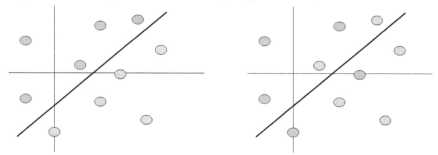

Figure 3. Set of linearly separable points.   **Figure 4.** Set of non-linearly separable points.

The limitations of the perceptron is that it is an one-layer feed-forward network (non-recurrent); it is only capable of learning solution of linearly separable problems; and its learning algorithm (delta rule) does not work with networks of more than one layer.

1.3. Neural network topology

In cerebral cortex, neurons are disposed in columns, and most synapses occur between different columns. See the famous drawing by Ramón y Cajal (figure 5). In the extremely simplified mathematical model, neurons are disposed in layers (representing columns), and there is communication between neurons in different layers (see figure 6).

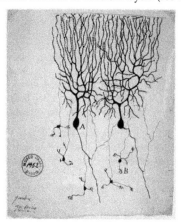

Figure 5. Drawing by Santiago Ramón y Cajal of neurons in the pigeon cerebellum. (A) denotes Purkinje cells, an example of a multipolar neuron, while (B) denotes granule cells, which are also multipolar [57].

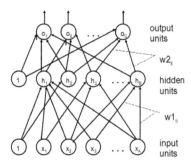

Figure 6. A 3-layer neural network. Notice that there are $A + 1$ input units, $B + 1$ hidden units, and C output units. w_1 and w_2 are the synaptic weight matrices between input and hidden layers and between hidden and output layers, respectively. The "extra" neurons in input and hidden layers, labeled 1, represent the presence of bias: the ability of the network to fire even in the absence of input signal.

1.4. Classical ANN models

Classical artificial neural networks models are based upon a simple description of the neuron, taking into account the presence of presynaptic cells and their synaptic potentials, the activation threshold, and the propagation of an action potential. So, they represent impoverished explanation of human brain characteristics.

As advantages, we may say that ANNs are naturally parallel solution, robust, fault tolerant, they allow integration of information from different sources or kinds, are adaptive systems, that is, capable of learning, they show a certain autonomy degree in learning, and display a very fast recognizing performance.

And there are many limitations of ANNs. Among them, it is still very hard to explain its behavior, because of lacking of transparency, their solutions do not scale well, and they are computationally expensive for big problems, and yet very far from biological reality.

ANNs do not focus on real neuron details. The conductivity delays are neglected. The output signal is either discrete (e.g., 0 or 1) or a real number (e.g., between 0 and 1). The network input is calculated as the weighted sum of input signals, and it is transformed in an output signal via a simple function (e.g., a threshold function). See the main differences between the biological neural system and the conventional computer on table 1.

Andy Clark proposes three types of connectionism [2]: (1) the *first-generation* consisting of perceptron and cybernetics of the 1950s. They are simple neural structures of limited applications [30]; (2) the *second generation* deals with complex dynamics with recurrent networks in order to deal with spatio-temporal events; (3) the *third generation* takes into account more complex dynamic and time properties. For the first time, these systems use biological inspired modular architectures and algorithms. We may add a fourth type: a network which considers populations of neurons instead of individual ones and the existence of chaotic oscillations, perceived by electroencephalogram (EEG) analysis. The K-models are examples of this category [30].

	Von Neumann computer	Biological neural system
Processor	Complex One or few Low speed	High speed Simple A large number
Memory	Separated from processor Non-content addressable Distributed	Localized Integrated with processor Content addressable
Computing	Centralized Stored programs Parallel	Sequential Distributed Self-learning
Reliability	Very vulnerable	Robust
Expertise	Numeric and symbolic manipulations	Perceptual problems
Operational environment	Well-defined, well-constrained	Poorly defined, unconstrained

Table 1. Von Neumann's computer versus biological neural system [26].

1.5. Learning

The Canadian psychologist Donald Hebb established the bases for current connectionist learning algorithms: "When an axon of cell A is near enough to excite a cell B and repeatedly or persistently takes part in firing it, some growth process or metabolic change takes place in one or both cells such that A's efficiency, as one of the cells firing B, is increased" [21]. Also, the word "connectionism" appeared for the first time: "The theory is evidently a form of connectionism, one of the switchboard variety, though it does not deal in direct connections between afferent and efferent pathways: not an 'S-R' psychology, if R means a muscular response. The connections server rather to establish autonomous central activities, which then are the basis of further learning" [21].

According to Hebb, knowledge is revealed by associations, that is, the plasticity in Central Nervous System (CNS) allows synapses to be created and destroyed. Synaptic weights change values, therefore allow learning, which can be through internal self-organizing: encoding of new knowledge and reinforcement of existent knowledge. How to supply a neural substrate to association learning among world facts? Hebb proposed a hypothesis: connections between two nodes highly activated at the same time are reinforced. This kind of rule is a formalization of the associationist psychology, in which associations are accumulated among things that happen together. This hypothesis permits to model the CNS plasticity, adapting it to environmental changes, through excitatory and inhibitory strength of existing synapses, and its topology. This way, it allows that a connectionist network learns correlation among facts.

Connectionist networks learn through synaptic weight change, in most cases: it reveals statistical correlations from the environment. Learning may happen also through network topology change (in a few models). This is a case of probabilistic reasoning without a statistical model of the problem. Basically, two learning methods are possible with Hebbian learning: unsupervised learning and supervised learning. In unsupervised learning there is no teacher, so the network tries to find out regularities in the input patterns. In supervised learning, the input is associated with the output. If they are equal, learning is called auto-associative; if they are different, hetero-associative.

1.6. Back-propagation

Back-propagation (BP) is a supervised algorithm for multilayer networks. It applies the generalized delta rule, requiring two passes of computation: (1) activation propagation (forward pass), and (2) error back propagation (backward pass). Back-propagation works in the following way: it propagates the activation from input to hidden layer, and from hidden to output layer; calculates the error for output units, then back propagates the error to hidden units and then to input units.

BP has a universal approximation power, that is, given a continuous function, there is a two-layer network (one hidden layer) that can be trained by Back-propagation in order to approximate as much as desired this function. Besides, it is the most used algorithm.

Although Back-propagation is a very known and most used connectionist training algorithm, it is computationally expensive (slow), it does not solve satisfactorily big size problems, and sometimes, the solution found is a local minimum - a locally minimum value for the error function.

BP is based on the error back propagation: while stimulus propagates forwardly, the error (difference between the actual and the desired outputs) propagates backwardly. In the cerebral cortex, the stimulus generated when a neuron fires crosses the axon towards its end in order to make a synapse onto another neuron input. Suppose that BP occurs in the brain; in this case, the error must have to propagate back from the dendrite of the postsynaptic neuron to the axon and then to the dendrite of the presynaptic neuron. It sounds unrealistic and improbable. Synaptic "weights" have to be modified in order to make learning possible, but certainly not in the way BP does. Weight change must use only local information in the synapse where it occurs. That's why BP seems to be so biologically implausible.

2. Dynamical systems

Neurons may be treated as *dynamical systems*, as the main result of Hodgkin-Huxley model [23]. A dynamical system consists of a set of variables that describe its state and a law that describes the evolution of state variables with time [25]. The Hodgkin-Huxley model is a dynamical system of four dimensions, because their status is determined solely by the membrane potential V and the variable opening (activation) and closing (deactivation) of ion channels n, m and h for persistent K^+ and transient Na^+ currents [1, 27, 28]. The law of evolution is given by a four-dimensional system of *ordinary differential equations* (ODE). Principles of neurodynamics describe the basis for the development of biologically plausible models of cognition [30].

All variables that describe the neuronal dynamics can be classified into four classes according to their function and time scale [25]:

1. *Membrane potential.*
2. *Excitation variables*, such as activation of a Na^+ current. They are responsible for lifting the action potential.
3. *Recovery variables*, such as the inactivation of a current Na^+ and activation of a rapid current K^+. They are responsible for re-polarization (lowering) of the action potential.

4. *Adaptation variables*, such as the activation of low voltage or current dependent on Ca^{2+}. They build prolonged action potentials and can affect the excitability over time.

2.1. The neurons are different

The currents define the type of neuronal dynamical system [20]. There are millions of different electrophysiological spike generation mechanisms. Axons are filaments (there are 72 km of fiber in the brain) that can reach from 100 microns (typical granule cell), up to 4.5 meters (giraffe primary afferent). And communication via spikes may be stereotypical (common pyramidal cells), or no communication at all (horizontal cells of the retina). The speed of the action potential (spike) ranges from 2 to 400 km/h. The input connections ranges from 500 (retinal ganglion cells) to 200,000 (purkinje cells). In about 100 billion neurons in the human brain, there are hundreds of thousands of different types of neurons and at least one hundred neurotransmitters. Each neuron makes on average 1,000 synapses on other neurons [8].

2.2. Phase portraits

The power of dynamical systems approach to neuroscience is that we can say many things about a system without knowing all the details that govern its evolution.

Consider a quiescent neuron whose membrane potential is at rest. Since there are no changes in their state variables, it is an equilibrium point. All incoming currents to depolarize the neuron are balanced or equilibrated by hyper-polarization output currents: stable equilibrium (figure 7(a) - top). Depending on the starting point, the system may have many trajectories, as those shown at the bottom of the figure 7. One can imagine the time along each trajectory. All of them are attracted to the equilibrium state denoted by the black dot, called *attractor* [25]. It is possible to predict the itinerant behavior of neurons through observation [10].

Regarding Freeman's neurodynamics (see section 2.5) the most useful state variables are derived from electrical potentials generated by a neuron. Their recordings allow the definition of one state variable for axons and another one for dendrites, which are very different. The axon expresses its state in frequency of action potentials (pulse rate), and dendrite expresses in intensity of its synaptic current (wave amplitude) [10].

The description of the dynamics can be obtained from a study of system phase portraits, which shows certain special trajectories (equilibria, separatrices, limit cycles) that determine the behavior of all other topological trajectory through the phase space.

The excitability is illustrated in figure 7(b). When the neuron is at rest (phase portrait = stable equilibrium), small perturbations, such as A, result in small excursions from equilibrium, denoted by PSP (post-synaptic potential). Major disturbances, such as B, are amplified by the intrinsic dynamics of neuron and result in the response of the action potential.

If a current strong enough is injected into the neuron, it will be brought to a pacemaker mode, which displays periodic spiking activity (figure 7(c)): this state is called the cycle stable limit, or stable periodic orbit. The details of the electrophysiological neuron only determine the position, shape and period of limit cycle.

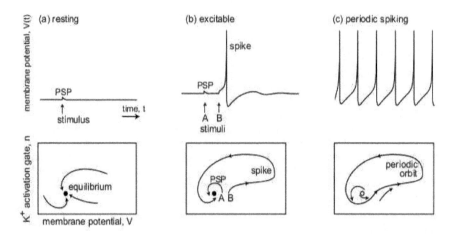

Figure 7. The neuron states: rest (a), excitable (b), and activity of periodic spiking (c). At the bottom, we see the trajectories of the system, depending on the starting point. Figure taken from [25], available at http://www.izhikevich.org/publications/dsn. pdf.

2.3. Bifurcations

Apparently, there is an injected current that corresponds to the transition from rest to continuous spiking, i.e. from the portrait phase of figure 7(b) to 7(c). From the point of view of dynamical systems, the transition corresponds to a *bifurcation* of the dynamical neuron, or a qualitative representation of the phase of the system.

In general, neurons are excitable because they are close to bifurcations from rest to spiking activity. The type of bifurcation depends on the electrophysiology of the neuron and determines its excitable properties. Interestingly, although there are millions of different electrophysiological mechanisms of excitability and spiking, there are only four different types of bifurcation of equilibrium that a system can provide. One can understand the properties of excitable neurons, whose currents were not measured and whose models are not known, since one can identify experimentally in which of the four bifurcations undergoes the rest state of the neuron [25].

The four bifurcations are shown in figure 8: saddle-node bifurcation, saddle-node on invariant circle, sub-critical Andronov-Hopf and supercritical Andronov-Hopf. In *saddle-node bifurcation*, when the magnitude of the injected current or other parameter of the bifurcation changes, a stable equilibrium correspondent to the rest state (black circle) is approximated by an unstable equilibrium (white circle). In *saddle-node bifurcation on invariant circle*, there is an invariant circle at the time of bifurcation, which becomes a limit cycle attractor. In *sub-critical Andronov-Hopf bifurcation*, a small unstable limit cycle shrinks to a equilibrium state and loses stability. Thus the trajectory deviates from equilibrium and approaches a limit cycle of high amplitude spiking or some other attractor. In the *supercritical Andronov-Hopf bifurcation*, the equilibrium state loses stability and gives rise to a small amplitude limit cycle attractor.

When the magnitude of the injected current increases, the limit cycle amplitude increases and becomes a complete spiking limit cycle [25].

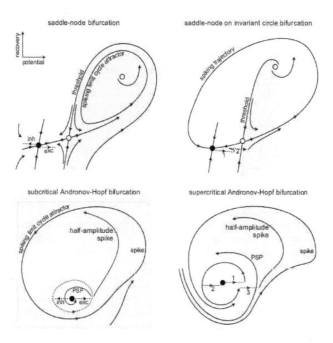

Figure 8. Geometry of phase portraits of excitable systems near the four bifurcations can exemplify many neurocomputational properties. Figure taken from [25], available at http://www.izhikevich.org/publications/dsn.pdf.

Systems with Andronov-Hopf bifurcations, either sub-critical or supercritical, exhibit low amplitude membrane potential oscillations, while systems with saddle bifurcations, both without and with invariant circle, do not. The existence of small amplitude oscillations creates the possibility of resonance to the frequency of the incoming pulses [25].

2.4. Integrators and resonators

Resonators are neurons with reduced amplitude sub-threshold oscillations, and those which do not have this property are *integrators*. Neurons that exhibit co-existence of rest and spiking states, are called *bistable* and those which do not exhibit this feature are *monostable*. See table 2.

2.4.1. Neurocomputational properties

Inhibition prevents spiking in integrators, but promotes it in resonators. The excitatory inputs push the state of the system towards the shaded region of figure 8, while the inhibitory inputs push it out. In resonators, both excitation and inhibition push the state toward the shaded region [25].

sub-threshold oscillations		co-existence of rest and spiking states	
		yes (bistable)	*no* (monostable)
no	(integrator)	saddle-node	saddle-node on invariant circle
yes	(resonator)	sub-critical Andronov-Hopf	supercritical Andronov-Hopf

Table 2. Neuron classification in integrators-resonators/monostable-bistable, according to the rest state bifurcation. Adapted from [25].

2.5. Freeman neurodynamics

Nowadays, two very different concepts co-exist in neuroscience, regarding the way how the brain operates as a whole [55]: (1) classical model, where the brain is described as consisting of a series of causal chains composed of nerve nets that operate in parallel (the conventional artificial neural networks [20]); (2) neurodynamical model, where the brain operates by non-linear dynamical chaos, which looks like noise but presents a kind of hidden order [10].

According to Freeman [10], in order to understand brain functioning, a foundation must be laid including brain imaging and non-linear brain dynamics, fields that digital computers make possible. Brain imaging is performed during normal behavior activity, and non-linear dynamics models these data.

In a dynamicist view, actions and choices made are responsible for creation of meanings in brains, and they are different from representations. Representations exist only in the world and have no meanings. The relation of neurons to meaning is not still well understood. In Freeman's opinion, although representations can be transferred between machines, meaning cannot be transferred between brains [10]. Brain activity is directed toward external objects, leading to creation of meaning through learning. Neuron populations are the key to understand the biology of intentionality.

Freeman argues that there are two basic units in brain organization: the *neuron* and the *neuron population*. Although neuron has been the base for neurobiology, masses of interacting neurons forming neuron populations are considered for a macroscopic view of the brain. Like neurons, neuron populations also have states and activity patterns, but they do (different) macroscopic things. Between the microscopic neuron and these macroscopic things, there are *mesoscopic* populations [10].

Neurobiologists usually claim that brains process information in a cause-and-effect manner: stimuli carry information that is conveyed in transformed information. What if stimuli are selected before appearance? This view fails in this case. This traditional view allowed the development of information processing machines. This simplified, or even mistaken, view of neuronal workings, led to the development of digital computers. Artificial Intelligence artifacts pose a challenge: how to attach meaning to the symbolic representations in machines?

Pragmatists conceive minds as dynamical systems, resulted from actions into the world. How are these actions generated? According to a cognitivist view, an action is determined by the form of a stimulus. Intentional action is composed by space-time processes, called short-term memory or cognitive maps, for materialists and cognitivists. In the pragmatism view there is no temporary storage of images and no representational map.

The neurons in the brain form dense networks. The balance of excitation and inhibition allow them to have intrinsic oscillatory activity and overall amplitude modulation (AM) [10, 55].

These AM patterns are expressions of non-linear chaos, not merely a summation of linear dendritic and action potentials. AM patterns create attractor basins and landscapes. In the neurodynamical model every neuron participates, to some extent, in every experience and every behavior, via non-linear chaotic mechanisms [10].

The concepts of non-linear chaotic neurodynamics are of fundamental importance to nervous system research. They are relevant to our understanding of the workings of the normal brain [55].

2.5.1. Neuron populations

Typical neuron have many dendrites (input) and one axon (output). The axon transmits information using *microscopic* pulse trains. Dendrites integrate information using continuous waves of ionic current. Neurons are connected by synapses. Each synapse drives electric current. The microscopic current from each neuron sums with currents from other neurons, which causes a *macroscopic* potential difference, measured with a pair of extracellular electrodes (E) as the electroencephalogram (EEG) [10, 18]. EEG records the activity patterns of *mesoscopic* neuron populations. The sum of currents that a neuron generates in response to electrical stimulus produces the post-synaptic potential. The strength of the post-synaptic potential decreases with distance between the synapse and the cell body. The attenuation is compensated by greater surface area and more synapses on the distal dendrites. Dendrites make waves and axons make pulses. Synapses convert pulses to waves. Trigger zones convert waves to pulses. See figure 9. Researchers who base their studies on single neurons think that population events such as EEG are irrelevant noise, because they do not have understanding of a mesoscopic state [10].

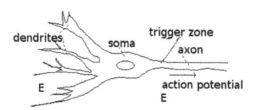

Figure 9. Typical neuron showing the dendrites (input), the soma (cell body), the axon (output), the trigger zone, and the direction of the action potential. Notice that letters "E" represent the pair of extracellular electrodes. Adapted from [45] and [10].

In single neurons, microscopic pulse frequencies and wave amplitudes are measured, while in populations, macroscopic pulse and wave densities are measured. The neuron is microscopic and ensemble is mesoscopic. The flow of the current inside the neuron is revealed by a change in the membrane potential, measured with an electrode inside the cell body, evaluating the dendritic wave state variable of the single neuron. Recall that extracellular electrodes are placed outside the neuron (see the Es in figure 9), so cortical potential provided by sum of dendritic currents in the neighborhood is measured. The same currents produce the membrane (intracellular) and cortical (extracellular) potentials, given two views of neural activity: the former, microscopic and the latter, mesoscopic [10].

Cortical neurons, because of their synaptic interactions, form neuron populations. Microscopic pulse and wave state variables are used to describe the activity of the single neurons that contribute to the population, and mesoscopic state variables (also pulse and wave) are used to describe the collective activities neurons give rise. Mass activity in the brain is described by a pulse density, instead of pulse frequency. This is done by recording from outside the cell the firing of pulses of many neurons simultaneously. The same current that controls the firings of neurons is measured by EEG, which does not allow to distinguish individual contributions. Fortunately, this is not necessary.

A population is a collection of neurons in a neighborhood, corresponding to a cortical column, which represents dynamical patterns of activity. The average pulse density in a population can never approach the peak pulse frequencies of single neurons. The activity of neighborhoods in the center of the dendritic sigmoid curve is very near linear. This simplifies the description of populations. Neuron populations are similar to mesoscopic ensembles in many complex systems [10]. The behavior of the microscopic elements is constrained by the embedding ensemble, and it cannot be understood outside a mesoscopic and macroscopic view.

The collective action of neurons forms activity patterns that go beyond the cellular level and approach the organism level. The formation of mesoscopic states is the first step for that. This way, the activity level is decided by the population, not by individuals [10]. The population is semi-autonomous. It has a point attractor, returning to the same level after its releasing. The state space of the neuron population is defined by the range of amplitudes that its pulse and wave densities can take.

2.5.2. Freeman K-sets

Regarding neuroscience at the mesoscopic level [10, 11], theoretical connection between the neuron activity at the microscopic level in small neural networks and the activity of cell assemblies in the mesoscopic scale is not well understood [16]. Katzir-Katchalsky suggests treating cell assemblies using thermodynamics forming a hierarchy of models of the dynamics of neuron populations [29] (*Freeman K-sets*): KO, KI, KII, KIII, KIV and KV. Katzir-Katchalsky is the reason for the K in Freeman K-sets.

The KO set represents a noninteracting collection of neurons. KI sets represent a collection of KO sets, which can be excitatory (KI_e) or inhibitory (KI_i). A KII set represents a collection of KI_e and KI_i. The KIII model consists of many interconnected KII sets, describing a given sensory system in brains. A KIV set is formed by the interaction of three KIII sets [30]. KV sets are proposed to model the scale-free dynamics of neocortex operating on KIV sets [16]. See the representation of KI and KII sets by networks of KO sets in figure 10 [9].

The K-sets mediate between the microscopic activity of small neural networks and the macroscopic activity of the brain. The topology includes excitatory and inhibitory populations of neurons and the dynamics is represented by ordinary differential equations (ODE) [16].

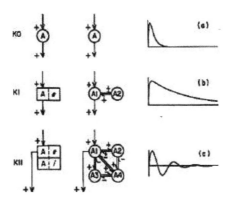

Figure 10. Representation of (b) KI and (c) KII sets by networks of (a) KO sets. Available at [9].

The advantages of KIII pattern classifiers on artificial neural networks are the small number of training examples needed, convergence to an attractor in a single step and geometric increase (rather than linear) in the number of classes with the number of nodes. The disadvantage is the increasing of the computational time needed to solve ordinary differential equations numerically.

The Katchalsky K-models use a set of ordinary differential equations with distributed parameters to describe the hierarchy of neuron populations beginning from micro-columns to hemispheres [31]. In relation to the standard KV, K-sets provide a platform for conducting analyzes of unified actions of the neocortex in the creation and control of intentional and cognitive behaviors [13].

2.5.3. Freeman's mass action

Freeman's mass action (FMA) [9] refers to collective synaptic actions neurons in the cortex exert on other neurons, synchronizing their firing of action potentials [17]. FMA expresses and conveys the meaning of sensory information in spatial patterns of cortical activity that resembles the frames in a movie [12, 13].

The prevailing concepts in neurodynamics are based on neural networks, which are Newtonian models, since they treated neural microscopic pulses as point processes in trigger zones and synapses. The FMA theory is Maxwellian because it treats the mesoscopic neural activity as a continuous distribution. The neurodynamics of the FMA includes microscopic neural operations that bring sensory information to sensory cortices and load the first percepts of the sensory cortex to other parts of the brain. The Newtonian dynamics can model cortical input and output functions but not the formation of percepts. The FMA needs a *paradigm shift*, because the theory is based on new experiments and techniques and new rules of evidence [17].

2.6. Neuropercolation

Neuropercolation is a family of stochastic models based on the mathematical theory of probabilistic cellular automata on lattices and random graphs, motivated by the structural and dynamical properties of neuron populations. The existence of phase transitions has been demonstrated both in discrete and continuous state space models, i.e., in specific probabilistic cellular automata and percolation models. Neuropercolation extends the concept of phase transitions for large interactive populations of nerve cells [31].

Basic bootstrap percolation [50] has the following properties: (1) it is a deterministic process, based on random initialization, (2) the model always progresses in one direction: from inactive to active states and never otherwise. Under these conditions, these mathematical models exhibit phase transitions with respect to the initialization probability p. Neuropercolation models develop neurobiologically motivated generalizations of bootstrap percolations [31].

2.6.1. Neuropercolation and neurodynamics

Dynamical memory neural networks is an alternative approach to pattern-based computing [18]. Information is stored in the form of spatial patterns of modified connections in very large scale networks. Memories are recovered by phase transitions, which enable cerebral cortices to build spatial patterns of amplitude modulation of a narrow band oscillatory wave. That is, information is encoded by spatial patterns of synaptic weights of connections that couple non-linear processing elements. Each category of sensory input has a Hebbian nerve cell assembly. When accessed by a stimulus, the assembly guides the cortex to the attractors, one for each category.

The oscillating memory devices are biologically motivated because they are based on observations that the processing of sensory information in the central nervous system is accomplished via collective oscillations of populations of globally interacting neurons. This approach provides a new proposal to neural networks.

From the theoretical point of view, the proposed model helps to understand the role of phase transitions in biological and artificial systems. A family of random cellular automata exhibiting dynamical behavior necessary to simulate feeling, perception and intention is introduced [18].

2.7. Complex networks and neocortical dynamics

Complex networks are at the intersection between graph theory and statistical mechanics [4]. They are usually located in an abstract space where the position of the vertexes has no specific meaning. However, there are several network vertexes where the position is important and influences the evolution of the network. This is the case of road networks or the Internet, where the position of cities and routers can be located on a map and the edges between them represent real physical entities, such as roads and optical fibers. This type of network is called a "geographic network" or spatial network. Neural networks are spatial networks [56].

From a computational perspective, two major problems that the brain has to solve is the extraction of information (statistical regularities) of the inputs and the generation of coherent states that allow coordinated perception and action in real time [56].

In terms of the theory of complex networks [4], the anatomical connections of the cortex show that the power law distribution of the connection distances between neurons is exactly optimal to support rapid phase transitions of neural populations, regardless of how great they are [31]. It is said that connectivity and dynamics are *scale-free* [13, 14], which states that the dynamics of the cortex is size independent, such that the brains of mice, men, elephants and whales work the same way [17].

Scale-free dynamics of the neocortex are characterized by self-similarity of patterns of synaptic connectivity and spatio-temporal neural activity, seen in power law distributions of structural and functional parameters and in rapid state transitions between levels of the hierarchy [15].

2.8. Brain-Computer Interfaces

A non-intrusive technique to allow direct *brain-computer interface* (BCI) can be a scalp EEG - an array of electrodes put on the head like a hat, which allows monitoring the cognitive behavior of animals and humans, by using brain waves to interact with the computer. It is a kind of a keyboard-less computer that eliminates the need for hand or voice interaction.

The Neurodynamics of Brain & Behavior group in the Computational Neurodynamics (CND) Lab at the University of Memphis's FedEx Institute of Technology is dedicated to research cognitive behavior of animals and humans including the use of molecular genetic or behavioral genetic approaches, to studies that involve the use of brain imaging techniques, to apply dynamical mathematical and computational models, to neuroethological studies. The research has three prongs of use for BCI: video/computer gaming; to support people with disabilities or physical constraints, such as the elderly; and to improve control of complex machinery, such as an aircraft and other military and civilian uses [24]. The direct brain-computer interface would give those with physical constraints or those operating complex machinery "extra arms" [3].

Similar to how they found seizure prediction markers, the plan is to use the data to analyze pre-motor movements, the changes in the brain that occur before there's actually movement, and apply that to someone who has a prosthetic device to allow them to better manipulate it. Since the brain is usually multitasking, the researchers will have to pick up the signal for the desired task from all the other things going on in the brain.

3. A biologically plausible connectionist system

Instead of the computationally successful, but considered to be biologically implausible supervised Back-propagation [5, 48], the learning algorithm BioRec employed in BioθPred [44, 46] is inspired by the Recirculation [22] and GeneRec [33] (GR) algorithms, and consists of two phases.

In the *expectation* phase[1] (figure 11), when input x, representing the first word of a sentence through semantic microfeatures, is presented to input layer α, there is propagation of these stimuli to the hidden layer β (*bottom-up propagation*) (step 1 in figure 11). There is also a propagation of the previous actual output o^p, which is initially empty, from output layer γ back to the hidden layer β (*top-down propagation*) (steps 2 and 3).[2] Then, a hidden expectation activation (h^e) is generated (Eq. (2)) for each and every one of the B hidden units, based on

---

[1] [33] employs the terms "minus" and "plus" phases to designate *expectation* and *outcome* phases respectively in his GeneRec algorithm.

[2] The superscript p is used to indicate that this signal refers to the *previous* cycle.

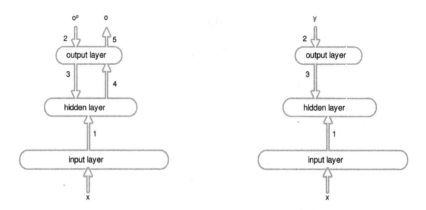

Figure 11. The expectation phase.   **Figure 12.** The outcome phase.

inputs and previous output stimuli o^p (sum of the bottom-up and top-down propagations - through the sigmoid logistic activation function σ). Then, these hidden signals propagate to the output layer γ (step 4), and an actual output o is obtained (step 5) for each and every one of the C output units, through the propagation of the hidden expectation activation to the output layer (Eq. (3)) [37]. w_{ij}^h are the connection (synaptic) weights between input (i) and hidden (j) units, and w_{jk}^o are the connection (synaptic) weights between hidden (j) and output (k) units[3].

$$h_j^e = \sigma\left(\Sigma_{i=0}^A w_{ij}^h . x_i + \Sigma_{k=1}^C w_{jk}^o . o_k^p\right) \qquad 1 \le j \le B \tag{2}$$

$$o_k = \sigma\left(\Sigma_{j=0}^B w_{jk}^o . h_j^e\right) \qquad 1 \le k \le C \tag{3}$$

In the *outcome* phase (figure 12), input x is presented to input layer α again; there is propagation to hidden layer β (bottom-up) (step 1 in figure 12). After this, expected output y (step 2) is presented to the output layer and propagated back to the hidden layer β (top-down) (step 3), and a hidden outcome activation (h^o) is generated, based on inputs and on expected outputs (Eq. (4)). For the other words, presented one at a time, the same procedure (*expectation* phase first, then *outcome* phase) is repeated [37]. Recall that the architecture is bi-directional, so it is possible for the stimuli to propagate either forwardly or backwardly.

---

[3] i, j, and k are the indexes for the input (A), hidden (B), and output (C) units respectively. Input (α) and hidden (β) layers have an extra unit (index 0) used for simulating the presence of a bias [20]. This extra unit is absent from the output (γ) layer. That's the reason i and j range from 0 to the number of units in the layer, and k from 1. x_0, h_0^e, and h_0^o are set to +1. w_{0j}^h is the bias of the hidden neuron j and w_{0k}^o is the bias of the output neuron k.

$$h_j^o = \sigma(\Sigma_{i=0}^{A} w_{ij}^h.x_i + \Sigma_{k=1}^{C} w_{jk}^o.y_k) \qquad 1 \leq j \leq \text{B} \qquad (4)$$

In order to make learning possible the synaptic weights are updated through the delta rule[4] (Eqs. (5) and (6)), considering only the local information made available by the synapse. The learning rate η used in the algorithm is considered an important variable during the experiments [20].

$$\Delta w_{jk}^o = \eta.(y_k - o_k).h_j^e \qquad 0 \leq j \leq \text{B}, \quad 1 \leq k \leq \text{C} \qquad (5)$$

$$\Delta w_{ij}^h = \eta.(h_j^o - h_j^e).x_i \qquad 0 \leq i \leq \text{A}, \quad 1 \leq j \leq \text{B} \qquad (6)$$

Figure 13 displays a simple application to digit learning which compares BP with GeneRec (GR) algorithms.

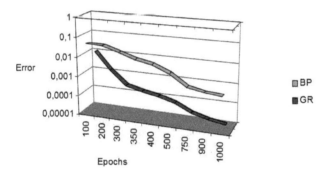

Figure 13. BP-GR comparison for digit learning.

Other applications were proposed using similar alleged biological inspired architecture and algorithm [34, 37–40, 42–44, 49].

---

[4] The learning equations are essentially the delta rule (Widrow-Hoff rule), which is basically error correction: "The adjustment made to a synaptic weight of a neuron is proportional to the product of the error signal and the input signal of the synapse in question." ([20], p. 53).

3.1. Intraneuron signaling

The Spanish Nobel laureate neuroscientist Santiago Ramón y Cajal, established at the end of the nineteenth century, two principles that revolutionized neuroscience: the Principle of connectional specificity, which states that "nerve cells do not communicate indiscriminately with one another or form random networks;" and the Principle of dynamic polarization, which says "electric signals inside a nervous cell flow only in a direction: from neuron reception (often the dendrites and cell body) to the axon trigger zone." Intraneuron signalling is based on the principle of dynamic polarization. The signaling inside the neuron is performed by four basic elements: receptive, trigger, signaling, and secretor. The Receptive element is responsible for input signals, and it is related to the dendritic region. The Trigger element is responsible for neuron activation threshold, related to the soma. The Signaling element is responsible for conducting and keeping the signal and its is related to the axon. And the Secretor element is responsible for signal releasing to another neuron, so it is related to the presynaptic terminals of the biological neuron.

3.2. Interneuron signaling

Electrical and chemical synapses have completely different morphologies. At electrical synapses, transmission occurs through gap junction channels (special ion channels), located in the pre and postsynaptic cell membranes. There is a cytoplasmatic connection between cells. Part of electric current injected in presynaptic cell escapes through resting channels and remaining current is driven to the inside of the postsynaptic cell through gap junction channels. At chemical synapses, there is a synaptic cleft, a small cellular separation between the cells. There are vesicles containing neurotransmitter molecules in the presynaptic terminal and when action potential reaches these synaptic vesicles, neurotransmitters are released to the synaptic cleft.

3.3. A biologically plausible ANN model proposal

We present here a proposal for a biologically plausible model [36] based on the microscopic level. This model in intended to present a mechanism to generate a biologically plausible ANN model and to redesign the classical framework to encompass the traditional features, and labels that model the binding affinities between transmitters and receptors. This model departs from a classical connectionist model and is defined by a restricted data set, which explains the ANN behavior. Also, it introduces T, R, and C variables to account for the binding affinities between neurons (unlike other models).

The following feature set defines the neurons:

$$N = \{\{w\}, \theta, g, T, R, C\} \tag{7}$$

where:

- w represents the connection weights,
- θ is the neuron activation threshold,
- g stands for the activation function,

- T symbolizes the transmitter,
- R the receptor, and
- C the controller.

θ, g, T, R, and C encode the genetic information, while T, R, and C are the labels, absent in other models. This proposal follows Ramón y Cajal's principle of connectional specificity, that states that each neuron is connected to another neuron not only in relation to $\{w\}$, θ, and g, but also in relation to T, R, and C; neuron i is only connected to neuron j if there is binding affinity between the T of i and the R of j. Binding affinity means compatible types, enough amount of substrate, and compatible genes. The combination of T and R results in C: C can act over other neuron connections.

The ordinary biological neuron presents many dendrites usually branched, which receive information from other neurons, an axon, which transmits the processed information, usually by propagation of an action potential. The axon is divided into several branches, and makes synapses onto the dendrites and cell bodies of other neurons (see figure 14). Chemical synapse is predominant is the cerebral cortex, and the release of transmitter substance occurs in active zones, inside presynaptic terminals. Certain chemical synapses lack active zones, resulting in slower and more diffuse synaptic actions between cells. The combination of a neurotransmitter and a receptor makes the postsynaptic cell releases a protein.

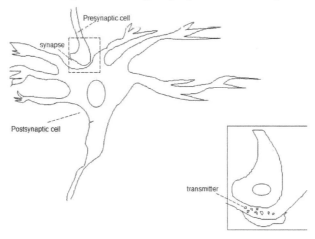

Figure 14. The chemical synapse. Figure taken from [45].

Although type I synapses seem to be excitatory and type II synapses inhibitory (see figure 15), the action of a transmitter in the postsynaptic cell does not depend on the chemical nature of the neurotransmitter, instead it depends on the properties of the receptors with which the transmitter binds. In some cases, it is the receptor that determines whether a synapse is excitatory or inhibitory, and an ion channel will be activated directly by the transmitter or indirectly through a second messenger.

Neurotransmitters are released by presynaptic neuron and they combine with specific receptor in membrane of postsynaptic neuron. The combination of neurotransmitter with

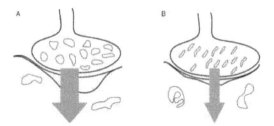

Figure 15. Morphological synapses type A and type B. In excitatory synapse (type A), neurons contribute to produce impulses on other cells: asymmetrical membrane specializations, very large synaptic vesicles (50 nm) with packets of neurotransmitters. In inhibitory synapse (type B), neurons prevent the releasing of impulses on other cells: symmetrical membrane specializations, synaptic vesicles are smaller and often ellipsoidal or flattened, contact zone usually smaller. Figure taken from [45].

receptor leads to intracellular release or production of a second messenger, which interacts (directly or indirectly) with ion channel, causing it to open or close. There are two types of resulting signaling : (1) propagation of action potential, and (2) production of a graded potential by the axon. Graded potential signaling does not occur over long distances because of attenuation.

Graded potentials can occur in another level. See, for instance, figure 16. Axon 1 making synapse in a given cell can receive a synapse from axon 2. Otherwise, the presynaptic synapse can produce only a local potential change, which is then restricted to that axon terminal (figure 17).

Figure 16. An axon-axon synapse [6].   **Figure 17.** A local potential change [6].

In view of these biological facts, it was decided to model through labels T and R, the binding affinities between Ts and Rs. And label C represents the role of the "second messenger,", the effects of graded potential, and the protein released by the coupling of T and R.

Controller C can modify the binding affinities between neurons by modifying the degrees of affinity of receptors, the amount of substrate (amount of transmitters and receptors), and gene expression, in case of mutation. The degrees of affinity are related to the way receptors gate ion channels at chemical synapses. Through ion channels transmitter material enters the postsynaptic cell: (1) in direct gating: receptors produce relatively fast synaptic actions, and (2) in indirect gating: receptors produce slow synaptic actions: these slower actions often serve to modulate behavior because they modify the degrees of affinity of receptors.

In addition, modulation can be related to the action of peptides[5]. There are many distinct peptides, of several types and shapes, that can act as neurotransmitters. Peptides are different from many conventional transmitters, because they "modulate" synaptic function instead of activating it, they spread slowly and persist for some time, much more than conventional transmitters, and they do not act where released, but at some distant site (in some cases).

As transmitters, peptides act at very restricted places, display a slow rate of conduction, and do not sustain the high frequencies of impulses. As neuromodulators, the excitatory effects of substance P (a peptide) are very slow in the beginning and longer in duration (more than one minute), so they cannot cause enough depolarization to excite the cells; the effect is to make neurons more readily excited by other excitatory inputs, the so-called "neuromodulation." In the proposed model, C explains this function by modifying the degrees of affinity of receptors.

In biological systems, the amount of substrate modification is regulated by the acetylcholine (a neurotransmitter). It spreads over a short distance, toward the postsynaptic membrane, acting at receptor molecules in that membrane, which are enzymatically divided, and part of it is taken up again for synthesis of a new transmitter. This will produce an increase in the amount of substrate. In this model, C represents substrate increase by a variable acting over initial substrate amount.

Peptides are a second, slower, means of communication between neurons, more economical than using extra neurons. This second messenger, besides altering the affinities between transmitters and receptors, can regulate gene expression, achieving synaptic transmission with long-lasting consequences. In this model, this is achieved by modification of a variable for gene expression, mutation can be accounted for.

3.3.1. The labels and their dynamic behaviors

In order to build the model, it is necessary to set the parameters for thew connectionist architecture. For the network genesis, the parameters are:

- number of layers;
- number of neurons in each layer;
- initial amount of substrate (transmitters and receptors) in each layer; and
- genetics of each layer:
  - type of transmitter and its degree of affinity,
  - type of receptor and its degree of affinity, and
  - genes (name and gene expression)).

For the evaluation of controllers and how they act, the parameters are:

- Controllers can modify:
  - the degree of affinity of receptors;
  - the initial substrate storage; and
  - the gene expression value (mutation).

---

[5] Peptides are a compound consisting of two or more amino acids, the building blocks of proteins.

The specifications stated above lead to an ANN with some distinctive characteristics: (1) each neuron has a genetic code, which is a set of genes plus a gene expression controller; (2) the controller can cause mutation, because it can regulate gene expression; (3) the substrate (amount of transmitter and receptor) is defined by layer, but it is limited, so some postsynaptic neurons are not activated: this way, the network favors clustering.

Also, the substrate increase is related to the gene specified in the controller, because the synthesis of a new transmitter occurs in the pre-synaptic terminal (origin gene) [36]. The modification of the genetic code, that is, mutation, as well as the modification of the degree of affinity of receptors, however, is related to the target gene. The reason is that the modulation function of controller is better explained at some distance of the emission of neurotransmitter, therefore at the target.

3.3.2. A network simulation

In table 3, a data set for a five-layer network simulation is presented [36]. For the specifications displayed in table 3, the network architecture and its activated connections are shown in figure 18. For the sake of simplicity, all degrees of affinity are set at 1 (the degree of affinity is represented by a real number in the range [0..1]; so that the greater the degree of affinity is the stronger the synaptic connection will be).

layer	1	2	3	4	5
number of neurons	10	10	5	5	1
amount of substrate	8	10	4	5	2
type of transmitter	1	2	1	2	1
degree of affinity of transmitter	1	1	1	1	1
type of receptor	2	1	2	1	2
degree of affinity of receptor	1	1	1	1	1
genes (name/gene expression)	abc/1	abc/1	abc/1, def/2	abc/1, def/2	def/2

Controllers: 1/1-2: abc/s/abc/1; 1/1-4: abc/e/abc/2; 2/2-3: abc/a/def/0.5. (Controller syntax: *number/origin layer-target layer*: *og/t/tg/res*, where *og* = origin gene (name); *t* = type of synaptic function modulation: a = degree of affinity, s = substrate, e = gene expression; *tg* = target gene (name); *res* = control result: for *t* = a: *res* = new degree of affinity of receptor (target), for *t* = s: *res* = substrate increasing (origin), for *t* = e: *res* = new gene expression controller (target). The controllers from layer 2 to 5, from layer 3 to 4, and from layer 4 to 5 are absent in this simulation.)

Table 3. The data set for a five-layer network. Adapted from [36].

In figure 18, one can notice that every unit in layer 1 (the input layer) is linked to the first nine units in layer 2 (first hidden layer). The reason why not every unit in layer 2 is connected to layer 1, although the receptor of layer 2 has the same type of the transmitter of layer 1, is that the amount of substrate in layer 1 is eight units. This means that, in principle, each layer-1 unit is able to connect to at most eight units. But controller 1, from layer 1 to 2, incremented by 1 the amount of substrate of the origin layer (layer 1). The result is that each layer 1 unit can link to nine units in layer 2. Observe that from layer 2 to layer 3 (the second hidden layer) only four layer-2 units are connected to layer 3, because also of the amount of substrate of layer 3, which is 4.

As a result of the compatibility of layer-2 transmitter and layer-5 receptor, and the existence of remaining unused substrate of layer 2, one could expect that the first two units in layer 2 should connect to the only unit in layer 5 (the output unit). However, this does

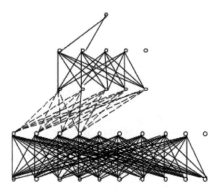

Figure 18. A five-layer neural network for the data set in table 3. In the bottom of the figure is the layer 1 (input layer) and in the top is the layer 5 (output layer). Between them, there are three hidden layers (layers 2 to 4). Figure taken from [36].

not occur because their genes are not compatible. Although gene compatibility exists, in principle, between layers 1 and 4, their units do not connect to each other because there is no remaining substrate in layer 1 and because controller 1 between layers 1 and 4 modified the gene expression of layer 4, making them incompatible. The remaining controller has the effect of modifying the degrees of affinity of receptors in layer 3 (target). Consequently, the connections between layers 2 and 3 became weakened (represented by dotted lines). Notice that, in order to allow connections, in addition to the existence of enough amount of substrate, the genes and the types of transmitters and receptors of each layer must be compatible.

Although the architecture shown in figure 18 is feed-forward, recurrence, or re-entrance, is permitted in this model. This kind of feedback goes along with Edelman and Tononi's "dynamic core" notion [7]. This up-to-date hypothesis suggests that there are neuronal groups underlying conscious experience, the dynamic core, which is highly distributed and integrated through a network of reentrant connections.

3.4. Other models

Other biological plausible ANN models are concerned with the connectionist architecture; related directly to the cerebral cortex biological structure, or focused on the neural features and the signaling between neurons. Always, the main purpose is to create a more faithful model concerning the biological structure, properties, and functionalities, including learning processes, of the cerebral cortex, not disregarding its computational efficiency. The choice of the models upon which the proposed description is based takes into account two main criteria: the fact they are considered biologically more realistic and the fact they deal with intra and inter-neuron signaling in electrical and chemical synapses. Also, the duration of action potentials is taken into account. In addition to the characteristics for encoding information regarding biological plausibility present in current spiking neuron models, a distinguishable feature is emphasized here: a combination of Hebbian learning and error driven learning [52–54].

4. Conclusions

Current models of ANN are in debt with human brain physiology. Because of their mathematical simplicity, they lack several biological features of the cerebral cortex. Also, instead of the individual behavior of the neurons, the mesoscopic information is privileged. The mesoscopic level of the brain could be described adequately by dynamical system theory (attractor states and cycles). The EEG waves reflect the existence of cycles in brain electric field. The objective here is to present biologically plausible ANN models, closer to human brain capacity. In the model proposed, still at the microscopic level of analysis, the possibility of connections between neurons is related not only to synaptic weights, activation threshold, and activation function, but also to labels that embody the binding affinities between transmitters and receptors. This type of ANN would be closer to human evolutionary capacity, that is, it would represent a genetically well-suited model of the brain. The hypothesis of the "dynamic core" [7] is also contemplated, that is, the model allows reentrancy in its architecture connections.

Acknowledgements

I am grateful to my students, who have collaborated with me in this subject for the last ten years.

Author details

João Luís Garcia Rosa

Bioinspired Computing Laboratory (BioCom), Department of Computer Science, University of São Paulo at São Carlos, Brazil

5. References

[1] B. Aguera y Arcas, A. L. Fairhall, and W. Bialek, "Computation in a Single Neuron: Hodgkin and Huxley Revisited," *Neural Computation* 15, 1715–1749 (2003), MIT Press.

[2] A. Clark, *Mindware: An introduction to the philosophy of cognitive science.* Oxford, Oxford University Press, 2001.

[3] CLION - Center for Large-Scale Integration and Optimization Networks, Neurodynamics of Brain & Behavior, FedEx Institute of Technology, University of Memphis, Memphis, TN, USA. http://clion.memphis.edu/laboratories/cnd/nbb/.

[4] L. da F. Costa, F. A. Rodrigues, G. Travieso, and P. R. Villas Boas, "Characterization of complex networks: A survey of measurements," *Advances in Physics*, vol. 56, No. 1, February 2007, pp. 167–242.

[5] F. H. C. Crick, "The Recent Excitement about Neural Networks," *Nature* **337** (1989) pp. 129–132.

[6] F. Crick and C. Asanuma, "Certain Aspects of the Anatomy and Physiology of the Cerebral Cortex," in J. L. McClelland and D. E. Rumelhart (eds.), *Parallel Distributed Processing*, Vol. 2, Cambridge, Massachusetts - London, England, The MIT Press, 1986.

[7] G. M. Edelman and G. Tononi, *A Universe of Consciousness - How Matter Becomes Imagination*, Basic Books, 2000.

[8] C. Eliasmith and C. H. Anderson, *Neural Engineering - Computation, Representation, and Dynamics in Neurobiological Systems*, A Bradford Book, The MIT Press, 2003.

[9] W. J. Freeman, *Mass action in the nervous system - Examination of the Neurophysiological Basis of Adaptive Behavior through the EEG*, Academic Press, New York San Francisco London 1975. Available at http://sulcus.berkeley.edu/.

[10] W. J. Freeman, *How Brains Make Up Their Minds*, Weidenfeld & Nicolson, London, 1999.

[11] W. J. Freeman, *Mesoscopic Brain Dynamics*, Springer-Verlag London Limited 2000.

[12] W. J. Freeman, "How and Why Brains Create Meaning from Sensory Information," *International Journal of Bifurcation & Chaos* 14: 513–530, 2004.

[13] W. J. Freeman, "Proposed cortical 'shutter' in cinematographic perception," in L. Perlovsky and R. Kozma (Eds.), *Neurodynamics of Cognition and Consciousness*, New York: Springer, 2007, pp. 11–38.

[14] W. J. Freeman, "Deep analysis of perception through dynamic structures that emerge in cortical activity from self-regulated noise," *Cogn Neurodyn* (2009) 3:105–116.

[15] W. J. Freeman and M. Breakspear, "Scale-free neocortical dynamics," *Scholarpedia* 2(2):1357. http://www.scholarpedia.org/article/Scale-free_neocortical_dynamics, 2007.

[16] W. J. Freeman and H. Erwin, "Freeman K-set," *Scholarpedia* 3(2):3238. http://www.scholarpedia.org/article/Freeman_K-set, 2008.

[17] W. J. Freeman and R. Kozma, "Freeman's mass action," *Scholarpedia* 5(1):8040. http://www.scholarpedia.org/article/Freeman's_mass_action, 2010.

[18] W. J. Freeman and R. Kozma, "Neuropercolation + Neurodynamics: Dynamical Memory Neural Networks in Biological Systems and Computer Embodiments," IJCNN2011 Tutorial 6, *IJCNN 2011 - International Joint Conference on Neural Networks*, San Jose, California, July 31, 2011.

[19] J. Guckenheimer, "Bifurcation," *Scholarpedia* 2(6):1517. http://www.scholarpedia.org/article/Bifurcation, 2007.

[20] S. Haykin, *Neural Networks - A Comprehensive Foundation. Second Edition.* Prentice-Hall, 1999.

[21] D. O. Hebb, *The Organization of Behavior: A Neuropsychological Theory*, Wiley, 1949.

[22] G. E. Hinton and J. L. McClelland, "Learning Representations by Recirculation," in D. Z. Anderson (ed.), *Neural Information Processing Systems*, American Institute of Physics, New York 1988, pp. 358–66.

[23] A. L. Hodgkin and A. F. Huxley, "A quantitative description of membrane current and its application to conduction and excitation in nerve," *J. Physiol.* (1952) 117, 500–544.

[24] S. Hoover, "Kozma's research is brain wave of the future," *Update - The newsletter for the University of Memphis*, http://www.memphis.edu/update/sep09/kozma.php, 2009.

[25] E. M. Izhikevich, *Dynamical Systems in Neuroscience: The Geometry of Excitability and Bursting*, The MIT Press, 2007.

[26] A. K. Jain, J. Mao, and K. M. Mohiuddin, "Artificial Neural Networks: A Tutorial," *IEEE Computer*, March 1996, pp. 31–44.

[27] E. R. Kandel, J. H. Schwartz, T. M. Jessell, *Essentials of Neural Science and Behavior*, Appleton & Lange, Stamford, Connecticut, 1995.

[28] E. R. Kandel, J. H. Schwartz, T. M. Jessell, *Principles of Neural Science*, Fourth Edition, McGraw-Hill, 2000.

[29] A. K. Katchalsky, V. Rowland and R. Blumenthal, *Dynamic patterns of brain cell assemblies*, MIT Press, 1974.

[30] R. Kozma, H. Aghazarian, T. Huntsberger, E. Tunstel, and W. J. Freeman, "Computational aspects of cognition and consciousness in intelligent devices," *IEEE Computational Intelligence Magazine*, August 2007, pp. 53–64.

[31] R. Kozma, "Neuropercolation," *Scholarpedia* 2(8):1360. http://www.scholarpedia.org/article/Neuropercolation, 2007.

[32] W. S. McCulloch and W. Pitts. "A logical calculus of the ideas immanent in nervous activity." *Bulletin of Mathematical Biophysics*, 5, 115-133, 1943.

[33] R. C. O'Reilly, "Biologically Plausible Error-driven Learning Using Local Activation Differences: the Generalized Recirculation Algorithm," *Neural Computation* 8:5 (1996) pp. 895–938.

[34] T. Orrú, J. L. G. Rosa, and M. L. Andrade Netto, "SABIO: A Biologically Plausible Connectionist Approach to Automatic Text Summarization," *Applied Artificial Intelligence*, 22(8), 2008, pp. 896–920. Taylor & Francis.

[35] J. Rinzel and G. B. Ermentrout, "Analysis of neuronal excitability and oscillations," in C. Koch and I. Segev (Eds.), *Methods In Neuronal Modeling: From Synapses To Networks*, MIT Press, 1989.

[36] J. L. G. Rosa, "An Artificial Neural Network Model Based on Neuroscience: Looking Closely at the Brain," in V. Kurková, N. C. Steele, R. Neruda, and M. Kárný (Eds.), *Artificial Neural Nets and Genetic Algorithms - Proceedings of the International Conference*

in Prague, Czech Republic, 2001 - ICANNGA-2001. April 22-25, Springer-Verlag, pp. 138-141. ISBN: 3-211-83651-9.

[37] J. L. G. Rosa, "A Biologically Inspired Connectionist System for Natural Language Processing," in *Proceedings of the 2002 VII Brazilian Symposium on Neural Networks* (SBRN 2002). 11-14 November 2002. Recife, Brazil. IEEE Computer Society Press.

[38] J. L. G. Rosa, "A Biologically Motivated Connectionist System for Predicting the Next Word in Natural Language Sentences," in *Proceedings of the 2002 IEEE International Conference on Systems, Man, and Cybernetics* - IEEE-SMC'02 - Volume 4. 06-09 October 2002. Hammamet, Tunísia.

[39] J. L. G. Rosa, "A Biologically Plausible and Computationally Efficient Architecture and Algorithm for a Connectionist Natural Language Processor," in *Proceedings of the 2003 IEEE International Conference on Systems, Man, and Cybernetics* - IEEE-SMC'03. 05-08 October 2003. Washington, District of Columbia, United States of America, pp. 2845–2850.

[40] J. L. G. Rosa, "A Biologically Motivated and Computationally Efficient Natural Language Processor," in R. Monroy, G. Arroyo-Figueroa, L. E. Sucar, and H. Sossa (Eds.), *Lecture Notes in Computer Science. Vol. 2972 / 2004. MICAI 2004: Advances in Artificial Intelligence: 3rd. Mexican Intl. Conf. on Artificial Intelligence*, Mexico City, Mexico, April 26-30, 2004. Proc., pp. 390–399. Springer-Verlag Heidelberg.

[41] J. L. G. Rosa, "Biologically Plausible Artificial Neural Networks," Two-hour tutorial at *IEEE IJCNN 2005 - International Joint Conference on Neural Networks*, Montréal, Canada, July 31, 2005. Available at http://ewh.ieee.org/cmte/cis/mtsc/ieeecis/contributors.htm.

[42] J. L. G. Rosa, "A Connectionist Thematic Grid Predictor for Pre-parsed Natural Language Sentences," in D. Liu, S. Fei, Z. Hou, H. Zhang, and C. Sun (Eds.), Advances in Neural Networks - ISNN2007 - *Lecture Notes in Computer Science*, Volume 4492, Part II, pp. 825–834. Springer-Verlag Berlin Heidelberg, 2007.

[43] J. L. G. Rosa, "A Hybrid Symbolic-Connectionist Processor of Natural Language Semantic Relations," *Proceedings of the 2009 IEEE Workshop on Hybrid Intelligent Models and Applications (HIMA2009), IEEE Symposium Series on Computational Intelligence, IEEE SSCI 2009*, March 30 - April 2, 2009. Sheraton Music City Hotel, Nashville, TN, USA. Pp. 64-71. IEEE Conference Proceedings.

[44] J. L. G. Rosa, "Biologically Plausible Connectionist Prediction of Natural Language Thematic Relations," *Proceedings of the WCCI 2010 - 2010 IEEE World Congress on Computational Intelligence, IJCNN 2010 - International Joint Conference on Neural Networks*, July 18-23, 2010. Centre de Convencions Internacional de Barcelona, Barcelona, Spain. IEEE Conference Proceedings, pp. 1127-1134.

[45] J. L. G. Rosa, *Fundamentos da Inteligência Artificial* (Fundamentals of Artificial Intelligence), Book in Portuguese, Editora LTC, Rio de Janeiro, 2011.

[46] J. L. G. Rosa and J. M. Adán-Coello, "Biologically Plausible Connectionist Prediction of Natural Language Thematic Relations," *Journal of Universal Computer Science*, J.UCS vol. 16, no. 21 (2010), pp. 3245-3277. ISSN 0948-6968.

[47] F. Rosenblatt, "The perceptron: A perceiving and recognizing automaton," *Report* 85-460-1, Project PARA, Cornell Aeronautical Lab., Ithaca, NY, 1957.

[48] D. E. Rumelhart, G. E. Hinton, and R. J. Williams, "Learning Internal Representations by Error Propagation," in D. E. Rumelhart and J. L. McClelland (eds.), *Parallel Distributed Processing, Volume 1 - Foundations*. A Bradford Book, MIT Press, 1986.

[49] M. O. Schneider and J. L. G. Rosa, "Application and Development of Biologically Plausible Neural Networks in a Multiagent Artificial Life System," *Neural Computing & Applications*, vol. 18, number 1, 2009, pp. 65–75. DOI 10.1007/s00521-007-0156-0.

[50] R. H. Schonmann, "On the Behavior of Some Cellular Automata Related to Bootstrap Percolation," *The Annals of Probability*, Vol. 20, No. 1 (Jan., 1992), pp. 174–193.

[51] G. M. Shepherd, *The synaptic organization of the brain*, fifth edition, Oxford University Press, USA, 2003.

[52] A. B. Silva and J. L. G. Rosa, "A Connectionist Model based on Physiological Properties of the Neuron," in *Proceedings of the International Joint Conference IBERAMIA/SBIA/SBRN 2006 - 1st Workshop on Computational Intelligence* (WCI'2006), Ribeirão Preto, Brazil, October 23-28, 2006. CD-ROM. ISBN 85-87837-11-7.

[53] A. B. Silva and J. L. G. Rosa, "Biological Plausibility in Artificial Neural Networks: An Improvement on Earlier Models," *Proceedings of The Seventh International Conference on Machine Learning and Applications* (ICMLA'08), 11-13 Dec. 2008, San Diego, California, USA. IEEE Computer Society Press, pp. 829-834. DOI 10.1109/ICMLA.2008.73.

[54] A. B. Silva and J. L. G. Rosa, "Advances on Criteria for Biological Plausibility in Artificial Neural Networks: Think of Learning Processes," *Proceedings of IJCNN 2011 - International Joint Conference on Neural Networks*, San Jose, California, July 31 - August 5, 2011, pp. 1394-1401.

[55] J. R. Smythies, Book review on "How Brains Make up Their Minds. By W. J. Freeman." *Psychological Medicine*, 2001, 31, 373–376. 2001 Cambridge University Press.

[56] O. Sporns, "Network Analysis, Complexity, and Brain Function," *Complexity*, vol. 8, no. 1, pp. 56–60. Willey Periodicals, Inc. 2003.

[57] Wikipedia - The Free Encyclopedia, available at http://en.wikipedia.org/wiki/Neuron

Chapter 2

Robust Design of Artificial Neural Networks Methodology in Neutron Spectrometry

José Manuel Ortiz-Rodríguez,
Ma. del Rosario Martínez-Blanco,
José Manuel Cervantes Viramontes and
Héctor René Vega-Carrillo

Additional information is available at the end of the chapter

1. Introduction

Applications of artificial neural networks (ANNs) have been reported in literature in various areas. [1–5] The wide use of ANNs is due to their robustness, fault tolerant and the ability to learn and generalize, through training process, from examples, complex nonlinear and multi input/output relationships between process parameters using the process data. [6–10] The ANNs have many other advantageous characteristics, which include: generalization, adaptation, universal function approximation, parallel data processing, robustness, etc.

Multilayer perceptron (MLP) trained with backpropagation (BP) algorithm is the most used ANN in modeling, optimization classification and prediction processes. [11, 12] Although BP algorithm has proved to be efficient, its convergence tends to be very slow, and there is a possibility to get trapped in some undesired local minimum. [4, 10, 11, 13]

Most literature related to ANNs focused on specific applications and their results rather than the methodology of developing and training the networks. In general, the quality of the developed ANN is highly dependable not only on ANN training algorithm and its parameters but also on many ANN architectural parameters such as the number of hidden layers and nodes per layer which have to be set during training process and these settings are very crucial to the accuracy of ANN model. [8, 14–19]

Above all, there is limited theoretical and practical background to assist in systematical selection of ANN parameters through entire ANN development and training process. Due to this the ANN parameters are usually set by previous experience in trial and error procedure which is very time consuming. In such a way the optimal settings of ANN parameters for achieving best ANN quality are not guaranteed.

The robust design methodology, proposed by Taguchi, is one of the appropriate methods for achieving this goal. [16, 20, 21] Robust design is a statistical technique widely used to study the relationship between factors affecting the outputs of the process. It can be used to systematically identify the optimum setting of factors to obtain the desired output. In this work, it was used to find the optimum setting of ANNs parameters in order to achieve minimum error network.

1.1. Artificial Neural Networks

The first ones works about neurology were carried out by Santiago Ramón y Cajal (1852-1934) and Charles Scott Sherrington (1852-1957). Starting from their studies it is known that the basic element that conforms the nervous system is the neuron. [2, 10, 13, 22] The model of an artificial neuron it is an imitation of a biological neuron. Thus, the ANNs try to emulate the processes carried out by biological neural networks trying to build systems capable to learn from experience, pattern recognition and to realize predictions. ANN are based on a dense interconnection of small processors called nodes, neuronodes, cells, unit or processing elements or neurons.

A simplified morphology of an individual biological neuron is showed in figure 1, where can be distinguished three fundamental parts: the soma or cell body, dendrites and the cylinder-axis or axon.

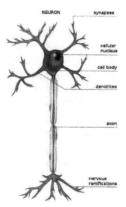

Figure 1. Simplified morphology of an individual biological neuron

Dendrites are fibers which receive the electric signals coming from other neurons and transmit them to the soma. The multiple signals coming from dendrites are processed by the soma and transmitted to the axon. The cylinder-axis or axon is a fiber of great longitude, compared with the rest of the neuron, connected to the soma for an end and divided in the other one in a series of nervous ramifications; the axon picks up the signal of the soma and transmits it to other neurons through a process known as synapses.

An artificial neuron it is a mathematical abstraction of the working of a biological neuron. [23] Figure 2, shows an artificial neuron. From a detailed observation of the biological process, the following analogies with the artificial system can be mentioned:

- The input X_i represents the signals that come from other neurons and are captured by dendrites.
- The weights W_i are the intensity of the synapses that connects two neurons; X_i and W_i are real values.
- θ is the threshold function that the neuron should exceed to be active; this process happens biologically in the body of the cell
- the input signals to the artificial neuron $X_1, X_2, ..., X_n$ are continuous variables instead of discrete pulses, as are presented in a biological neuron. Each input signal passes through a gain or weight called synaptic weight or strength of the connection whose function is similar to the synaptic function of the biological neuron.
- Weights can be positive (excitatory) or negatives (inhibitory), the summing node accumulates all the input signals multiplied by the weights and pass to the output through a threshold or transfer function.

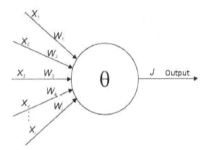

Figure 2. Artificial neuron model

An idea of this process is shown in figure 3, where can be observed a group of inputs entering to an artificial neuron.

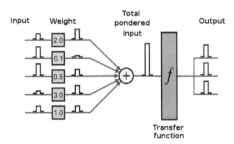

Figure 3. Analogies of an artificial neuron with a biological model

The input signals are pondered multiplying them for the corresponding weight that would correspond in the biological version of the neuron to the strength of the synaptic connection; the pondered signals arrive to the neuronal node that acts as a summing of the signals; the output of the node is denominated net output, and it is calculated as the summing of the pondered entrances plus a b value denominated gain. The net outpu is used as entrance to the transfer function providing the total output or answer of the artificial neuron.

The representation of figure 3 can be simplified as is shown in figure 4. From this figure, the net output of neuron n, can be mathematically represented as follows:

$$n = \sum_{i=1}^{r} p_i w_i + b \tag{1}$$

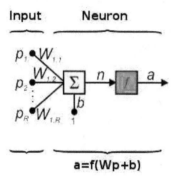

Figure 4. Didactic model of an artificial neuron

The neuronal response to the input signals a, can be represented as:

$$a = f(n) = \sum_{i=1}^{r} p_i w_i + b \tag{2}$$

A more didactic model, showed in figure 5, facilitates the study of a neuron.

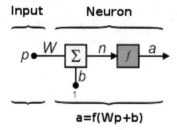

Figure 5. Didactic model of a single artificial neuron

From this figure can be seen that the net inputs are present in the vector p, an alone neuron only has one element; W represents the weights and the new input b is a gain that reinforce the output of the summing n, which is the net output of the network; the net output it is determined by the transfer function which can be a lineal or non-lineal function of n, and is chosen depending of the specifications of the problem that the neuron wants to solve.

Generally, a neuron has more than one entrance. In figure 4, can be observed a neuron with R inputs; the individual inputs $p_1, p_2, ..., p_R$ are multiplied by the corresponding weights $w_{1,1}, w_{1,2}, ..., w_{1,R}$ belonging to the weight matrix W. The sub-indexes of the weigh matrix represent the terms involved in the connection. The first sub-index represents the neuron destination, and the second represents the source of the signal that feeds to the neuron. For example, the $w_{1,2}$ indexes indicate that this weight is the connection from the second entrance to the first neuron.

This convention becomes more useful when there is a neuron with too many parameters; in this case the notation of figure 4, can be inappropriate and it is preferred to use the abbreviated notation represented in figure 6.

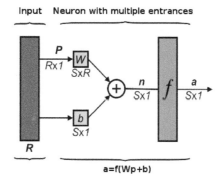

Figure 6. Abbreviated didactic model of an artificial neuron

The entrance vector p is represented by the vertical solid bar to the left. The dimensions of p are shown in the inferior part of the variable as $Rx1$, indicating that the entrance vector is a vectorial row of R elements. The entrances go to the weight matrix W, which has R columns and just one row for the case of a single neuron. A constant 1 enters to the neuron multiplied by the scalar gain b. The exit of the net a it is a scalar in this case. If the net had more than a neuron a would be a vector.

ANN are highly simplified models of the working of the brain. [10, 24] An ANN is a biologically inspired computational model which consists of a large number of simple processing elements or neurons which are interconnected and operate in parallel. [2, 13] Each neuron is connected to other neurons by means of directed communication links, which constitute the neuronal structure, each with an associated weight. [4] The weights represent information being used by the net to solve a problem.

ANNs are usually formed by several interconnected neurons. The disposition and connection varies from one type of nets to other, but in a general way the neurons are grouped by layers. A layer is a collection of neurons; according to the location of the layer in the neural net, this receives different names:

- **Input later:** receives the input signals from the environment. In this layer the information is not processed, for this reason, it is not considered as a layer of neurons.

- **Hidden layers:** these layers do not have contact with the exterior environment; the hidden layers pick up and process the information coming from the input layer; the numbers of hidden layers and neurons per layer and the form in that are connected, vary from some nets to others. Their elements can have different connections and these determine the different topologies of the net.

- **Output layer:** receives the information from the hidden layers and transmits the answer to the external means.

Figure 7 shows an ANN with two hidden layers. The outputs of first hidden layer are the entrances of the second hidden layer. In this configuration, each layer have its own weight matrix W, the summing, a gain vector b, net inputs vector n, the transfer function and the output vector a. This ANN can be observed in abbreviated notation in figure 8.

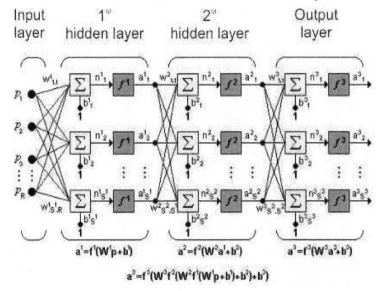

Figure 7. Artificial Neural Network with two hidden layers

Figure 8 shows a three-layer network using abbreviated notation. From this figure can be seen that the network has R^1 inputs, S^1 neurons in the first layer, S^2 neurons in the second layer, etc. A constant input 1 is fed to the bias for each neuron. The outputs of each intermediate layer are the inputs to the following layer. Thus layer 2 can be analyzed as a one-layer network with S^1 inputs, S^2 neurons, and an $S^2 x S^1$ weight matrix W^2. The input to layer 2 is a^1; the output is a^2. Now that all the vectors and matrices of layer 2 have been identified, it can be treated as a single-layer network on its own. This approach can be taken with any layer of the network.

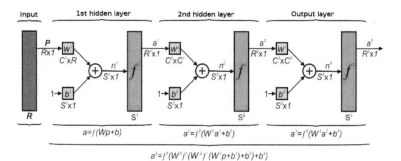

$$a^3 = f^3(W^3 f^2(W^2 f(W^1 p + b^1) + b^2) + b^3)$$

Figure 8. Artificial Neural Network with two hidden layers in abreviated notation

The arrangement of neurons into layers and the connection patterns within and between layers is called the *net architecture* [6, 7]. According to the absence or presence of feedback connections in a network, two types of architectures are distinguished:

- **Feedforward architecture**. There are no connections back from the output to the input neurons; the network does not keep a memory of its previous output values and the activation states of its neurons; the perceptron-like networks are feedforward types.

- **Feedback architecture**. There are connections from output to input neurons; such a network keeps a memory of its previous states, and the next state depends not only on the input signals but on the previous states of the network; the Hopfield network is of this type.

Back propagation feed forward neural nets is a network with supervised learning which uses a propagation-adaptation cycle of two phases. Once a pattern has been applied to the input of the network as a stimulus, this is propagated from the first layer through the superior layers of the net until generate an output. The output signal is compared with the desired output and a signal error is calculated for each one of the outputs.

The outputs errors are back propagated from the output layer toward all the neurons of the hidden layer that contribute directly with the output. However, the neurons of the hidden layer only receive a fraction of the signal from the whole error signal, based on the relative contribution that has contributed each neuron to the original output. This process is repeated for each layer until all neurons of the network have received an error signal which describes its relative contribution to the total error. Based on the perceived signal error the connection synaptic weights of each neuron are upgrade to make that the net converges toward a state that allows to classify correctly all the patterns of training.

The importance of this process consists in that as trains the net, those neurons of the intermediate layers are organized themselves in such a way that the neurons learn how to recognize different features of the whole entrance space. After the training, when they are presented an arbitrary pattern of entrance that contain noise or that it is incomplete, the neurons of the hidden layer of the net will respond with an active output if the new entrance contains a pattern that resembles each other to that characteristic that the individual neurons have learned how to recognize during their training. And to the inverse one, the units of the hidden layers have one tendency to inhibit their output if the entrance pattern does not contain the characteristic to recognize, for which they have been trained.

During the training process, the Backpropagation net tends to develop internal relationships among neurons with the purpose to organize the training data in classes. This tendency can be extrapolated to arrive to the hypothesis that all the units of the hidden layer of a Backpropagation are associated somehow to specific characteristic of the entrance pattern as consequence of the training. That the association is or not exact, it cannot be evident for the human observer, the important thing it is that the net has found one internal representation that allows him to generate the wanted outputs when are given the entrances in the training process. This same internal representation can be applied to entrances that the net has not seen before, and the net will classify these entrances according to the characteristics that share with the examples of training.

In recent years, there is increasing interest in using ANNs for modeling, optimization and prediction. The advantages that ANNs offer are numerous and are achievable only by developing an ANN model of high performance. However, determining suitable training and architectural parameters of an ANN still remains a difficult task mainly because it is very hard to know beforehand the size and the structure of a neural network one needs to solve a given problem. An ideal structure is a structure that independently of the starting weights of the net, always learns the task, i.e. makes almost no error on the training set and generalizes well.

The problem with neural networks is that a number of parameter have to be set before any training can begin. Users have to choose the architecture and determine many of the parameters in a selected network. However, there are no clear rules how to set these parameters. Yet, these parameters determine the success of the training.

As can be appreciated in figure 9, the current practice in the selection of design parameters for ANN is based on the trial and error procedure, where a large number of ANN models are developed and compared to one another. If the level of a design parameter is changed and does not have effect in the performance of the net, then a different design parameter is varied, and the experiment is repeated in a series of approaches. The observed answers are examined in each phase, to determine the best level in each design parameter.

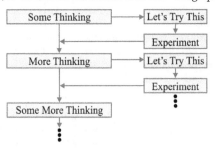

Figure 9. Trial-and-error procedure in the selection of ANN parameters

The serious inconvenience of this method is that a parameter is evaluated while the other ones are maintained in an only level. Of here, the best selected level in a design variable in particular, could not necessarily be the best at the end of the experimentation, since those other parameters could have changed. Clearly, this method cannot evaluate interactions among parameters since only combines one at the same time it could lead to an ANN impoverished design in general.

All of these limitations have motivated researchers to generate ideas of merging or hybridizing ANN with other approaches in the search for better performance. A form of overcoming this disadvantage, is to evaluate all the possible level combinations of the design parameters, i.e., to carry out a complete factorial design. However, since the number of combinations can be very big, even for a small number of parameters and levels, this method is very expensive and consumes a lot of time. The number of experiments to be carried out can be decreased making use of the factorial fractional method, a statistical method based on the robust design of Taguchi philosophy.

The Taguchi technique is a methodology for finding the optimum setting of the control factors to make the product or process insensitive to the noise factors. Taguchi based optimization technique has produced a unique and powerful optimization discipline that differs from traditional practices.[16, 20, 21]

1.2. Taguchi philosophy of robust design

Designs of experiments involving multiple factors was first proposed by R. A. Fisher, in the 1920s to determine the effect of multiple factors on the outcome of agricultural trials (Ranjit 1990). This method is known as *factorial design of experiments*. A full factorial design identifies all possible combinations for a given set of factors. Since most experiments involve a significant number of factors, a full factorial design may involve a large number of experiments.

Factors are the different variables which determines the functionality or performance of a product or system as for example, design parameters that influence the performance or input that can be controlled.

Dr. Genichi Taguchi is considered the author of the robust design of parameters. [8, 14–21] This is an engineering method for the design of products or processes focused in diminishing the variation and/or sensibility to the noise. When it is used appropriately, Taguchi design provides a powerful and efficient method for the design of products that operate consistent and optimally about a variety of conditions. In the robust design of parameters, the primary objective is to find the selection of the factors that decrease the variation of the answer, while the processes are adjusted on the objective.

The distinct idea of Taguchi's robust design that differs from the conventional experimental design is the simultaneous modeling of both mean and variability in the designing. However, Taguchi methodology is based on the concept of fractional factorial design.

By using Orthogonal Arrays (OAs) and fractional factorial instead of full factorial, Taguchi's approach allows to study the entire parameter space with a small number of experiments. An OA is a small fraction of full factorial design and assures a balanced comparison of levels of any factor or interaction of factors. The columns of an OA represent the experimental parameters to be optimized and the rows represent the individual trials (combinations of levels).

Taguchi's robust design can be divided into two classes: static and dynamic characteristics. The static problem attempts to obtain the value of a quality characteristic of interest as close as possible to a single specified target value. The dynamic problem, on the other hand, involves situations where a system's performance depends on a signal factor.

Taguchi also proposed a two-phase procedure to determine the factors level combination. First, the control factors that are significant for reducing variability are determined and their settings are chosen. Next, the control factors that are significant in affecting the sensitivity are identified and their appropriate levels are chosen. The objective of the second phase is to adjust the responses to the desired values.

The Taguchi method is applied in four steps.

1. **Brainstorm the quality characteristics and design parameters important to the product/process.**

   In Taguchi methods there are variables that are under control and variables that are not. These are called design and noise factors, respectively, which can influence a product and operational process. The design factors, as controlled by the designer, can be divided into: (1) signal factor, which influences the average of the quality response and (2) control factor, which influences the variation of the quality response. The noise factors are uncontrollable such as manufacturing variation, environmental variation and deterioration.

   Before designing an experiment, knowledge of the product/process under investigation is of prime importance for identifying the factors likely to influence the outcome. The aim of the analysis is primarily to seek answers to the following three questions:

   (a) What is the optimum condition?

   (b) Which factors contribute to the results and by how much?

   (c) What will be the expected result at the optimum condition?

2. **Design and conduct the experiments.**

   Taguchi's robust design involves using an OA to arrange the experiment and selecting the levels of the design factors to minimize the effects of the noise factors. That is, the settings of the design factors for a product or a process should be determined so that the product's response has the minimum variation, and its mean is close to the desired target.

   To design an experiment, the most suitable OA is selected. Next, factors are assigned to the appropriate columns, and finally, the combinations of the individual experiments (called the trial conditions) are described. Experimental design using OAs is attractive because of experimental efficiency.

   The array is called orthogonal because for every pair of parameters, all combinations of parameter levels occur an equal number of times, which means the design is balanced so that factor levels are weighted equally. The real power in using an OA is the ability to evaluate several factors in a minimum of tests. This is considered an efficient experiment since much information is obtained from a few trials. The mean and the variance of the response at each setting of parameters in OA are then combined into a single performance measure known as the signal-to-noise (S/N) ratio.

3. **Analyze the results to determine the optimum conditions.**

The S/N ratio is a quality indicator by which the experimenters can evaluate the effect of changing a particular experimental parameter on the performance of the process or product. Taguchi used S/N ratio to evaluate the variation of the system's performance, which is derived from quality loss function. For static characteristic, Taguchi classified them into three types of S/N ratios:

(a) Smaller-the-Better (STB)

(b) Larger-the-Better (LTB)

(c) Nominal-the-Best (NTB)

For the STB and LTB cases, Taguchi recommended direct minimization of the expected loss. For the NTB case, Taguchi developed a two-phase optimization procedure to obtain the optimal factor combinations.

For the dynamic characteristics the SN ratio

$$SN_i = 10log_{10}(\beta_i/MSE_i) \tag{3}$$

is used for evaluating the S/N ratio, where the mean square error (MSE) represents the mean square of the distance between the measured response and the best fitted line; denotes the sensitivity.

4. **Run a confirmatory test using the optimum conditions.**

The two major goals of parameter design are to minimize the process or product variation and to design robust and flexible processes or products that are adaptable to environmental conditions. Taguchi methodology is useful for finding the optimum setting of the control factors to make the product or process insensitive to the noise factors.

In this stage, the value of the robustness measure is predicted at the optimal design condition; a confirmation experiment at the optimal design condition is conducted, calculating the robustness measure for the performance characteristic and checking if the robustness prediction is close to the predicted value.

Today, ANN can be trained to solve problems that are difficult for conventional computers or human beings, and have been trained to perform complex functions in various fields, including pattern recognition, identification, classification, speech, vision, and control systems. Recently, the use of ANN technology has been applied with relative success in the research area of nuclear sciences,[3] mainly in the neutron spectrometry and dosimetry domains. [25–31]

1.3. Neutron spectrometry with ANNs

The measurement of the intensity of a radiation field with respect to certain quantity like angle, energy, frequency, etc., is very important in radiation spectrometry having, as a final result, the radiation spectrum. [32–34] The radiation spectrometry term can be used to describe measurement of the intensity of a radiation field with respect to energy, frequency or momentum. [35] The distribution of the intensity with one of these parameters is commonly referred to as the "spectrum". [36] A second quantity is the variation of the intensity of these radiations as a function of angle of incidence on a body situated in the radiation field and is referred as "dose". The neutron spectra and the dose are of great importance in radiation protection physics. [37]

Neutrons are found in the environment or are artificially produced by different ways; these neutrons have a wide energy range extending from few thousandths of eV to several hundreds of MeV. [38] Also, they are in a broad variety of energy distributions, named neutron-fluence spectrum or simply neutron spectrum, $\Phi_E(E)$.

Determination of neutron dose received by those exposed to workplaces or accidents in nuclear facilities, generally requires knowledge of the neutron energy spectrum incident on the body. [39] Spectral information must generally be obtained from passive detectors which respond to different ranges of neutron energies such as the multispheres Bonner system or Bonner spheres system (BSS). [40–42]

BSS system, has been used to unfold the neutron spectra mainly because it has an almost isotropic response, can cover the energy range from thermal to GeV neutrons, and is easy to operate. However, the weight, time consuming procedure, the need to use an unfolding procedure and the low resolution spectrum are some of the BSS drawbacks. [43, 44]

As can be seen from figure 10, BSS consists of a thermal neutron detector such as $^6LiI(Eu)$, Activation foils, pairs of thermoluminiscent dosimeters or track detectors, which is placed at the centre of a number of moderating spheres made of polyethylene of different diameter to obtain, through an unfolding process the neutron energy distribution, also known as spectrum, $\Phi_E(E)$. [42, 45]

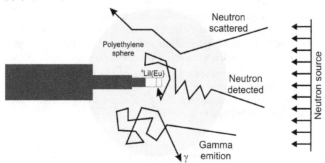

Figure 10. Bonner spheres system for a $^6LiI(Eu)$ neutrons detector

The derivation of the spectral information is not simple; the unknown neutron spectrum is not given directly as a result of the measurements. [46] If a sphere d has a response function $R_d(E)$, and is exposed in a neutron field with spectral fluence $\Phi_E(E)$, the sphere reading M_d is obtained by folding $R_d(E)$ with $\Phi_E(E)$, this means to solve the Fredholm integral equation of the first kind shown in equation 4.

$$M_d = \int R_d(E)\Phi_E(E)dE \qquad (4)$$

This folding process takes place in the sphere itself during the measurement. Although the real $\Phi_E(E)$ and $R_d(E)$ are continuous functions of neutron energy, they cannot be described by analytical functions, and, as a consequence, a discretised numerical form is used, showed in the following equation:

$$C_j = \sum_{i=1}^{N} R_{i,j} \Phi_i \ --- > j = 1, 2, ..., m \tag{5}$$

where C_j is j^{th} detector's count rate; $R_{i,j}$ is the jth detector's response to neutrons at the ith energy interval; Φ_i is the neutron fluence within the ith energy interval and m is the number of spheres utilized.

Once the neutron spectrum, $\Phi_E(E)$, has been obtained, the dose $\triangle$ can be calculated using the fluence-to-dose conversion coefficients $\delta_\Phi E$, as shown in equation 3.

$$\triangle = \int_{E_{min}}^{E_{max}} \delta_\Phi E \Phi_E(E) dE \tag{6}$$

Equation 5 is an ill-conditioned equations system with an infinite number of solutions which have motivated researches to propose new and complementary approaches. To unfold the neutron spectrum, Φ, several methods are used. [43, 44, 47] ANN technology is a useful alternative to solve this problem; [25–31] however, several drawbacks must be solved in order to simplify the use of these procedures.

Besides many advantages that ANNs offer, there are some drawbacks and limitations related to ANN design process. In order to develop an ANN which generalizes well and be robust, a number of issues must be taken into consideration, particularly related to architecture and training parameters. [8, 14–21] The trial-and-error technique is the usual way to get a better combination of these vales. This method cannot identify interactions between the parameters and do not use systematic methodologies for the identification of the "best" values, consuming much time and does not systematically target a near optimal solution, which may lead to a poor overall neural network design.

Even though the BP learning algorithm provides a method for training multilayer feed forward neural nets, is not free of problems. Many factors affect the performance of the learning and should be treated for having a successful learning process. Those factors include the synaptic weight initialization, the learning rate, the momentum, the size of the net and the learning database. A good election of these parameters could speed up and improve in great measure the learning process to reach the goal, although a universal answer does not exist for such topics.

Choosing the ANN architecture followed by selection of training algorithm and related parameters is rather a matter of the designer past experience since there are no practical rules which could be generally applied. This is usually a very time consuming trial and error procedure where a number of ANNs are designed and compared to one another. Above all, the design of optimal ANN is not guaranteed. It is unrealistic to analyze all combination of ANN parameters and parameter's levels effects on the ANN performance.

To deal economically with the many possible combinations, the Taguchi method can be applied. Taguchi's techniques have been widely used in engineering design, and can be applied to many aspects such as optimization, experimental design, sensitivity analysis, parameter estimation, model prediction, etc.

This work is concerned with the application of Taguchi method for the optimization of ANN models. The integration of ANN and Taguchi's optimization provides a tool for designing robust network parameters and improving their performance. The Taguchi method offers considerable benefits in time and accuracy when is compared with the conventional trial and error neural network design approach.

In this work, for the robust design of multilayer feedforward neural networks trained by backpropagation algorithm in the neutron spectrometry field, a systematic and experimental strategy called *Robust Design of Artificial Neural Networks* (RDANN) methodology was designed. This computer tool, emphasizes simultaneous ANNs parameters optimization under various noise conditions. Here, we make a comparison among this method and conventional training methods. The attention is drawing on the advantages on Taguchi methods which offer potential benefits in evaluating the network behavior.

2. Robust design of artificial neural networks methodology

Neutron spectrum unfolding is an ill-conditioned system with an infinite number of solutions. [27] Researchers have using ANNs to unfold neutron spectra from BSS. [48] Figure 11, shows the classical approach of neutron spectrometry by means ANN technology starting from rate counts measured with BSS.

As can be appreciated in figure 11, neutron spectrometry by means of ANN technology is done by using a neutron spectra data set compiled by the International Atomic Energy Agency (IAEA). [49] This compendium contains a large collection of detector responses and spectra. The original spectra in this report were defined per unit lethargy in 60 energy groups ranging from thermal to 630 MeV.

One challenge in neutron spectrometry using neural nets is the pre-processing of the information in order to create suitable pair input-output training data sets. [50] The generation of a suitable data set is a non trivial task. Because the novelty of this technology in this research area, the researcher spent a lot of time in this activity mainly because all the work is done by hand and a lot of effort is required. From the anterior, it is evident the need to have technological tools that automate this process. At present, work is being realized in order to alleviate this drawback.

In order to use the response matrix known as UTA4, expressed en 31 energy groups, ranging from 10^{-8} up to 231.2 MeV in the ANN training process, the energy range of neutrons spectra was changed through a re-binning process by means of MCNP simulations. [50] 187 neutrons spectra from IAEA compilation, expressed in energy units and in 60 energy bins, were re-binned into the thirty-one energy groups of the UTA4 response matrix, and at the same time, 13 different equivalent doses were calculated per spectra by using the International Commission on Radiological Protection (ICRP) fluence-to-dose conversion factors.

Figure 12, shows the re-binned neutron spectra data set used for training and testing the optimum ANN architecture designed with RDANN methodology.

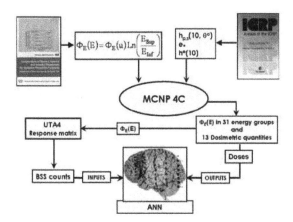

Figure 11. Classical Neutron spectrometry with ANN technology

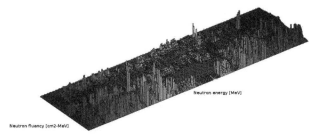

Figure 12. Re-binned neutron spectra data set used to train the optimum ANN architecture designed with RDANN methodology

Multiplying re-binned neutron spectra by UTA4 response matrix, the rate counts data set was calculated. Re-binned spectra and equivalent doses are the desired output of ANN and its corresponding calculated rate counts the entrance data.

The second one challenge in neutron spectrometry by means ANN, is the determination of the net topology. In the ANN design process, the choice of the ANN's basic parameters often determines the success of the training process. The selection of these parameters follows in practical use no rules, and their value is at most arguable. This method consuming much time and does not systematically target a near optimal solution to select suitable parameter values. The ANN designers have to choose the architecture and determine many of the parameters through the trial and error technique, which produces ANN with poor performance and low generalization capability, spending often large amount of time.

An easier and more efficient way to overcome this disadvantage is to use the RDANN methodology, showed in figure 13, which has become in a new approach to solve this problem.

RDANN is a very powerful method based on parallel processes where all the experiments are planed a priori and the results are analyzed after all the experiments are completed. This is a

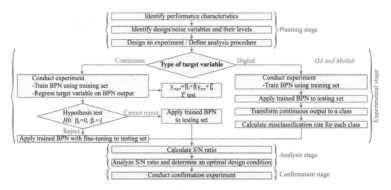

Figure 13. Robust design of artificial neural networks methodology

systematic and methodological approach of ANN design, based on the Taguchi philosophy, which maximize the ANN performance and generalization capacity.

The integration of neural networks and optimization provides a tool for designing ANN parameters improving the network performance and generalization capability. The main objective of the proposed methodology is to develop accurate and robust ANN models. In other words, the goal is to select ANN training and architectural parameters, so that the ANN model yields best performance.

From figure 13 can be seen that in ANN design using Taguchi philosophy in RDANN methodology, the designer must recognize the application problem well and choose a suitable ANN model. In the selected model, the design parameters, factors, which need to be optimized need to be determined (Planning stage). Using OAs, simulations, i.e., training of ANNs with different net topologies can be executed in a systematic way (experimentation stage). From simulation results, the response can be analyzed by using S/N ratio from Taguchi method (Analysis stage). Finally, a confirmation experiment at the optimal design condition is conducted, calculating the robustness measure for the performance characteristic and checking if the robustness prediction is close to the predicted value (Confirmation stage).

To provide scientific discipline to this work, in this research the systematic and methodological approach called RDANN methodology was used to obtain the optimum architectural and learning values of an ANN capable to solve the neutron spectrometry problem.

According figure 13, the steps followed to obtain the optimum design of the ANN are described:

1. **Planning stage**

   In this stage it is necessary to identify the objective function and the design and noise variables.

   (a) *The objective function.* The objective function must be defined according to the purpose and requirements of the problem.

   In this research, the objective function is the prediction or classification errors between the target and the output values of BP ANN at testing stage, i.e., the performance or mean square error (MSE) output of the ANN is used as the objective function as is showed in the following equation:

$$MSE = \sqrt{\frac{1}{N} \sum_{i=1}^{N} (\Phi_E(E)_i^{ANN} - \Phi_E(E)_i^{ORIGINAL})^2} \qquad (7)$$

Where N is the number of trials, $\Phi_E(E)_i^{ORIGINAL}$ is the original spectra and $\Phi_E(E)_i^{ANN}$ is the spectra unfolded with ANN.

(b) *Design and noise variables.* Based in the requirements of the physical problem, users can choose some factors as design variables, which can be varied during the optimization iteration process, and some factors as fixed constants.

Among the various parameters that affect the ANN performance, four design variables were selected, as is showed in the table 1:

Design Var.	Level 1	Level 2	Level 3
A	L1	L2	L3
B	L1	L2	L3
C	L1	L2	L3
D	L1	L2	L3

Table 1. Design variables and their levels

where **A** is the number of neurons in the first hidden layer, **B** is the number of neurons in the second hidden layer, **C** is the momentum and **D** is the learning rate.

Noise variables are shown in table 2. These variables in most cases are not controlled by the user. The initial set of weights, U, usually is randomly selected; In the training and testing data sets, V, the designer must decide how much of the whole data should be allocated to the training and testing data sets. Once V is determined, the designer must decide which data of the whole data set to include in the training and testing data set, W.

Design Var.	Level 1	Level 2
U	Set 1	Set 2
V	6:4	8:2
W	Tr-1/Tst-1	Tr-2/Tst-2

Table 2. Noise variables and their levels

where **U** is the initial set of random weights, **V** is the size of training set versus size of testing set, i.e., **V** = 60% / 40%, 80% / 20% and **W** is the selection of training and testing sets, i.e., **W** = Training1/Test1, Training2/Test2.

In practice, these variables are randomly determined, and are not controlled by designer. Because the random nature of this selection processes, the ANN designer must create these data sets starting from the whole data set. This procedure is very time consuming when is done by hand without the help of technological tools.

RDANN methodology was designed in order to fully automate in a computer program, developed under Matlab environment and showed in figure 14, the creation of the noise variables and their levels. This work is done before the training of the several net topologies tested at experimentation stage.

Besides the automatic generation of noise variables, another programming routines were created in order to train the different net architectures, and to statistically analyze and graph the obtained data. When this procedure is done by hand, is very time consuming. The use of the designed computer tool saves a lot of time and effort to ANN designer.

Figure 14. Robust Design of Artificicial Neural Networks Methodology

After the factors and levels are determined, a suitable OA can be selected for training process. The Taguchi OAs are denoted by $L_r(s^c)$ where r is the number of rows, c is the number of columns and s is the number of levels in each column.

2. **Experimentation stage**. The choice of a suitable OA is critical for the success of this stage. OA allow to compute the main interaction effects via a minimum number of experimental trails. In this research, the columns of OA represent the experimental parameters to be optimized and the rows represent the individual trials, i.e., combinations of levels.

For a robust experimental design, Taguchi suggest to use two crossed OAs with a $L_9(3^4)$ y $L_4(3^2)$ configuration, as is showed in table 3.

From table 3, can be seen that a design variable is assigned to a column of the OA. Then, each row of the design OA represents a specific design of ANN. Similarly, a noise variable is assigned to a column of the noise OA, each row corresponds to a noise condition.

3. **Analysis stage**.

The S/N ratio is a measure of both, the location and dispersion of the measured responses. It transforms the row data to allow quantitative evaluation of the design parameters considering their mean and variation. It is measured in decibels using the formula:

$$S/N = 10log_{10}(MSD) \tag{8}$$

where MSD is a measure of the mean square deviation in performance, since in every design, more signal and less noise is desired. The best design will have the highest S/N ratio. In this stage, the statistical program JMP was used to select the best values of the ANN being designed.

Trial No.	A	B	C	D	S1	S2	S3	S4	Mean	S/N
1	1	1	1	1						
2	1	2	2	2						
3	1	3	3	3						
4	2	1	2	3						
5	2	2	3	1						
6	2	3	1	2						
7	3	1	3	2						
8	3	2	1	3						
9	3	3	2	1						

Table 3. ANN measured responses with a crossed OA with $L_9(3^4)$ y $L_4(3^2)$ configuration

4. **Confirmation stage**.

In this stage, the value of the robustness measure is predicted at the optimal design condition; a confirmation experiment at the optimal design condition is conducted, calculating the robustness measure for the performance characteristic and checking if the robustness prediction is close to the predicted value.

3. Results and discussion

RDANN methodology was applied in nuclear sciences in order to solve the neutron spectrometry problem starting from the count rates of BSS System with a ^{6}LiI(Eu) thermal neutrons detector, 7 polyethylene spheres and the UTA4 response matrix expressed 31 energy bins.

In this work, a feed-forward ANN trained with BP learning algorithm was designed. For ANN training, the *"trainscg"* training algorithm and mse = $1E^{-4}$ were selected. In RDANN methodology an OA with $L_9(3^4)$ and $L_4(3^2)$ configuration, corresponding to design and noise variables respectively, was used. The optimal net architecture was designed in short time and has high performance and generalization capability.

The obtained results after applying RDANN methodology are:

3.1. Planning stage

Tables 4 and 5 shown the design and noise variables selected and their levels.

Design Var.	Level 1	Level 2	Level 3
A	14	28	56
B	0	28	56
C	0.001	0.1	0.3
D	0.1	0.3	0.5

Table 4. Design variables and their levels

where **A** is the number of neurons in the first hidden layer, **B** is the number of neurons in the second hidden layer, **C** is the momentum, **D** is the learning rate.

Design Var.	Level 1	Level 2
U	Set 1	Set 2
V	6:4	8:2
W	Tr-1/Tst-1	Tr-2/Tst-2

Table 5. Noise variables and their levels

where **U** is the initial set of random weights, **V** is the size of training set versus size of testing set, i.e., **V** = 60% / 40%, 80% / 20% and **W** is the selection of training and testing sets, i.e., **W** = Training1/Test1, Training2/Test2.

3.2. Experimentation Stage

In this stage by using a crossed OA with $L_9(3^4)$, $L_4(3^2)$ configuration, 36 different ANNs architectures were trained and tested as is showed in table 6.

Trial No.	Resp-1	Resp-2	Resp-3	Resp-4	Median	S/N
1	3.316E-04	2.416E-04	2.350E-04	3.035E-04	2.779E-04	3.316E-04
2	2.213E-04	3.087E-04	3.646E-04	2.630E-04	2.894E-04	2.213E-04
3	4.193E-04	3.658E-04	3.411E-04	2.868E-04	3.533E-04	4.193E-04
4	2.585E-04	2.278E-04	2.695E-04	3.741E-04	2.825E-04	2.585E-04
5	2.678E-04	3.692E-04	3.087E-04	3.988E-04	3.361E-04	2.678E-04
6	2.713E-04	2.793E-04	2.041E-04	3.970E-04	2.879E-04	2.713E-04
7	2.247E-04	7.109E-04	3.723E-04	2.733E-04	3.953E-04	2.247E-04
8	3.952E-04	5.944E-04	2.657E-04	3.522E-04	4.019E-04	3.952E-04
9	5.425E-04	3.893E-04	3.374E-04	4.437E-04	4.282E-04	5.425E-04

Table 6. ANN measured responses with a corssed OA with L9,L4 configuration

The signal-to-noise ratio was analyzed by means of Analysis of Variance (ANOVA) by using the statistical program JMP. Since an error of $1E^{-4}$ was established for the objective function, from table 6, can be seen that all ANN performances reach this value. This means that this particular OA has a good performance.

3.3. Analysis stage

The signal-to-noise ratio is used in this stage to determine the optimum ANN architecture. The best ANN's design parameters are showed in table 7.

Trial No.	A	B	C1	C2	C3	D
1	14	0	0.001	0.001	0.001	0.1
2	14	0	0.001	**0.1**	0.3	**0.1**
3	56	56	0.001	0.1	0.1	0.1

Table 7. Best values used in the confirmation stage to design the ANN

3.4. Confirmation stage

Once optimum design parameters were determined, the confirmation stage was performed to determine the final optimum values, highlighted in table 7. After the best ANN topology was determined a final training and testing was made to validate the data obtained with the ANN designed. At final ANN validation and using the designed computational tool, correlation and Chi square statistical tests were carried out as shown in figure 15.

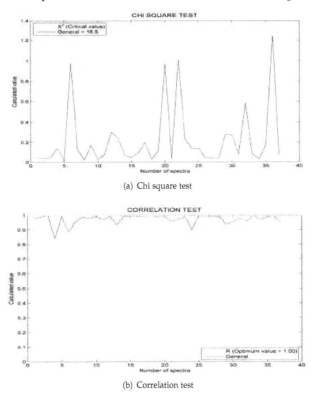

(a) Chi square test

(b) Correlation test

Figure 15. Subfigure with four images

From figure 15(a), can be seen that all neutron spectra pass the Chi square statistical test, which demonstrate that statistically there is not difference among the neutron spectra reconstructed by the designed ANN and the target neutron spectra. Similarly from figure 15(b), can be seen that the whole data set of neutron spectra is near of the optimum value equal to one, which demonstrate that this is an OA with high quality.

Figure 16 and 17 shown the best and worst neutron spectra unfolded at final testing stage of the designed ANN compared with the target neutron spectra, along with the correlation and chi sqare tests applied to each spectra.

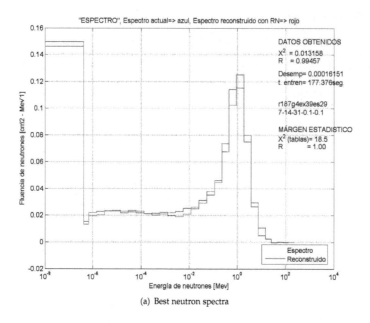

(a) Best neutron spectra

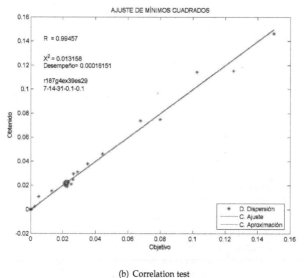

(b) Correlation test

Figure 16. RDANN: Best neutron spectra and correlation test

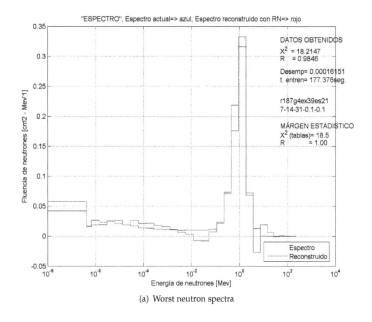

(a) Worst neutron spectra

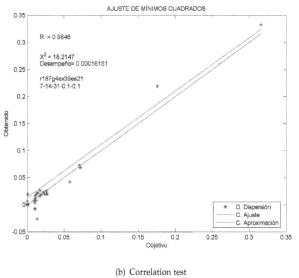

(b) Correlation test

Figure 17. RDANN: Worst neutron spectra and correlation test

In ANNs design, the use of the RDANN methodology can help provide answers to the following critical design and construction issues:

- **What is the proper density for training samples in the input space?**. The proper density for training samples in the input space was: 80% for ANN training stage and 20% for testing stage.

- **When is the best time to stop training to avoid over-fitting?**. The best time to stop training to avoid over-fitting is variable and depends of the proper selection of the ANN parameters. In the optimum ANN designed, the best time to train the network avoiding the over-fitting was 120 seconds average.

- **Which is the best architecture to use?**. The best architecture to use is 7 : 14 : 31, a learning rate = 0.1 and a momentum = 0.1, a *trainscg* training algorithm and an mse = $1E^{-4}$.

- **Is it better to use a large architecture and stop training optimally or to use an optimum architecture, which probably will not over-fit the data, but may require more time to train?**. It is better to use an optimum architecture, designed with the RDANN methodology, which not overfit the data and do not require more training time instead of using a large architecture stopping the training over the time or trials which produce a poor ANN.

- **If noise is present in the training data, is best to reduce the amount of noise or gather additional data?, and what is the effect of noise in the testing data on the performance of the network?**. In the random weight initialization is introduced a great amount of noise in training data. Such initialization introduces large negative numbers which is very harmful for the neutron spectra unfolded. The effect of noise in the random weight initialization in the testing data, affects significantly the performance of the network. In this case, the noise produced results negatives in the unfolded neutrons, which has not physics meaning. In consequence, can be concluded that it is necessary to reduce the noise introduced in the random weight initialization.

4. Conclusions

ANNs is a theory that still is in development process; its true potentiality has not still been reached; although researchers have developed potent learning algorithms of great practical value, representations and procedures that the brain is served, are even unknown. The integration of ANN and optimization provides a tool for designing neural network parameters and improving the network performance. In this work, a systematic, methodological and experimental approach called RDANN methdology was introduced to obtain the optimum design of artificial neural networks. The Taguchi method is the main technique used to simplify the optimization problem.

RDANN methdology was applied with success in nuclear sciences to solve the neutron spectra unfolding problem. The factors that are found to be significant in the case study were number of hidden neurons in hidden layer 1 and 2, learning rate and momentum term. The near optimum ANN topology was: 7:14:31 whit a momentum = 0.1 and a learning rate = 0.1, mse = $1E^{-4}$ and a *"trainscg"* learning function. The optimal net architecture was designed in short time and has high performance and generalization capability.

The proposed systematic and experimental approach is a useful alternative for the robust design of ANNs. It offers a convenient way of simultaneously considering design and noise variables, and incorporates the concept of robustness in the ANN design process. The computer program developed to implement the experimental and confirmation stages of the RDANN methodology, reduces significantly the time required to prepare, to process and to present the information in an appropriate way to de designer, and in the search of the optimal net topology being designed. This gives to the researcher time to solve the problem in which he is interested.

The results show that RDANN methodolgy can be used to find better setting of ANNs, which not only results in minimum error, but also significantly reduces training time and effort in the modeling phases.

The optimum setting of ANNS parameters are largely problem-dependent. Ideally and optimization process should be performed for each ANNs application, as the significant factors might be different for ANNs trained for different purpose.

When compared with the trial-and-error approach, which can spent from several days to months to prove different ANN architectures and parameters which may lead to a poor overall ANN design, RDANN methodology reduces significantly the time spent in determining the optimum ANN architecture. With RDANN it takes from minutes to a couple of hours to determine the best and robust ANN architectural and learning parameters allowing to researches more time to solve the problem in question.

Acknowledgements

This work was partially supported by Fondos Mixtos CONACYT - Gobierno del Estado de Zacatecas (México) under contract ZAC-2011-C01-168387.

This work was partially supported by PROMEP under contract PROMEP/103.5/12/3603.

Author details

José Manuel Ortiz-Rodríguez[1,*],
Ma. del Rosario Martínez-Blanco[2],
José Manuel Cervantes Viramontes[1] and
Héctor René Vega-Carrillo[2]

* Address all correspondence to: morvymm@yahoo.com.mx

Universidad Autónoma de Zacatecas, Unidades Académicas, 1-Ingeniería Eléctrica, 2-Estudios Nucleares, México

5. References

[1] C.R. Alavala. *Fuzzy logic and neural networks basic concepts & applications*. New Age International Publishers, 1996.

[2] J. Lakhmi and A. M. Fanelli. *Recent advances in artificial neural networks design and applications*. CRC Press, 2000.

[3] R. Correa and I. Requena. Aplicaciones de redes neuronales artificiales en la ingeniería nuclear. *XII congreso Español sobre Tecnologías y Lógica Fuzzy*, 1:485–490, 2004.

[4] G. Dreyfus. *Neural networks, methodology and applications*. Springer, 2005.

[5] B. Apolloni, S. Bassis, and M. Marinaro. *New directions in neural networks*. IOS Press, 2009.

[6] J. Zupan. Introduction to artificial neural network methods: what they are and how to use them. *Acta Chimica Slovenica*, 41(3):327–352, month 1994.

[7] A. K. Jain, J. Mao, and K. M. Mohiuddin. Artificial neural networks: a tutorial. *IEEE: Computer*, 29(3):31–44, month 1996.

[8] T. Y. Lin and C. H. Tseng. Optimum design for artifcial neural networks: an example in a bicycle derailleur system", journal = "engineering applications of artificial inteligence. 13:3–14, 2000.

[9] M.M. Gupta, L. Jin, and N. Homma. *Static and dynamic neural networks: from fundamentals to advanced theory*. 2003.

[10] D. Graupe. *Principles of artificial neural networks*. World Scientific, 2007.

[11] M. Kishan, K. Chilukuri, and R. Sanjay. *Elements of artificial neural networks*. The MIT Press, 2000.

[12] L. Fausett. *Fundamentals of neural networks, architectures, algorithms and applications*. Prentice Hall, 1993.

[13] A.I. Galushkin. *Neural networks theory*. Springer, 2007.

[14] J.A. Frenie and A. Jiju. Teaching the taguchi method to industrial engineers. *MCB University Press*, 50(4):141–149, 2001.

[15] S. C. Tam, W. L. Chen, Y. H. Chen, and H. Y. Zheng. Application of taguchi method in the optimization of laser micro-engraving of photomasks. *International Journal of Materials & Product Technology*, 11(3-4):333–344, 1996.

[16] G. E. Peterson, D. C. St. Clair, S. R. Aylward, and W. E. Bond. Using taguchi's method of experimental design to control errors in layered perceptrons. *IEEE Transactions on Neural Networks*, 6(4):949–961, month 1995.

[17] Y.K. Singh. *Fundamentl of research methodology and statistics*. New Age International Publishers, 2006.

[18] M.N. Shyam. Robust design. Technical report, 2002.

[19] T.T. Soong. *Fundamentals of probability and statistics for engineers*. John Wiley & Sons, Inc., 2004.

[20] M. S. Packianather, P. R. Drake, and Rowlands H. Optimizing the parameters of multilayered feedforward neural networks through taguchi design of experiments. *Quality and Reliability Engineering International*, 16:461–473, month 2000.

[21] M. S. Packianather and P. R. Drake. Modelling neural network performance through response surface methodology for classifying wood veneer defects. *Proceedings of the Institution of Mechanical Engineers, Part B*, 218(4):459–466, month 2004.

[22] M.A. Arbib. *Brain theory and neural networks*. The Mit Press, 2003.

[23] M. H. Beale, M. T Hagan, and H. B. Demuth. *Neural networks toolbox, user's guide*. Mathworks, 1992. www.mathworks.com/help/pdf_doc/nnet/nnet.pdf.

[24] N. K. Kasabov. *Foundations of neural networs, fuzzy systems, and knowledge engineering*. MIT Press, 1998.

[25] M.R. Kardan, R. Koohi-Fayegh, S. Setayeshi, and M. Ghiassi-Nejad. Neutron spectra unfolding in Bonner spheres spectrometry using neural networks. *Radiation Protection Dosimetry*, 104(1):27–30, 2004.

[26] H. R. Vega-Carrillo, V. M. Hernández-Dávila, E. Manzanares-Acuña, G. A. Mercado Sánchez, E. Gallego, A. Lorente, W. A. Perales-Muñoz, and J. A. Robles-Rodríguez. Artificial neural networks in neutron dosimetry. *Radiation Protection Dosimetry*, 118(3):251–259, month 2005.

[27] H. R. Vega-Carrillo, V. M. Hernández-Dávila, E. Manzanares-Acuña, G. A. Mercado-Sánchez, M. P. Iñiguez de la Torre, R. Barquero, S. Preciado-Flores, R. Méndez-Villafañe, T. Arteaga-Arteaga, and J. M. Ortiz-Rodríguez. Neutron spectrometry using artificial neural networks. *Radiation Measurements*, 41:425–431, month 2006.

[28] H. R. Vega-Carrillo, M. R. Martínez-Blanco, V. M. Hernández-Dávila, and J. M. Ortiz-Rodríguez. Ann in spectroscopy and neutron dosimetry. *Journal of Radioanalytical and Nuclear Chemistry*, 281(3):615–618, month 2009a.

[29] H.R. Vega-Carrillo, J.M. Ortiz-Rodríguez, M.R. Martínez-Blanco, and V.M. Hernández-Dávila. Ann in spectrometry and neutron dosimetry. *American Institute of Physics Proccedings*, 1310:12–17, 2010.

[30] H. R. Vega-Carrillo, J. M. Ortiz-Rodríguez, V. M. Hernández-Dávila, M .R. Martínez-Blanco, B. Hernández-Almaraz, A. Ortiz-Hernández, and G. A. Mercado. Different spectra with the same neutron source. *Revista Mexicana de Física S*, 56(1):35–39, month 2009b.

[31] H.R. Vega-Carrillo, M.R. Martínez-Blanco, V.M. Hernández-Dávila, and J.M. Ortiz-Rodríguez. Spectra and dose with ANN of 252Cf, 241Am-Be, and 239Pu-Be. *Journal of Radioanalytical and Nuclear Chemistry*, 281(3):615–618, 2009.

[32] R.R. Roy and B.P. Nigam. *Nuclear physics, theory and experiment*. John Wiley & Sons, Inc., 1967.

[33] R.N. Cahn and G. Goldhaber. *The experimental fundations of particle physics.* Cambridge University Press, 2009.

[34] R.L. Murray. *Nuclear energy, an introduction to the concepts, systems, and applications of nuclear processes.* World Scientific, 2000.

[35] D. J. Thomas. Neutron spectrometry for radiation protection. *Radiation Protection Dosimetry*, 110(1-4):141–149, month 2004.

[36] B.R.L. Siebert, J.C. McDonald, and W.G. Alberts. Neutron spectrometry for radiation protection purposes. *Nuclear Instruments and Methods in Physics Research A*, 476(1-2):347–352, 2002.

[37] P. Reuss. *Neutron physics.* EDP Sciences, 2008.

[38] F. D. Brooks and H. Klein. Neutron spectrometry, historical review and present status. *Nuclear Instruments and Methods in Physics Research A*, 476:1–11, month 2002.

[39] M. Reginatto. What can we learn about the spectrum of high-energy stray neutorn fields from bonner sphere measurements. *Radiation Measurements*, 44:692–699, 2009.

[40] M. Awschalom and R.S. Sanna. Applications of bonner sphere detectors in neutron field dosimetry. *Radiation Protection Dosimetry*, 10(1-4):89–101, 1985.

[41] V. Vylet. Response matrix of an extended bonner sphere system. *Nuclear Instruments and Methods in Physics Research A*, 476:26–30, month 2002.

[42] V. Lacoste, V. Gressier, J. L. Pochat, F. Fernández, M. Bakali, and T. Bouassoule. Characterization of bonner sphere systems at monoenergetic and thermal neutron fields. *Radiation Protection Dosimetry*, 110(1-4):529–532, month 2004.

[43] M. Matzke. Unfolding procedures. *Radiation Protection Dosimetry*, 107(1-3):155–174, month 2003.

[44] M. El Messaoudi, A. Chouak, M. Lferde, and R. Cherkaoui. Performance of three different unfolding procedures connected to bonner sphere data. *Radiation Protection Dosimetry*, 108(3):247–253, month 2004.

[45] R.B. Murray. Use of 6LiI(Eu) as a scintillation detector and spectrometer for fast neutrons. *Nuclear Instruments*, 2:237–248, 1957.

[46] V. Lacoste, M. Reginatto, B. Asselineau, and H. Muller. Bonner sphere neutron spectrometry at nuclear workplaces in the framework of the evidos project. *Radiation Protection Dosimetry*, 125(1-4):304–308, month 2007.

[47] H. Mazrou, T. Sidahmed, Z. Idiri, Z. Lounis-Mokrani, , Z. Bedek, and M. Allab. Characterization of the crna bonner sphere spectrometer based on 6lii scintillator exposed to an 241ambe neutron source. *Radiation Measurements*, 43:1095–1099, month 2008.

[48] H. R. Vega-Carrillo, V. M. Hernández-Dávila, E. Manzanares-Acuña, E. Gallego, A. Lorente, and M. P. Iñiguez. Artificial neural networks technology for neutron spectrometry and dosimetry. *Radiation Protection Dosimetry*, 126(1-4):408–412, month 2007b.

[49] IAEA. Compendium of neutron spectra and detector responses for radiation protection purposes. Technical Report 403, 2001.

[50] M. P. Iñiguez de la Torre and H. R. Vega Carrillo. Catalogue to select the initial guess spectrum during unfolding. *Nuclear Instruments and Methods in Physics Research A*, 476(1):270–273, month 2002.

Chapter 3

Weight Changes for Learning Mechanisms in Two-Term Back-Propagation Network

Siti Mariyam Shamsuddin,
Ashraf Osman Ibrahim and Citra Ramadhena

Additional information is available at the end of the chapter

1. Introduction

The assignment of value to the weight commonly brings the major impact towards the learning behaviour of the network. If the algorithm successfully computes the correct value of the weight, it can converge faster to the solution; otherwise, the convergence might be slower or it might cause divergence. To prevent this problem occurring, the step of gradient descent is controlled by a parameter called the learning rate. This parameter will determine the length of step taken by the gradient to move along the error surface. Moreover, to avoid the oscillation problem that might happen around the steep valley, the fraction of last weight update is added to the current weight update and the magnitude is adjusted by a parameter called momentum. The inclusion of these parameters aims to produce a correct value of weight update which later will be used to update the new weight. The correct value of weight update can be seen in two aspects: sign and magnitude. If both aspects are properly chosen and assigned to the weight, the learning process can be optimized and the solution is not hard to reach. Owing to the usefulness of two-termBP and the adaptive learning method in learning the network, this study is proposing the weights sign changes with respect to gradient descent in BP networks, with and without the adaptive learning method.

2. Related work

Gradient descent technique is expected to bring the network closer to the minimum error without taking for granted the convergence rate of the network. It is meant to generate the slope that moves downwardsalong the error surface to search for the minimum point. During its movement, the points passed by the slope throughout the iterations affect the magnitude of the value of weight update and its direction. Later, the updated weight is used for training the network at each epoch until the predefined iteration is achieved or the minimum error has been reached. Despite the general success of BP in learning, several major deficiencies still need to be solved. The most notable deficiencies, according to reference [1], are the existence of temporary local minima due to the saturation behaviour of activation function. The slow rates of convergence are due to the existence of local minima and the convergence rate is relatively slow for a network with more than one hidden layer. These drawbacks are also acknowledged by several scholars [2-5].

Error function plays a vital role in the learning process of two-termBP algorithm. A side from calculating the actual error from the training, it assists the algorithm in reaching the minimum point where the solution converges by calculating its gradient and back propagation to the network for weight adjustment and error minimization. Hence, the problem of being trapped in local minima can be avoided and the desired solution can be achieved.

The movement of the gradient on the error surface may vary in term of its direction and magnitude. The sign of the gradient indicates the direction it moves and the magnitude of the gradient indicates the step size taken by the gradient to move on the error surface. This temporal behaviour of the gradient provides insight about conditions on the error surface. This information will then be used to perform a proper adjustment of the weight, which is carried out by implementing a weight adjustment method. Once the weight is properly adjusted, the learning process takes only a short time to converge to the solution. Hence, the problem faced by two-termBP is solved. The term "proper adjustment of weight" here refers to the proper assignment of magnitude and sign to the weight, since both of these factors affect the internal learning process of the network.

Aside from the gradient, there are some factors that play an important role in the assignment of proper change to the weight specifically in term of its sign. These factors are the learning parameters such as learning rate and momentum. Literally, learning rate and momentum parameters hold an important role in the two-term BP training process. Respectively, they control the step size taken by the gradient along the error surface and speed up the learning process. In a conventional BP algorithm, the initial value of both parameters is very critical since it will be retained throughout all the learning iterations. The assignment of fixed value to both parameters is not always a good idea,bearing in mind that the error surface is not always flat or never flat. Thus, the step size taken by the gradient cannot be similar over time. It needs to take into account the characteristics of the error surface and the direction of movement. This is a very important condition to be taken into consideration to generate the proper value and direction of the weight. If this can be achieved, the network can reach the minimum in a shorter time and the desired output is obtained.

Setting a larger value for the learning rate may assist the network to converge faster. However, owing to the larger step taken by the gradient, the oscillation problem may occur and cause divergence or in some cases, we might overshoot the minimum. On the other hand, if the smaller value is assigned to the learning rate, the gradient will move in the correct direction and gradually reach the minimum point. However, the convergence rate is compromised owing to the smaller steps taken by the gradient. On the other hand, the momentum is used to overcome the oscillation problem. It pushes the gradient to move up the steep valley in order to escape the oscillation problem, otherwise the gradient will bounce from one side of the surface to another. Under this condition, the direction of gradient changes rapidly and may cause divergence. As a result, the computed weight update value and direction will be incorrect, which affects the learning process. It is obviously seen that the use of a fixed parameter value is not efficient. The obvious way to solve this problem is to implement an adaptive learning method to produce the dynamic value of learning parameters.

In addition, the fact that the two-term BP algorithm uses the uniform value of learning rate may lead to the problem of overshooting minima and slow movement on the shallow surface. This phenomenon may cause the algorithm to diverge or converge very slowly to the solution owing to the different step size taken by each slope to move in a different direction. In [6] has proposed a solution to these matters, called the Delta-Bar-Delta (DBD) algorithm. The method proposed by the author focuses on the setting of a learning rate value for each weight connection. Thus, each connection will have its own learning rate. However, this method still suffers from certain drawbacks. The first drawback is that the method is not efficient to be used together with the momentum since sometimes it causes divergence. The second drawback is the assignment of the increment parameter which causesa drastic increment on the learning rate so that the exponential decrement does not bring a significant impact to overcome a wild jump. For these reasons, [7] proposed an improved DBD algorithm called the Extended Delta-Bar-Delta (EDBD) algorithm. EDBD implements a similar notion of DBD and adds some modifications to it to alleviate the drawbacks faced by DBD, and demonstrates a satisfactory learning performance. Unlike DBD, EDBD provides a way to adjust both learning rate and momentum for individual weight connection, and its learning performance is thus superior to DBD. EDBD is one of many adaptive learning methods proposed to improve the performance of standard BP. The author has proven that the EDBD algorithm outperforms the DBD algorithm. The satisfactory performance tells us that the algorithm performssuccessfully and well in generating proper weight with the inclusion of momentum.

[8] has proposed the batch gradient descent method momentum, by combining the momentum with the batch gradient descent algorithm. Any sample in the network cannot have an immediate effect, however; it has to wait until all the input samples are in attendance. If that happens, then we accumulate the sum of all errors, and finally focus on the right to modify the weights to enhance the convergence rate accordingto the totalerror. The advantages of this method are faster speed, fewer iterations and smoother convergence. On the other hand, [9] has presented a new learning algorithm for a feed-forward neural network based on the two-termBP method using an adaptive learning rate. The adaptation is based on the error criteria where error is measured in the validation set instead of the training set to dynamically adjust the global learning rate. The proposed algorithm consists of two phases. In the first phase, the learning rate is adjusted after each iterationso that the minimum error is quickly attained. In the second phase, the search algorithm is refined by repeatedly reverting to previous weight configurations and decreasing the global learning rate. The experi-

mental result shows that the proposed method quickly converges and outperforms two-term BP in terms of generalization when the size of the training set is reduced. [10] has improved the convergence rates of the two-term BP model with some modifications in learning strategies. The experiment results show that the modified BP improved much better compared with standard BP.

Meanwhile, in [11] proposed a differential adaptive learning rate method for BP to speed up the learning rate. The proposed method employs the large learning rate at the beginning of training and gradually decreases the value of learning rate using differential adaptive method. The comparison made between this method and other methods, such as two-term BP, Nguyen-Widrow Weight Initialization and Optical BP shows that the proposed method outperforms the competing method in terms of learning speed.

[5] proposed a new BP algorithm with adaptive momentum for feed-forward training. Based on the information of current descent direction and last weight increment, the momentum coefficient is adjusted iteratively. Moreover, while maintaining the stability of the network, the range for the learning rate is widened after the inclusion of the adaptable momentum. The simulation results show that the proposed method is superior to the conventional BP method where fast convergence is achieved and the oscillation is smoothed.

[12] presented an improved training algorithm of BP with a self-adaptive learning rate. The function relationship between the total quadratic training error change and the connection weight and bias change is acquired based on the Taylor formula. By combining it with weight and bias change in a batch BP algorithm, the equations to calculate a self-adaptive learning rate are obtained. The learning rate will be adaptively adjusted based on the average quadratic error and the error curve gradient. Moreover, the value of the self-adaptive learning rate depends on neural network topology, training samples, average quadratic error and gradient but not artificial selection. The result of the experiment shows the effectiveness of the proposed training algorithm.

In [13] a fast BP learning method is proposed using optimization of the learning rate for pulsed neural networks (PNN). The proposed method optimized the learning rate so as to speed up learning in every learning cycle, during connection weight learning and attenuation rate learning for the purpose of accelerating BP learningina PNN.The authors devised an error BP learning method using optimization of the learning rate. The results showed that the average number of learning cycles required in all of the problems was reduced by optimization of the learning rate during connection weight learning, indicating the validity of the proposed method.

In [14], the two-term BP is improvedso that it can overcome the problems of slow learning and is easy to trap into the minimum by adopting an adaptive algorithm.The method divides the whole training process into many learning phases. The effects will indicate the direction of the network globally. Different ranges of effect values correspond to different learning models. The next learning phase will adjust the learning model based on the evaluation effects according to the previous learning phase.

We can infer from previous literature that the evolution of the improvement of BP learning for more than 30 years still points towards the openness of contribution in enhancing the BP algorithm in training and learning the network especially in terms of weight adjustments. The modification of the weight adjustment aims to update the weight with the correct value to obtain a better convergence rate and minimum error. This can be seen from various studies that significantly control the proper sign and magnitude of the weight.

3. Two-TermBack-Propagation (BP) Network

The architecture of two-term BP is deliberately built in such away that it resembles the structure of neuron. It contains several layers where each layer interacts with the upper layer connected to it by connection link. Connection link is specifically connecting the nodes with in the layers with the nodes in the adjacent layer that builds a highly inter connected network. The bottom-most layer, called the input layer, will accept and process the input and pass the output to the next adjacent layer, called the hidden layer. The general architecture of ANN is depicted in Figure1 [15].

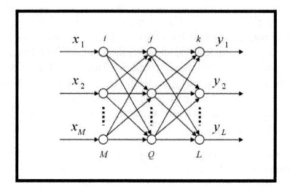

Figure 1. ANN architecture

where,

i is the input layer.

j is the hidden layer and

k is the output layer.

The input layer has M neurons and input vector $X = [\, x_1 \,,\, x_2 \,,...,\, x_M \,]$ and the output layer has L neurons and has output vector $Y=[\, y_1 \,,\, y_2 \,,...,\, y_L \,]$ while the hidden layer has Q neurons.

The output received from the input layer will be processed and computed mathematically in the hidden layer and the output will be passed to the output layer. In addition, BP can have more than one hidden layer but it creates complexity in training the network. One reason for this complexity is the existence of local minima compared with the one with one hidden layer. The learning depends greatly on the initial weight choice to lead to convergence.

Nodes in BP can be thought of a sun its that process in put to produce output. The output produced by the node is affected largely by the weight associated with each link. In this process, each input will be multiplied with weight associated with connection link connected to the node and added with bias. Weight is used to determine the strength of the output to be closer to the desired output. The greater the weight, the greater the chance of the output being closer to the desired output. The relationship between the weight, connection link and the layers can be shown in Figure 2 in reference [16].

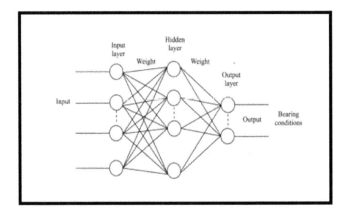

Figure 2. Connection links, weights and layers.

Once the output arrives at the hidden layer, it will be summed up to create a net.This is called linear combination. The net is fed to activation function and the output will be passed to the output layer. To ensure the learning takes place continuously, in the sense that the derivative of error function can keep moving down hillon the error surface in searching for the minimum, the activation function needs to be a continuous differentiable function. The most commonly used activation function is the sigmoid function, which limits the output between 0 and 1.

$$net_j = \sum_i W_{ij}O_i + \theta_i \tag{1}$$

$$O_j = \frac{1}{1 + e^{-net_j}} \tag{2}$$

where,

net $_j$ is the summation of the weighted input added with bias,

W_{ij} is the weight associated at the connection link between nodes in the input layer*i*and nodes in

hidden layer *j*,

O_i is the input at the nodes in input layer*i*,

θ_i is the bias associated at each connection link between input layer*i*andhidden layer*j*,

O_j is the output of activation functionat hidden layer *j*

Other activation functions that are commonly used are the logarithmic,tangent, hyperbolic tangent functions and many more.

The output generated by activation functionis forwarded to the output layer. Similar to input and hidden layers, the connection link that connects the hidden and output layers is associated with weight. Activated output received from the hidden layer is multiplied by weight. Depending on the application, the number of nodes in the output layer may vary. In a classification problem, the output layer only consists of one node to produce the result of either yes or no or abinary numbers. All the weighted outputs are added together and this value will be fed to the activation function togener ate the final output. Mean Square Error is used as an error function to calculate the error at each iteration using the target output and the final calculated output of the learning at each iteration. If the error is still larger than the predefined acceptable error value, the training process continues to the next iteration.

$$net_k = \sum_j W_{jk} O_j + \theta_k \qquad (3)$$

$$O_k = \frac{1}{1 + e^{-net_k}} \qquad (4)$$

$$E = \frac{1}{2} \sum_k \left(t_k - o_k \right)^2 \qquad (5)$$

where,

net $_k$ is the summation of weighted output at the output layer *k*,

O_j isthe output at nodes in hidden layer *j*,

W_{jk} is the weight associated to connection link between the hidden layer *j* and

the output layer *k*,

E is the error function of the network (Mean Square Error),

t_k is the target output at output layer k,

θ_k is the bias associated to each connection link between the hidden layer

j and the output layer k,

O_k is the final output at the output layer.

A large value of error obtained at the end of each iteration denotes the deviation of learning where the desired output has not been achieved. To solve this problem, the derivative of error function with respect to weight is computedand back-propagated to the layers to compute the new weight value at each connection link. This algorithm is known as the delta rule, which employs the gradient descent method. The new weight is expected to be a correct weight that can produce the correct output. For weight associated to each connection link between output layer k to hidden layer j, the weight incremental value is computed using a weight adjustment equation as follows:

$$\Delta W_{kj}(t) = -\eta \frac{\partial E}{\partial W_{kj}} + \beta \Delta W_{kj}(t-1) \tag{6}$$

where,

$\Delta W_{kj}(t)$ is the weight incremental value at tth iteration

$\eta$is the learning rate parameter

$-\frac{\partial E}{\partial W_{kj}}$ is the negative derivative of error function with respect to weight

β is the momentum parameter

$\Delta W_{kj}(t-1)$ is the previous weight incremental value at $(t-1)$th iteration

By applying the chain rule,we can simplify the negative derivative of error function with respect to weight as follows:

$$\frac{\partial E}{\partial W_{kj}} = \frac{\partial E}{\partial net_k} \bullet \frac{\partial net_k}{\partial W_{kj}} \tag{7}$$

Substituting Equation (3) into Equation (6), we get,

$$\frac{\partial E}{\partial W_{kj}} = \frac{\partial E}{\partial net_k} \bullet O_j \tag{8}$$

$$\frac{\partial E}{\partial net_k} = \delta_k \tag{9}$$

Thus, by substituting Equation (9) into Equation (8), we get,

$$\frac{\partial E}{\partial W_{kj}} = \delta_k \bullet O_j \tag{10}$$

Simplifying Equation (9) to be as follows:

$$\delta_k = \frac{\partial E}{\partial net_k} = \frac{\partial E}{\partial O_k} \bullet \frac{\partial O_k}{\partial net_k} \tag{11}$$

$$\frac{\partial O_k}{\partial net_k} = O_k(O_k - 1) \tag{12}$$

Substituting Equation (12) into Equation (11) yields,

$$\frac{\partial E}{\partial net_k} = \frac{\partial E}{\partial O_k} \bullet O_k(O_k - 1) \tag{13}$$

$$\frac{\partial E}{\partial O_k} = -(t_k - O_k) \tag{14}$$

Substituting Equation (14) in to Equation (13), we get error signal at output layer

$$\delta_k = \frac{\partial E}{\partial net_k} = -(t_k - O_k) \bullet O_k(O_k - 1) \tag{15}$$

Thus, by substituting Equation (15) into Equation (6), we get the weight adjustment equation forweight associated to each connection link between output layer k to hidden layer j with simplified negative derivative error function with respect to weight,

$$\Delta W_{kj}(t) = \eta(t_k - O_k) \bullet O_k(O_k - 1) \bullet O_j + \beta \Delta W_{kj}(t - 1) \tag{16}$$

On the other side, the error signal is back-propagated to bring impact to the weight between input layer i and hidden layer j. The error signal at hidden layer$j$can be written as follows:

$$\delta_j = \left(\sum_k \delta_k W_{kj}\right) O_j(1 - O_j) \tag{17}$$

Based on Equation(10) and the substitution of Equation(17) in to Equation(6),the weight adjustment equation for the weights associated to each connection link between input layer I and hidden layer j is as follows:

$$\Delta W_{ji}(t) = \eta\left(\sum_k \delta_k W_{kj}\right) O_j(1 - O_j) \bullet O_i + \beta \Delta W_{ji}(t - 1) \tag{18}$$

Where,

$\Delta W_{ji}(t)$ is the weight incremental value at tth iteration,

O_i is the input at nodes in input layer i.

The values obtained from Equation (16) and Equation (18) are used to update the value of weights at each connection link. Let t refer to tth iteration of training; the new weight value at $(t+1)$th iteration associated to each connection link between output layer to hidden layer j is calculated as follows:

$$W_{kj}(t+1) = \Delta W_{kj}(t) + W_{kj}(t) \qquad (19)$$

Where,

$W_{kj}(t+1)$ is the new value for weight associated to each connectionlinkbetween output layer k and hidden layer j,

$W_{kj}(t)$ is the current value of weight associated to each connection linkbetween output layer k and hidden layer j at t th iteration

Meanwhile, the new weight value at $(t-1)$th iteration for the weight associated at each connection link between hidden layer j and the input layer i can be written as follows:

$$W_{ji}(t+1) = \Delta W_{ji}(t) + W_{ji}(t) \qquad (20)$$

Where,

$W_{ji}(t+1)$ is the new value for the weight associated to each connection linkbetween hidden layer j and input layer i,

$W_{ji}(t)$ is the current value of weight associated to each connection link between hidden layer j and input layer i.

The gradient of error function is expected to move down the error surface and reach the minima point where the global minimum resides. Owing to the temporal behaviour of gradient descent and the shape of the error surface, the step taken to move down the error surface may lead to the divergence of the training. Many reasons can cause this problem but one of the misovershooting the local minima where the desired output lies. This may happen when the step taken by the gradient is large. However, a large step can lead the network to converge faster but when it moves down along the narrow and steep valley, the algorithm might go in the wrong direction and bounce from one side across to the other side.In contrast, a small step can direct the algorithm to the correct direction but the convergencerate is compromised. The learning time becomes slower since more instances of training are needed to achieve minimum error. Thus, the difficulty of this algorithm lies in controlling the step and direction of the gradient along the error surface. For this reason a parameter called the learning rate is used in weight adjustment computation. The choice of learning rate value is application-dependent and most cases are based on experiments. Once the correct learning rate is obtained, the gradient movement can produce the correct new weight value to produce the correct output.

Owing to the problem of oscillation in the narrow valley, another parameter is needed to keep the gradient moving in the correct direction so that the algorithm will not suffer from wide oscillation. This parameter is called momentum. Momentum brings the impact of previous weight change to the current weight change by which the gradient will move uphill escaping the oscillation along the valley. The incorporation of two parameters in the weight adjustment calculation produces a great impact on the convergence of the algorithm and problem of local minima if they are tuned to the correct value.

4. Weight Sign and Adaptive Methods

The previous sections have discussed the role of parameters in producing the increment value of weight through the implementation of a weight adjustment equation. As discussed before, learning rate and momentum coefficient are the most commonly used parameters in two-term BP. The use of a constant value of parameter is not always a good idea. In the case of learning rate, setting up a smaller value to learning rate may decelerate the convergence speed even though it can guarantee that the gradient will move in the correct direction. On the contrary, setting up a larger value to learning rate may fasten the convergence speed but is prone to an oscillation problem that may lead to divergence. On the other hand, the momentum parameter is introduced to stabilize the movement of gradient descentin the steepest valley by overcoming the oscillation problem. In [15] stated that assigning too small a value to the momentum factor may decelerate the convergence speed and the stability of the network is compromised, while too large a value for the momentum factor results in the algorithm giving excessive emphasis to the previous derivatives that weaken the gradient descent of BP. Hence, the author suggested the use of a dynamic adjustment method for momentum. Like the momentum parameter, the value of the learning rate also needs to be adjusted at each iteration to avoid the problem produced by having a constant value throughout all iterations.

The adaptive parameters (learning rate and momentum) used in this study are implemented to assist the network in controlling the movement of gradient descent on the error surface which primarily aims to attain the correct value of the weight.

The correct increment value of weight will be used later to update the new value of weight. This method will be implemented to two-term BP algorithmwith MSE. The adaptive method assists in generating the correct sign value for the weight, which is the primary concern of this study.

The choice of the adaptive method focuses on the learning characteristic of the algorithm used in this study, which is batch learning. In [17] gave a brief definition of online learning and the difference with batch learning. The author defined online learningas a scheme for updating weight that updates weight after every input-output case, while batch learning accumulates error signals over all input-output cases before updatingweight.In otherwords, online learningupdates weight after the presentation of each input and target data. The batch learning method reflects the true gradient descent where, asstated in reference [18], each weight update tries to minimize the error.The author also stated that the summed gradient information for the whole pattern set provides reliable information regarding the shape of the whole error function.

With the task of pointing out the temporal behaviour of gradient of error functionanditsrelationtothechangeofweightsign,theadaptivelearning method used in this study is adopted from the paper written by reference [7]entitled "Back-Propagation Heuristics: A Study of the Extended Delta-Bar-Delta Algorithm". The author proposed an improvement of the DBD algorithm proposed in reference [6], called the Extended Delta-Bar-Delta (EDBD) algorithm, where the improved method provide sa way of updating the value of momentum for each weight connection a teach iteration. Since EDBD is anextension of DBD, it implements a similar notion to DBD. It exploits the information of the sign of past and current gradients. The sign information of past and current gradients becomes the condition for learning rate and momentum adaptation. Moreover,the improved algorithm also providesace iling to prevent the value of learning rate and momentum becoming too large. The detail edequations of the method are described below:

$$\Delta w_{ji}(t) = -\eta_{ji}(t)\frac{\partial E(t)}{\partial w_{ji}} + \beta_{ji}(t)\Delta w_{ji}(t-1) \tag{21}$$

Where,

η_{ji} is the learning rate between ith input layer and jth hidden layer a t $t$thiteration

$\beta_{ji}(t)$ is the momentum between ith input layer and$j$th hidden layer at t th iteration

The updated value for learning rate and momentum can be written as follows.

$$\Delta\eta_{ji}(t) = \begin{cases} k_l\,exp\left(-y_l\left|\bar{\delta}_{ji}(t)\right|\right) & if\ \bar{\delta}_{ji}(t-1)\delta_{ji}(t)>0 \\ -\varnothing_l\,\eta_{ji}(t) & if\ \bar{\delta}_{ji}(t-1)\delta_{ji}(t)<0 \\ 0 & otherwise \end{cases} \tag{22}$$

$$\Delta\beta_{ji}(t) = \begin{cases} k_m\,exp\left(-y_m\left|\bar{\delta}_{ji}(t)\right|\right) & if\ \bar{\delta}_{ji}(t-1)\delta_{ji}(t)>0 \\ -\varnothing_m\beta_{ji}(t) & if\ \bar{\delta}_{ji}(t-1)\delta_{ji}(t)<0 \\ 0 & otherwise \end{cases} \tag{23}$$

$$\bar{\delta}_{ij}(t) = (1-\theta)\delta_{ij}(t) + \theta\bar{\delta}_{ij}(t-1) \tag{24}$$

$$\eta_{ji}(t+1) = MIN[\eta_{max}, \ \eta_{ji}(t) + \Delta\eta_{ji}(t)] \qquad (25)$$

$$\beta_{ji}(t+1) = MIN[\beta_{max}, \ \beta_{ji}(t) + \Delta\beta_{ji}(t)] \qquad (26)$$

Where,

k_l, y_l, $\varnothing_l$ are parameters for learning rate adaptive equation,

k_m, y_m, $\varnothing_m$ are parameters for momentum adaptive equation,

θ is the weighting on the exponential average of the past derivatives,

$\bar{\delta}_{ij}$ is the exponentially decaying trace of gradient values,

δ_{ij} is gradient value between i th input layer andj th hidden layer

at ^{t} th iteration,

β_{max} is the maximum value of momentum,

η_{max} is the maximum value of learning rate.

The algorithm calculates the exponential average of past derivatives to obtain information about the recent history of the direction in which the error is decreasing up to iteration t. This information together with the current gradient is used to adjust the parameters' value based on their sign. When the current and past derivatives possess the same sign, it shows that the gradient is moving in the same direction. One can assume that in this situation, the gradient is moving in the flat area at which the minimum lies ahead. In contrast, when the current and past derivatives possess an opposite sign, it shows that the gradient is moving ina different direction.

One can assume that in this situation,the gradient has jumped over the minimuma nd weight needs to be decreased to solve this.

The increment of learning rate value is made proportional to exponentially decaying trace so that the learning rate will increase significantly at a flat region and decrease at a steep slope. To prevent the unbounded increment of parameters, the maximum value for learning rate and momentum are set to act as a ceiling to both parameters.

Owing to the excellent idea and performance of the algorithmas has been proven in reference [7], this method is proposed to assist the network in producing proper weight sign change and achieving the purpose of this study.

5. Weights Performance in Terms of Sign Change and Gradient Descent

Mathematically, the adaptivemethodandtheBPalgorithm, specifically the weight adjustment method described in Equations (19) and (20) used in this study, will assist the algorithm in producing the proper weight. Basically, the adaptive methods are the transformation of the author's idea of an optimization conceptinto a mathematical concept. The measurement of the success of the method and the algorithm as a whole can be done in many ways. Some of them are carried out by analysing the convergence rate, the accuracy of the result, the error value it produces and the change of the weight sign as a response to the temporal behaviour of the gradient, etc. Hence, the role of the adaptive method that is constructed by using a mathematical concept to improve the weight adjustment computation in order to yield the proper weights will be implemented and examined in this study to check the efficiency and the learning behaviour of both algorithms. The efficiency can be drawn from the criteria of the measurement of success described earlier.

A simplicitly depicted from the algorithm, the process of generating the proper weight stems from calculating it sup date value. This process is affected by various variables start-ing from the parameters up to the controlled variable such as gradient, previous weight in-crement value and error. They all play a great part in affecting the sign of the weight produced, especially the partial derivative of error function with respectto weight (gradi-ent). In reference [15] briefly described the relationship between error curvature, gradient and weight. The author mentioned that when the error curve enters the flat region, the change of derivative and error curve are smaller and as a result, the change of the weight will not be optimized. Moreover, when it enters the high curvature region, the derivative change is large especially if the minimum point exists at this region, and the adjustment of weight value is large which sometimes overshoots the minima. This problem can be alleviat-ed by adjusting the step size of the gradient and this can be done by adjusting the learning rate. The momentum coefficient can be used to control the oscillation problem and its imple-mentation along with the proportional factor can speed up the convergence. In addition, in [15] also gave the proper condition for the rate of weight and the temporal behaviour of the gradient. The author wrote that if the derivative has the same symbol as the previous one, then the sum of the weight is in creased, which makes the weight increment value larger and yields the increment of weight rate. On the contrary, if the derivative has the opposite sign to the previous one, the sum of the weight is decreased to stabilize the network. In [19] also emphasized the causes of the slow convergence which in volve the magnitude and the direction component of the gradient vector. The author stated that when the error surface is fairly flat along the weight dimension, the magnitude of derivative of weight is small yields small adjustment value of weight and many steps are required to reduce the error. Mean-while, when the error surface is highly curved along the weight dimension, the derivative of weight is large in magnitude yields a large value of weight which may over shoot the mini-mum. The author also briefly discussed the performance of BP with momentum. The author stated that when the consecutive derivatives of a weight possess the same sign, the exponen-tially weighted sum grows large in magnitude and the weight is adjusted by a large value.

On the contrary, when the signs of the consecutive derivatives of the weight are opposite, the weighted sum is small in magnitude and the weight is adjusted by a small amount. Moreover, the author raised the implementation of local adaptive methods such as Delta-Bar-Delta which is originally proposed in reference [6]. From the descriptiongivenin [6], the

learning behaviour of the network can be justified as follows: The consecutive weight increment value that possesses the opposite sign indicates the oscillation of weight value which
requires the learning rate to be reduced. Similarly, the consecutive weight increment value
that possesses the same sign requires the incremental of the value of the learning rate. This
information will be used in studying the weight sign change of both algorithms.

6. Experimental Result and Analysis

This section discusses the result of the experiment and its analysis. The detailed discussion
of the experiment process covers its initial phase until the analysis is summarized.

The point of learning occurs when the difference between the calculate do utput and the desired output exists,otherwise there is no point of learning to take place. When the difference
does exist, the error signal is propagated back into the network to be minimized. The network will then adjust itself to compensate the lost during the training to learn better. This
procedure is carried out by calculating the gradient of error which mainly aimed to adjust
the value of the weight to be used for the next feed-forward training procedure.

By looking at the feed-forward computation in Equation (1) through Equation (5), the next
data train is fed again into the network and multiplied by the new weight value. The similar
feed-forward and backward procedures are performed until the minimum value of error is
achieved. A sa result,thetraining may take fewer or more iterations depending on the proper
adjustment of weight. There is no doubt that weight plays important role intraining. Its role
lies in determining the strength of the incoming signal (input) in the learning process.This
weighted signal will be accumulated and forwarded to the next adjacent upper layer.

Based on the influence of weight, this signal can bring a bigger or smaller influence to the
learning. When the weight is negative, the weight connection inhibits the input signal, and
thus it does not bring significant influence to the learning and output. As are sult, the other
nodes with positive weight will dominate the learning and the output. On the other hand,
when the weight is positive, the weight exhibits the input signal to bring significant impact
to the learning and the output and the respective node makes a contribution to the learning
and output. If the assignment results in large error, the corresponding weight needs to be
adjusted to reduce the error. The adjustment comprises magnitude and sign change.By
properly adjusting the weight, the algorithm can converge to the solution faster.

To have the clear idea of the impact of the weight sign in the learning,the assumption is
used: Let all value of weights be negative and using the equation written below, we obtain
the negative value of *net*.

$$net = \sum_i W_i O + \theta \qquad\qquad (27)$$

$$O = \frac{1}{1 + e^{-net}} \tag{28}$$

Feeding *net* into the sigmoid activation function Equation (28), we obtain the value of O close to 0. On the other hand, Letall value of weights be negative and using the equation below, we obtain the positive value of*net*.

Feeding *net* into the sigmoid activation function at equation (28), we obtain the value of O close to1. From the assumption above, we can infer that by adjusting the weight with the proper value and sign, the network can learn better and faster. Mathematically, the adjustment of weight is carried out by using the weight update method in and the current weight value as written below.

$$\Delta W(t) = \eta(t) \nabla E(W(t)) + \beta(t) \Delta W(t - 1) \tag{29}$$

$$W(t + 1) = \Delta W(t) + W(t) \tag{30}$$

It can be seen from Equation (29) and (30) that the rear evarious factors which influence the calculation of the weight update value. The most notable factor is gradient descent. Each gradient with respect to each weight in the network will be calculated and the weight update value is computed to update the corresponding weight. The negative sign is assigned to a gradient to force it to move downhill along the error surface in the weight space. This is meant to find the minimum point of the error surface where the set of optimal weight resides. With this optimal value, the goal of learning can be achieved. Another factor is the previous weight update value.

According to reference [20], the role of the previous weight update value in the weight is to bring in the fraction of the previous weight update value into the current weight to smooth out the new weight value.

To have a significant impact on the weight update value, the magnitude of gradient and the previous weight update value are controlled by learning parameters such as learning rate and momentum. As in two-termBP, the values of learning rate and parameters are acquired through experiments.The correct tuning of learning a parameter's value can assist in obtaining the correct value and sign of weight update. Afterwards, it effects the calculation of the new value of weight by using the weight adjustment method in Equation (30).

In experiments,a few authors have observed that the temporal behaviour of the gradient does make a contribution to the learning. This temporal behaviour can be seen as the changing of the gradient's sign during its movement on the error surface. Owing to the curvature on the error surface, the gradient behaves differently under certain conditions. In [6] stated that when the gradient possesses the same sign in several consecutive iterations, it indicates that the minimum lies ahead but when the gradient changes its sign in several consecutive iterations, it indicates that the minimum has been passed. By using this information, we can improve our wayto update the weight.

To sum up, based on the heuristic that has been discussed, the value of weight should be increased when the several consecutive signs of gradient remain the same and decreased if the opposite condition occurs. However, that is not the sole determination of the sign. Other factors such as LR,gradient, momentum, previous weight value and current weight value also play a greater role in affecting the weight changing sign and magnitude. The heuristic given previously is merelyan indicator and information about gradient movement on the surface and the surface itself by which we get a better understanding about the gradient and the error surface so that we can arrive at the enhancement on gradient movement in the weight space.

Through a thorough study on the weight change sign processon both algorithms, it can be concluded that the information about the sign of past and current gradient is very helpful in guiding us to improve the training performance which in this case refers to the movement of gradienton the error surface. However, factors like gradient, learning rate, momentum, previous weight update value and current weight value do have greater influence on the sign and magnitude of the new value of weight. Besides that, the assignment of initial weight value also needs to be addressed further.The negative as sign one at fifth iteration. value of weight may lead the weight to remain negative on consecutive occasions when the gradient possesses a negatives ign. As a result the node will not contribute much to the learning and output. This can be observed from the weight update equation as follows.

$$\Delta W(t) = \eta(t) \nabla E(W(t)) + \beta(t) \Delta W(t-1) \tag{31}$$

At the initial training iteration,the errort end stobe large and so does the gradient. This large value of gradient together with its sign will dominate the weight update calculation and thus will bring a large change to the sign and magnitude of the weight. The influence of the gradient through the weight update value can be seen from Equation (31) and the weight adjustment calculation below.

$$W(t+1) = \Delta W(t) + W(t) \tag{32}$$

If the value of initial weight is smallert han the gradient, the new weight update value will be more likely affected by the gradient. As a result, the magnitude and sign of the weight will be changed according to the fraction of the gradient since at this initial iteration,the previous weight update value is set to 0 and leaves the gradient to dominate the computation of weight up date value as shown by Equation (31). The case discussed before can be viewed in this way. Assume that the random function assigns a negative value for one of the weight connections at the hidden layer. Afterperforming the feed-forward process, the difference between the output at output layer with the desired output is large. Thus, theminimization method is performed by calculating the gradient with respect to the weight at hidden layer. Since the error is large, the value of the computed gradient becomes large also. This can be seen in the equation below.

$$\delta_k = -\left(t_k - O_k\right) \bullet O_k \left(O_k - 1\right) \qquad (33)$$

$$\nabla E(W(t)) = \left(\sum_k \delta_k W_{kj}\right) O_j \left(1 - O_j\right) \qquad (34)$$

Assume that from Equation (34), the gradient at hidden layer has a large positive value and since it is at the initial state, the previous weight update value is set to 0 and according to Equation (31), it does not contribute anything to the weight update computation. As the result, the weight update value is largely influenced by the magnitude and sign of the gradient (including the contribution of the learning rate in adjusting the step size of the gradient). By performing the weight adjustment method described by Equation (32), the value of weight update which is mostly affected by gradient will dominate the change of weight magnitude and sign. However, this can be applied also to weight adjustment in the middle of training, where the gradient and error are still large and the previous weight update value is set to a certain amount.

We can see that the large value of error will affect the value of gradient where it will be assigned with a relatively large value. This value will be used to fix the weight in the network by propagating back the error signal to the network. As a result, the value and the sign of weight will be adjusted to compensate the error. Another notice able conclusion attained from the experiment is that when for consecutive iterations the gradient retains the same signs,the weight value over the iterations is in creased while when the gradient changes its signs for several consecutive iterations, the weight value is decreased. However,the change of weight sign and magnitude is still affected by the parameters and factors included in Equation (33) and (34) as explained before.

The following examples show the change of weight affected by the sign of gradient at consecutive iterations and its value.The change of the weight is represented by a Hinton diagram. The following Hinton diagram is the representation of the weights in standard BP with adaptive learning network on a balloon dataset.

The Hinton diagram in Figure 3 illustrates the sign and magnitude of all weights connection between hidden and input layer as well as hidden and output layer at first iteration where the light colour indicates the positive sign of weight and the dark colour indicates the negative sign of weight.The size of the rectangle indicates the magnitude of the weight. The fifth rectangles in Figure 3 are the bias connection between the input layer to the hidden layer; however, the bias connection to the first hidden layer carries a small value so that its representation is not clearly shown in the diagram and its sign is negative. The biases have the value of 1. The resulting error at the first iteration is still large, which is 0.1243.

The error decreases gradually from the first iteration until the fifth iteration. The changes on the gradient are shown in the table below.

Designs and Applied Principles of Artificial Neural Networks

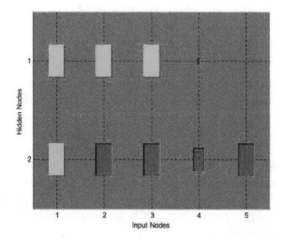

Figure 3. Hinton diagram of all weights connection between input layer and hidden layer at first iteration on Balloon dataset

		Input node 1	Input node 2	Input node 3	Input node 4	Bias
Iteration 1	Hidden node1	0.004	0.0029	0.0019	0.004	0.0029
	Hidden node2	-0.007	-0.005	-0.0033	-0.0068	-0.005
Iteration 2	Hidden node1	0.0038	0.0027	0.0017	0.0039	0.0025
	Hidden node2	-0.0063	-0.0044	-0.0028	-0.0062	-0.0042
Iteration 3	Hidden node1	0.0037	0.0025	0.0015	0.0039	0.0022
	Hidden node2	-0.0053	-0.0037	-0.0022	-0.0055	-0.0032
Iteration 4	Hidden node1	0.0035	0.0023	0.0012	0.0038	0.0016
	Hidden node2	-0.0043	-0.0029	-0.0016	-0.0046	-0.0021
Iteration 5	Hidden node1	0.0031	0.0019	0.0009	0.0036	0.0009
	Hidden node2	-0.0032	-0.0021	-0.0009	-0.0037	-0.001

Table 1. The gradient value between input layer and hidden layer at iterations 1 to 5.

		Hidden node 1	Hidden node 2	Bias
Iteration 1	Output node	0.0185	0.0171	0.0321
Iteration 2	Output node	0.0165	0.0147	0.0279
Iteration 3	Output node	0.0135	0.0117	0.0222
Iteration 4	Output node	0.0097	0.008	0.0151
Iteration 5	Output node	0.0058	0.0042	0.0078

Table 2. The gradient value between hidden layer and output layer at iterations 1 to 5.

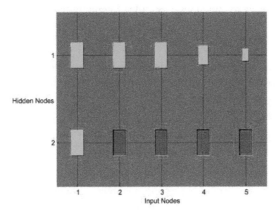

Figure 4. Hinton diagram of weightconnections between inputlayer and hidden layer at fifth iteration.

From the table above we can infer that the gradient in the hidden layer moves in a different direction while the one in the output layer moves in the same direction. Based on the heuristic,when each gradient moves in the same iteration for these consecutive iterations, the value of weight needs to be increased. However, it still depends on the factors that have been mentioned before. The impact on weight is given in the diagram below.

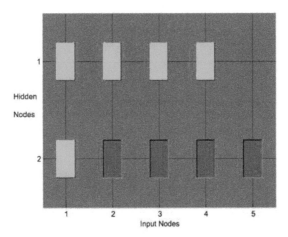

Figure 5. Hinton diagramof weight connections between inputlayer and hidden layer at 12th iteration.

Comparing the value of the weight in the fifth iteration with the first iteration, we can infer that most of the magnitude of weight on the connection between input and hidden layers in the fifth iteration becomes greater compared with that inthe first iteration. This shows that the value of weight is increased over iterations according to the sign of gradient that is similar over several iterations. However, it is noticeable that the sign of the weight between input node 4 and the first hidden node as well as bias at input layer to first hidden node changes. This is due to the influence of the result of the multiplication of large positive gradient and LR which dominates the weight update calculation, and hence increases its magnitude and switches the weight direction. As a result, the error decreases to 0.1158 from 0.1243.

Atiterations 12 and 16 the error gradient moves slowly along the shallow slope in the same direction and brings smaller changes in gradient, weight and of course error itself. The change in the gradient is shown in the table below.

It can be seen from the sign of the gradient that it differs from the one at iterations 1-5, which means that the gradient at bias connection moves in a different direction. The same thing happens with the gradient at the third node of input layer to all hidden nodes where the sign changes from the one at fifth iteration. Another change occurs at the gradient in second input node to the first hidden node at iteration 16.

		Input node 1	Input node 2	Input node 3	Input node 4	Bias
Iteration 12	Hidden node1	0.0017	0.0007	-0.0003	0.0026	-0.0013
	Hidden node2	-0.0017	-0.001	0.0001	-0.0025	0.0006
Iteration 13	Hidden node1	0.0014	0.0005	-0.0006	0.0024	-0.0017
	Hidden node2	-0.0016	-0.001	0.0003	-0.0025	0.0009
Iteration 14	Hidden node1	0.0011	0.0003	-0.0009	0.0022	-0.0021
	Hidden node2	-0.0015	-0.0009	0.0005	-0.0025	0.0013
Iteration 15	Hidden node1	0.0008	0.0001	-0.0012	0.0021	-0.0028
	Hidden node2	-0.0012	-0.0008	0.0009	-0.0025	0.0018
Iteration 16	Hidden node1	0.0005	-0.0001	-0.0016	0.0019	-0.0035
	Hidden node2	-0.001	-0.0007	0.0013	-0.0025	0.0025

Table 3. The gradient value between input and hidden layer at iterations 12 to 16.

Owing to the change of gradient sign that has been discussed before, the change on weight at this iteration is clearly seen in its magnitude. The weights are large in magnitude compared with the one at fifth iteration since some of the gradients have moved in the same direction. The bias connection to the first hidden node is not clearly seen since its value is very small. However,its value is negative. For some of the weights, the changes in sign of the gradient have less effect on the new weight value since its value is very small. Thus, the sign of the weights remains the same. Moreover, although the gradient sign of the third input node and the first hidden node changes, the weight sign remains the same since the positive weight updateat the previous iteration and the changes of gradient are very small. Thus, it has a smaller impact on the change of weight although the weight update value is negative or decreasing. At this iteration, the error decreases to 0.1116.

Besides the magnitude change, the obvious change is seen in the sign of weight of the first input node to the second hidden node. It is positive at the previous iteration, but now it turns to negative.

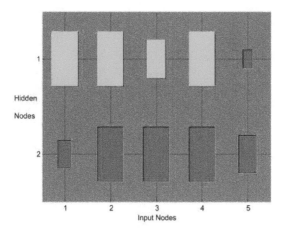

Figure 6. Hinton diagram of weight connections between input layer and hidden layer at 14th iteration.

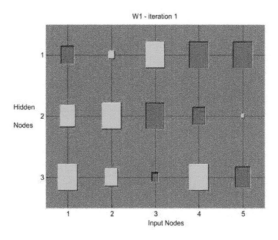

Figure 7. Hinton diagram of weight connections between input layer and hidden layer at 1st iteration.

From the experiment, the magnitude of this weight decreases gradually in small numbers over several iterations. This is due to the negative value of gradient at the first iteration.

Since its initial value is quite big, thus, the decrement does not have a significant effect on the sign. Moreover, since its value is getting smaller after several iterations, the impact of the negative gradient can be seen in the change of the weight sign. The error at this iteration decreases to 0.1089.

The next example is the Hinton diagram representing weights in standard BP with fixed parameters network on Iris dataset.

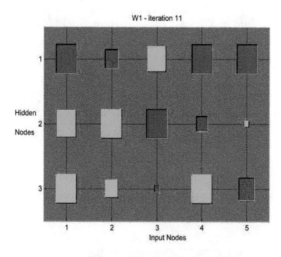

Figure 8. Hinton diagram of weight connections between input layer and hidden layer at 11th iteration.

		Input Node 1	Input Node 2	Input Node 3	Input Node 4	Bias
Iteration 1	Hidden Node 1	-0.018303748	-0.011141395	-0.008590033	-0.002383615	-0.003356197
	Hidden Node 2	0.001416033	0.000224827	0.002969737	0.001394722	2.13E-05
	Hidden Node 3	-0.001842087	-0.001514775	0.000163215	0.000251155	-0.000430432
Iteration 2	Hidden Node 1	-0.01660207	-0.010163722	-0.007711067	-0.002135194	-0.00304905
	Hidden Node 2	0.001824512	0.000525327	0.003040339	0.001392819	0.000106987
	Hidden Node 3	-0.001355907	-0.001195881	0.000330876	0.000285222	-0.000335039
Iteration 3	Hidden Node 1	-0.014965571	-0.009227058	-0.006852751	-0.001889934	-0.002755439
	Hidden Node 2	0.002207694	0.000812789	0.003095022	0.001386109	0.000188403
	Hidden Node 3	-0.000932684	-0.000914026	0.000466302	0.000309974	-0.000251081
Iteration 4	Hidden Node 1	-0.013416363	-0.008340029	-0.006036264	-0.00165541	-0.002478258
	Hidden Node 2	0.002525449	0.001063613	0.003111312	0.001367368	0.000258514
	Hidden Node 3	-0.000557761	-0.000660081	0.000576354	0.000327393	-0.000175859

Table 4. The gradient value between input and hidden layer at iterations 1-4

		Input Node 1	Input Node 2	Input Node 3	Input Node 4	Bias
Iteration 11	Hidden Node 1	-0.006205968	-0.004164878	-0.002294527	0.000583307	-0.001184916
	Hidden Node 2	0.003261605	0.001956214	0.00242412	0.000995646	0.000485827
	Hidden Node 3	0.000946822	0.00043872	0.00083246	0.000312944	0.000141871
Iteration 12	Hidden Node 1	-0.00559575	-0.003804835	-0.001989824	-0.000497406	-0.001074373
	Hidden Node 2	0.003205306	0.001986585	0.002247662	0.000920457	0.000488935
	Hidden Node 3	0.001041566	0.000519475	0.000821693	0.000299802	0.000164175
Iteration 13	Hidden Node 1	-0.005055156	-0.003484476	-0.001722643	-0.000422466	-0.000976178
	Hidden Node 2	0.003122239	0.001999895	0.002060602	0.00084271	0.000486953
	Hidden Node 3	0.001115805	0.000586532	0.000804462	0.000285504	0.000182402
Iteration 14	Hidden Node 1	-0.004575005	-0.003198699	-0.001487817	-0.000356958	-0.000888723
	Hidden Node 2	0.003016769	0.001998522	0.001865671	0.000763285	0.000480617
	Hidden Node 3	0.001172258	0.000641498	0.000782111	0.000270422	0.000197051

Table 5. The gradient value between input and hidden layer at iterations 11-14

Atiteration 11 ,the most obvious change in sign is on the weight between the second input node and the first hidden node. Based on the table of gradient, we might know that the gradient at this connection moves in the same direction through out iterations 1-4 and 11-14. However, due to the negative value of the gradient, the weight update value carries a negative sign that causes the value to decrease until its sign is negative. At this iteration, the error value decreases.

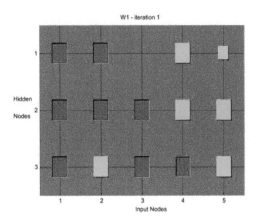

Figure 9. Hinton diagram of weight connections between input layer and hidden layer at 1st iteration.

The next example is the Hinton diagram representing weights in standard BPwith an adaptive learning parameter network on Iris dataset.

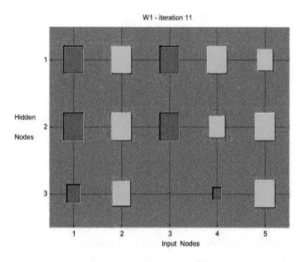

Figure 10. Hinton diagram of weight connections between input layer and hidden layer at 11th iteration.

		Input Node 1	Input Node 2	Input Node 3	Input Node 4	Bias
Iteration 1	Hidden Node 1	-0.002028133	0.001177827	-0.006110183	-0.002515178	6.16E-05
	Hidden Node 2	0.00327263	0.002733914	-0.000166769	-0.000344516	0.000749096
	Hidden Node 3	-0.004784699	-0.003919529	-0.000360459	0.000140134	-0.001022238
Iteration 2	Hidden Node 1	-0.002754283	0.000759663	-0.006493288	-0.00262835	-7.00E-05
	Hidden Node 2	0.003322116	0.002868889	-0.00034058	-0.000417257	0.000772938
	Hidden Node 3	-0.003433234	-0.003331085	0.000673172	0.000468549	-0.000802899
Iteration 3	Hidden Node 1	-0.002109624	0.001068822	-0.006027406	-0.002476693	3.47E-05
	Hidden Node 2	0.003299403	0.002898428	-0.00043867	-0.000457266	0.000775424
	Hidden Node 3	-0.002239138	-0.002627843	0.001246792	0.000621859	-0.000583171
Iteration 4	Hidden Node 1	-0.001150779	0.001525718	-0.005325608	-0.002246529	0.000189476
	Hidden Node 2	0.003268854	0.002945653	-0.000588941	-0.000519753	0.000780289
	Hidden Node 3	-0.000746758	-0.001700258	0.001868946	0.000774123	-0.000301095

Table 6. The gradient value between input and hidden layer at iterations 1-4 .

		Input Node 1	Input Node 2	Input Node 3	Input Node 4	Bias
Iteration 11	Hidden Node 1	0.001907574	0.002986261	-0.002973391	-0.001440144	0.00065675
	Hidden Node 2	0.000812331	0.002899602	-0.004647719	-0.002073105	0.000546702
	Hidden Node 3	-0.002190841	-0.000838811	-0.002332771	-0.000908119	-0.000280471
Iteration 12	Hidden Node 1	0.003681706	0.004088069	-0.002210031	-0.001245223	0.000986844
	Hidden Node 2	0.002483971	0.003929436	-0.003913207	-0.001884712	0.000855605
	Hidden Node 3	-0.002708979	-0.001126258	-0.002636196	-0.001002275	-0.000370089
Iteration 13	Hidden Node 1	0.00439905	0.004702491	-0.002255431	-0.001321819	0.001149609
	Hidden Node 2	0.002580744	0.004096122	-0.004087027	-0.00196994	0.000891341
	Hidden Node 3	-0.003069687	-0.001361618	-0.002782251	-0.001041828	-0.00043751
Iteration 14	Hidden Node 1	0.001502568	0.003228589	-0.004165255	-0.00193001	0.000663654
	Hidden Node 2	-0.000869554	0.002112189	-0.005859167	-0.002472493	0.00027103
	Hidden Node 3	-0.003177038	-0.001479172	-0.002727358	-0.001012298	-0.000466909

Table 7. The gradient value between input and hidden layer at iterations 11-12.

At the 11 th iteration, all weights change their magnitude and some have different signs from before. The weight between the second input node to the first and second hidden layers changes its sign to positive because of the positive incremental value since the gradient moves along the same direction over time. The positive incremental value gradually change the magnitude and sign of the weight from negative to positive.

7. Conclusions

This study is performed through experimental results achieved by constructing programs for both algorithms which are implemented on various datasets. The dataset comprises a small and medium dataset which will be broken down into two datasets, training and testing, with ratio percentages of 70% and 30% respectively. The result from both algorithms will be examined and studied based on its accuracy, convergence time and error. In addition, this study also studies the weight change sign with respect to the temporal behaviour of gradient to study the learning behaviour of the network and also to measure the performance of the algorithm. However, two-term BP with an adaptive algorithm works better in producing proper change of weight so that the time needed to converge is shorter compared with two-term BP without an adaptive learning method. This can be seen from the result of the convergence rate of the network. Moreover, the study on weight sign change of both algorithms shows that the gradient sign and magnitude and error have greater influence on the weight adjustment process.

Acknowledgements

Authors would like to thanks Universiti Teknologi Malaysia (UTM) for the support in Research and Development, and Soft Computing Research Group (SCRG) for the inspiration in making this study a success. This work is supported by The Ministry of Higher Education (MOHE) under Long Term Research Grant Scheme (LRGS/TD/2011/UTM/ICT/03 - VOT 4L805).

Author details

Siti Mariyam Shamsuddin*, Ashraf Osman Ibrahim and Citra Ramadhena

*Address all correspondence to: mariyam@utm.my

Soft Computing Research Group, Faculty of Computer Science and Information Systems, UniversitiTeknologi Malaysia, Malaysia

References

[1] Ng, S., Leung, S., & Luk, A. (1999). Fast convergent generalized back-propagation algorithm with constant learning rate. *Neural processing letters*, 13-23.

[2] Zweiri, Y. H., Whidborne, J. F., & Seneviratne, L. D. (2003). A three-term backpropagation algorithm. *Neurocomputing*, 305-318.

[3] Yu, C. C. B., & Liu, D. (2002). A backpropagation algorithm with adaptive learning rate and momentum coefficient. in 2002 International Joint Conference on Neural Networks (IJCNN 2002). May 12-May 17, 2002, *Honolulu, HI, United states: Institute of Electrical and Electronics Engineers Inc.*

[4] Dhar, V. K., et al. (2010). Comparative performance of some popular artificial neural network algorithms on benchmark and function approximation problems. *Pramana-Journal of Physics*, 74(2), 307-324.

[5] Hongmei, S., & Gaofeng, Z. (2009). A new BP algorithm with adaptive momentum for FNNs training. in 2009 WRI Global Congress on Intelligent Systems GCIS 2009. May 19, 2009-May 21, 2009. Xiamen, China: , *IEEE Computer Society.*

[6] Jacobs, R. A. (1988). Increased Rates of Convergence Through Learning Rate Adaptation. *Neural Networks*, 1(4), 295-307.

[7] Minai, A. A., & Williams, R. D. (1990). Back-propagation heuristics: A study of the extended Delta-Bar-Delta algorithm. in 1990 International Joint Conference on Neu-

ral Networks- IJCNN 90. June 17, 1990-June 21, 1990, *San Diego, CA, USA: Publ by IEEE*.

[8] Jin, B., et al. (2012). The application on the forecast of plant disease based on an improved BP neural network. in 2011 International Conference on Material Science and Information Technology, MSIT2011 September 16-September 18, 2011. Singapore, Singapore: Trans Tech Publications.

[9] Duffner, S., & Garcia, C. (2007). An online backpropagation algorithm with validation error-based adaptive learning rate. Artificial Neural Networks-ICANN 2007 , 249-258.

[10] Shamsuddin, S. M., Sulaiman, M. N., & Darus, M. (2001). An improved error signal for the backpropagation model for classification problems. *International Journal of Computer Mathematics*, 297-305.

[11] Iranmanesh, S., & Mahdavi, M. A. (2009). A differential adaptive learning rate method for back-propagation neural networks. World Academy of Science, Engineering and Technology , 38, 289-292.

[12] Li, Y., et al. (2009). The improved training algorithm of back propagation neural network with selfadaptive learning rate. in 2009 International Conference on Computational Intelligence and Natural Computing, CINC 2009. June 6-June 7, 2009Wuhan, China: IEEE Computer Society.

[13] Yamamoto, K., et al. (2011). Fast backpropagation learning using optimization of learning rate for pulsed neural networks. *Electronics and Communications in Japan*, 27-34.

[14] Hua, Li. C., Xiangji, J., & Huang, . (2012). Spam filtering using semantic similarity approach and adaptive BPNN. *Neurocomputing*.

[15] Xiaoyuan, L., Bin, Q., & Lu, W. (2009). A new improved BP neural network algorithm. in 2009 2nd International Conference on Intelligent Computing Technology and Automation, ICICTA 2009. October 10-October 11, 2009., *Changsha, Hunan, China: IEEE Computer Society*.

[16] Yang, H., Mathew, J., & Ma, L. (2007). Basis pursuit-based intelligent diagnosis of bearing faults. *Journal of Quality in Maintenance Engineering*, 152-162.

[17] Fukuoka, Y., et al. (1998). A modified back-propagation method to avoid false local minima. *Neural Networks*, 1059-1072.

[18] Riedmiller, M. (1994). Advanced supervised learning in multi-layer perceptrons-from backpropagation to adaptive learning algorithms. *Computer Standards and Interfaces*, 16(3), 265-278.

[19] Sidani, A., & Sidani, T. (1994). Comprehensive study of the back propagation algorithm and modifications. in Proceedings of the 1994 Southcon Conference,. March 29-March 31, 1994Orlando, FL, USA: IEEE.

[20] Samarasinghe, S. (2007). Neural networks for applied sciences and engineering: from fundamentals to complex pattern recognition. *Auerbach Publications.*

Chapter 4

Improved Kohonen Feature Map Probabilistic Associative Memory Based on Weights Distribution

Shingo Noguchi and Osana Yuko

Additional information is available at the end of the chapter

1. Introduction

Recently, neural networks are drawing much attention as a method to realize flexible information processing. Neural networks consider neuron groups of the brain in the creature, and imitate these neurons technologically. Neural networks have some features, especially one of the important features is that the networks can learn to acquire the ability of information processing.

In the field of neural network, many models have been proposed such as the Back Propagation algorithm [1], the Kohonen Feature Map (KFM) [2], the Hopfield network [3], and the Bidirectional Associative Memory [4]. In these models, the learning process and the recall process are divided, and therefore they need all information to learn in advance.

However, in the real world, it is very difficult to get all information to learn in advance, so we need the model whose learning process and recall process are not divided. As such model, Grossberg and Carpenter proposed the ART (Adaptive Resonance Theory) [5]. However, the ART is based on the local representation, and therefore it is not robust for damaged neurons in the Map Layer. While in the field of associative memories, some models have been proposed [6 - 8]. Since these models are based on the distributed representation, they have the robustness for damaged neurons. However, their storage capacities are small because their learning algorithm is based on the Hebbian learning.

On the other hand, the Kohonen Feature Map (KFM) associative memory [9] has been proposed. Although the KFM associative memory is based on the local representation as similar as the ART[5], it can learn new patterns successively [10], and its storage capacity is larger than that of models in refs.[6 - 8]. It can deal with auto and hetero associations and the associations for plural sequential patterns including common terms [11, 12]. Moreover, the KFM associative memory with area representation [13] has been proposed. In the model, the area representation [14] was introduced to the KFM associative memory, and it has robustness for damaged neurons. However, it can not deal with one-to-many associations, and associations of analog patterns. As the model which can deal with analog patterns and one-to-many associations, the Kohonen Feature Map Associative Memory with Refractoriness based on Area Representation [15] has been proposed. In the model, one-to-many associations are realized by refractoriness of neurons. Moreover, by improvement of the calculation of the internal states of the neurons in the Map Layer, it has enough robustness for damaged neurons when analog patterns are memorized. However, all these models can not realize probabilistic association for the training set including one-to-many relations.

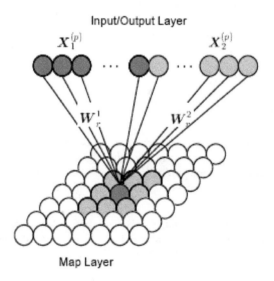

Figure 1. Structure of conventional KFMPAM-WD.

As the model which can realize probabilistic association for the training set including one-to-many relations, the Kohonen Feature Map Probabilistic Associative Memory based on Weights Distribution (KFMPAM-WD) [16] has been proposed. However, in this model, the weights are updated only in the area corresponding to the input pattern, so the learning considering the neighborhood is not carried out.

In this paper, we propose an Improved Kohonen Feature Map Probabilistic Associative Memory based on Weights Distribution (IKFMPAM-WD). This model is based on the conventional Kohonen Feature Map Probabilistic Associative Memory based on Weights Distribution [16]. The proposed model can realize probabilistic association for the training set including one-to-many relations. Moreover, this model has enough robustness for noisy input and damaged neurons. And, the learning considering the neighborhood can be realized.

2. KFM Probabilistic Associative Memory based on Weights Distribution

Here, we explain the conventional Kohonen Feature Map Probabilistic Associative Memory based on Weights Distribution (KFMPAM-WD)(16).

2.1. Structure

Figure 1 shows the structure of the conventional

KFMPAM-WD. As shown in Fig. 1, this model has two layers; (1) Input/Output Layer and (2) Map Layer, and the Input/Output Layer is divided into some parts.

2.2. Learning process

In the learning algorithm of the conventional KFMPAM-WD, the connection weights are learned as follows:

1. The initial values of weights are chosen randomly.

2. The Euclidian distance between the learning vector $X^{(p)}$ and the connection weights vector W_i, $d(X^{(p)}, W_i)$ is calculated.

3. If $d(X^{(p)}, W_i) \theta^t$ is satisfied for all neurons, the input pattern $X^{(p)}$ is regarded as an unknown pattern. If the input pattern is regarded as a known pattern, go to (8).

4. The neuron which is the center of the learning area r is determined as follows:

$$r = \underset{\substack{i : D_{iz}+D_{zi}<d_{iz} \\ (for\ \forall z \in F)}}{\operatorname{argmin}}\ d\left(X^{(p)}, W_i\right) \tag{1}$$

where F is the set of the neurons whose connection weights are fixed. d_{iz} is the distance between the neuron i and the neuron z whose connection weights are fixed. In Eq.(1), D_{ij} is the radius of the ellipse area whose center is the neuron i for the direction to the neuron j, and is given by

$$D_{ij}=\begin{cases} a_i, & (d_{ij}^y=0)\\ b_i, & (d_{ij}^x=0)\\ \sqrt{\dfrac{a_i^2 b_i^2}{b_i^2+m_{ij}^2 a_i^2}(m_{ij}^2+1)}, & (otherwise) \end{cases} \tag{2}$$

where a_i is the long radius of the ellipse area whose center is the neuron i and b_i is the short radius of the ellipse area whose center is the neuron i. In the KFMPAM-WD, a_i and b_i can be set for each training pattern. m_{ij} is the slope of the line through the neurons i and j. In Eq.(1), the neuron whose Euclidian distance between its connection weights and the learning vector is minimum in the neurons which can be take areas without overlaps to the areas corresponding to the patterns which are already trained. In Eq.(1), a_i and b_i are used as the size of the area for the learning vector.

5. If $d(X^{(p)}, W_r) > \theta^t$ is satisfied, the connection weights of the neurons in the ellipse whose center is the neuron r are updated as follows:

$$W_i(t+1) = \begin{cases} W_i(t) + \alpha(t)(X^{(p)} - W_i(t)), & (d_{ri} \leq D_{ri}) \\ W_i(t), & (\text{otherwise}) \end{cases} \qquad (3)$$

where $\alpha(t)$ is the learning rate and is given by

$$\alpha(t) = \frac{-\alpha_0(t-T)}{T}. \qquad (4)$$

Here, α_0 is the initial value of $\alpha(t)$ and T is the upper limit of the learning iterations.

6. (5) is iterated until $d(X^{(p)}, W_r) \leq \theta^t$ is satisfied.

7. The connection weights of the neuron r W_r are fixed.

8. (2)~ (7) are iterated when a new pattern set is given.

2.3. Recall process

In the recall process of the KFMPAM-WD, when the pattern X is given to the Input/Output Layer, the output of the neuron i in the Map Layer, x_i^{map} is calculated by

$$x_i^{map} = \begin{cases} 1, & (i=r) \\ 0, & (\text{otherwise}) \end{cases} \qquad (5)$$

where r is selected randomly from the neurons which satisfy

$$\frac{1}{N^{in}} \sum_{k \in C} g(X_k - W_{ik}) > \theta^{map} \qquad (6)$$

where θ^{map} is the threshold of the neuron in the Map Layer, and $g(\cdot)$ is given by

$$g(b) = \begin{cases} 1, & (|b| < \theta^d) \\ 0, & (\text{otherwise}). \end{cases} \qquad (7)$$

In the KFMPAM-WD, one of the neurons whose connection weights are similar to the input pattern are selected randomly as the winner neuron. So, the probabilistic association can be realized based on the weights distribution.

When the binary pattern X is given to the Input/Output Layer, the output of the neuron k in the Input/Output Layer x_k^{io} is given by

$$x_k^{io} = \begin{cases} 1, & (W_{rk} \geq \theta_b^{no}) \\ 0, & (\text{otherwise}) \end{cases} \tag{8}$$

where θ_b^{io} is the threshold of the neurons in the Input/Output Layer.

When the analog pattern X is given to the Input/Output Layer, the output of the neuron k in the Input/Output Layer x_k^{io} is given by

$$x_k^{io} = W_{rk} \tag{9}$$

3. Improved KFM Probabilistic Associative Memory based on Weights Distribution

Here, we explain the proposed Improved Kohonen Feature Map Probabilistic Associative Memory based on Weights Distribution (IKFMPAM-WD). The proposed model is based on the conventional Kohonen Feature Map Probabilistic Associative Memory based on Weights Distribution (KFMPAM-WD) [16] described in 2.

3.1. Structure

Figure 2 shows the structure of the proposed IKFMPAM-WD. As shown in Fig. 2, the proposed model has two layers; (1) Input/Output Layer and (2) Map Layer, and the Input/Output Layer is divided into some parts as similar as the conventional KFMPAM-WD.

3.2. Learning process

In the learning algorithm of the proposed IKFMPAM-WD, the connection weights are learned as follows:

1. The initial values of weights are chosen randomly.

2. The Euclidian distance between the learning vector $X^{(p)}$ and the connection weights vector W_i, $d(X^{(p)}, W_i)$, is calculated.

3. If $d(X^{(p)}, W_i)$ θ^t is satisfied for all neurons, the input pattern $X^{(p)}$ is regarded as an unknown pattern. If the input pattern is regarded as a known pattern, go to (8).

4. The neuron which is the center of the learning area r is determined by Eq.(1). In Eq.(1), the neuron whose Euclid distance between its connection weights and the learning vector is minimum in the neurons which can be take areas without overlaps to the areas

corresponding to the patterns which are already trained. In Eq.(1), a_i and b_i are used as the size of the area for the learning vector.

5. If $d(X^{(p)}, W_r)\,\theta^{\,t}$ is satisfied, the connection weights of the neurons in the ellipse whose center is the neuron r are updated as follows:

$$W_i(t+1)=\begin{cases}X^{(p)}, & (\theta_1^{learn}\le H(\overline{d_{ri}}))\\ W_i(t)+H(\overline{d_{ri}})(X^{(p)}-W_i(t)), & (\theta_2^{learn}\le H(\overline{d_{ri}})<\theta_1^{learn}\\ & \text{and} H(\overline{d_{i\,*_i}})<\theta_1^{learn})\\ W_i(t), & (\text{otherwise})\end{cases}\tag{10}$$

where θ_1^{learn} are thresholds. $H(\overline{d_{ri}})$ and $H(\overline{d_{i\,*_i}})$ are given by Eq.(11) and these are semi-fixed function. Especially, $H(\overline{d_{ri}})$ behaves as the neighborhood function. Here, i^* shows the nearest weight-fixed neuron from the neuron i.

$$H(\overline{d_{ij}})=\frac{1}{1+\exp\left(\dfrac{\overline{d_{ij}}-D}{\varepsilon}\right)}\tag{11}$$

where $\overline{d_{ij}}$ shows the normalized radius of the ellipse area whose center is the neuron i for the direction to the neuron j, and is given by

$$\overline{d_{ij}}=\frac{d_{ij}}{D_{ij}}.\tag{12}$$

In Eq.(11), D $(1\ D)$ is the constant to decide the neighborhood area size and is the steepness parameter. If there is no weight-fixed neuron,

$$H(\overline{d_{i\,*_i}})=0\tag{13}$$

is used.

6. (5) is iterated until $d(X^{(p)}, W_r)\le \theta^{\,t}$ is satisfied.

7. The connection weights of the neuron r W_r are fixed.

8. (2)~ (7) are iterated when a new pattern set is given.

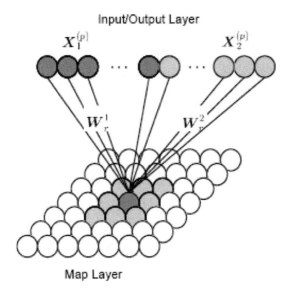

Input/Output Layer

$X_1^{(p)}$ $X_2^{(p)}$

W_r^1 W_k^2

Map Layer

Figure 2. Structure of proposed IKFMPAM-WD.

3.3. Recall process

The recall process of the proposed IKFMPAM-WD is same as that of the conventional KFMPAM-WD described in 2.3.

4. Computer experiment results

Here, we show the computer experiment results to demonstrate the effectiveness of the proposed IKFMPAM-WD.

4.1. Experimental conditions

Table 1 shows the experimental conditions used in the experiments of 4.2 ~ 4.6.

4.2. Association results

4.2.1. Binary patterns

In this experiment, the binary patterns including one-to-many relations shown in Fig. 3 were memorized in the network composed of 800 neurons in the Input/Output Layer and 400 neurons in the Map Layer. Figure 4 shows a part of the association result when "crow" was given to the Input/Output Layer. As shown in Fig. 4, when "crow" was given to the network, "mouse" (t=1), "monkey" (t=2) and "lion" (t=4) were recalled. Figure 5 shows a part of the association result when "duck" was given to the Input/Output Layer. In this case, "dog" (t=251), "cat" (t=252) and "penguin" (t=255) were recalled. From these results, we can confirmed that the proposed model can recall binary patterns including one-to-many relations.

Parameters for Learning		
Threshold for Learning	θ_t^{learn}	10^{-4}
Neighborhood Area Size	D	3
Steepness Parameter in Neighborhood Function	ε	0.91
Threshold of Neighborhood Function (1)	θ_1^{learn}	0.9
Threshold of Neighborhood Function (2)	θ_2^{learn}	0.1
Parameters for Recall (Common)		
Threshold of Neurons in Map Layer	θ^{map}	0.75
Threshold of Difference between Weight Vector and Input Vector	θ_d	0.004
Parameter for Recall (Binary)		
Threshold of Neurons in Input/Output Layer	θ_b^{in}	0.5

Table 1. Experimental Conditions.

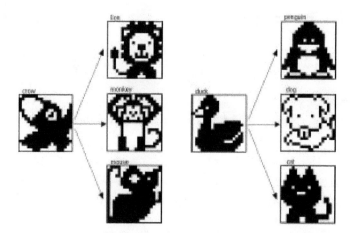

Figure 3. Training Patterns including One-to-Many Relations (Binary Pattern).

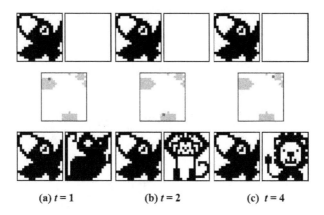

(a) $t = 1$ (b) $t = 2$ (c) $t = 4$

Figure 4. One-to-Many Associations for Binary Patterns (When "crow" was Given).

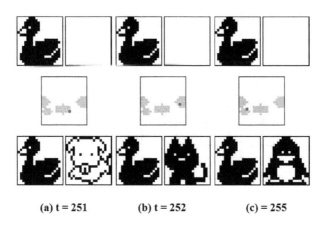

(a) t = 251   (b) t = 252   (c) = 255

Figure 5. One-to-Many Associations for Binary Patterns (When "duck" was Given).

Figure 6 shows the Map Layer after the pattern pairs shown in Fig. 3 were memorized. In Fig. 6, red neurons show the center neuron in each area, blue neurons show the neurons in areas for the patterns including "crow", green neurons show the neurons in areas for the patterns including "duck". As shown in Fig. 6, the proposed model can learn each learning pattern with various size area. Moreover, since the connection weights are updated not only in the area but also in the neighborhood area in the proposed model, areas corresponding to the pattern pairs including "crow"/"duck" are arranged in near area each other.

Learning Pattern	Long Radius a_i	Short Radius b_i
"crow"–"lion"	2.5	1.5
"crow"–"monkey"	3.5	2.0
"crow"–"mouse"	4.0	2.5
"duck"–"penguin"	2.5	1.5
"duck"–"dog"	3.5	2.0
"duck"–"cat"	4.0	2.5

Table 2. Area Size corresponding to Patterns in Fig. 3.

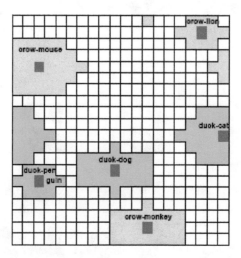

Figure 6. Area Representation for Learning Pattern in Fig. 3.

Input Pattern	Output Pattern	Area Size	Recall Times
crow	lion	11 (1.0)	43 (1.0)
	monkey	23 (2.1)	87 (2.0)
	mouse	33 (3.0)	120 (2.8)
duck	penguin	11 (1.0)	39 (1.0)
	dog	23 (2.1)	79 (2.0)
	cat	33 (3.0)	132 (3.4)

Table 3. Recall Times for Binary Pattern corresponding to "crow" and "duck".

Table 3 shows the recall times of each pattern in the trial of Fig. 4 ($t=1 \sim 250$) and Fig. 5 ($t=251 \sim 500$). In this table, normalized values are also shown in ( ). From these results, we can confirmed that the proposed model can realize probabilistic associations based on the weight distributions.

4.2.2. Analog patterns

In this experiment, the analog patterns including one-to-many relations shown in Fig. 7 were memorized in the network composed of 800 neurons in the Input/Output Layer and 400 neurons in the Map Layer. Figure 8 shows a part of the association result when "bear" was given to the Input/Output Layer. As shown in Fig. 8, when "bear" was given to the network, "lion" ($t=1$), "raccoon dog" ($t=2$) and "penguin" ($t=3$) were recalled. Figure 9 shows a part of the association result when "mouse" was given to the Input/Output Layer. In this case, "monkey" ($t=251$), "hen" ($t=252$) and "chick" ($t=253$) were recalled. From these results, we can confirmed that the proposed model can recall analog patterns including one-to-many relations.

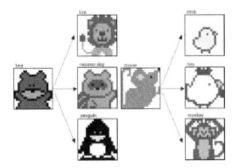

Figure 7. Training Patterns including One-to-Many Relations (Analog Pattern).

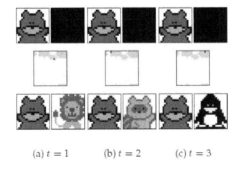

(a) $t = 1$ (b) $t = 2$ (c) $t = 3$

Figure 8: One-to-Many Associations for Analog Patterns (When "bear" was Given).

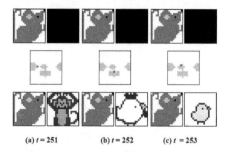

(a) $t = 251$ (b) $t = 252$ (c) $t = 253$

Figure 9. One-to-Many Associations for Analog Patterns (When "mouse" was Given).

Learning Pattern	Long Radius a_i	Short Radius b_i
"bear"–"lion"	2.5	1.5
"bear"–"raccoon dog"	3.5	2.0
"bear"–"penguin"	4.0	2.5
"mouse"–"chick"	2.5	1.5
"mouse"–"hen"	3.5	2.0
"mouse"–"monkey"	4.0	2.5

Table 4. Area Size corresponding to Patterns in Fig. 7.

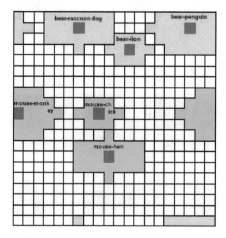

Figure 10. Area Representation for Learning Pattern in Fig. 7.

Input Pattern	Output Pattern	Area Size	Recall Times
bear	lion	11 (1.0)	40 (1.0)
	raccoon dog	23 (2.1)	90 (2.3)
	penguin	33 (3.0)	120 (3.0)
mouse	chick	11 (1.0)	38 (1.0)
	hen	23 (2.1)	94 (2.5)
	monkey	33 (3.0)	118 (3.1)

Table 5. Recall Times for Analog Pattern corresponding to "bear" and "mouse".

Figure 10 shows the Map Layer after the pattern pairs shown in Fig. 7 were memorized. In Fig. 10, red neurons show the center neuron in each area, blue neurons show the neurons in the areas for the patterns including "bear", green neurons show the neurons in the areas for the patterns including "mouse". As shown in Fig. 10, the proposed model can learn each learning pattern with various size area.

Table 5 shows the recall times of each pattern in the trial of Fig. 8 ($t=1\sim 250$) and Fig. 9 ($t=251\sim 500$). In this table, normalized values are also shown in ( ). From these results, we can confirmed that the proposed model can realize probabilistic associations based on the weight distributions.

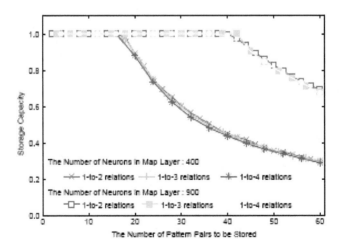

Figure 11. Storage Capacity of Proposed Model (Binary Patterns).

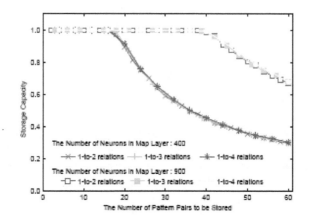

Figure 12. Storage Capacity of Proposed Model (Analog Patterns).

4.3. Storage capacity

Here, we examined the storage capacity of the proposed model. Figures 11 and 12 show the storage capacity of the proposed model. In this experiment, we used the network composed of 800 neurons in the Input/Output Layer and 400/900 neurons in the Map Layer, and 1-to-P ($P=2,3,4$) random pattern pairs were memorized as the area ($a_i=2.5$ and $b_i=1.5$). Figures 11 and 12 show the average of 100 trials, and the storage capacities of the conventional model(16) are also shown for reference in Figs. 13 and 14. From these results, we can confirm that the storage capacity of the proposed model is almost same as that of the conventional model(16). As shown in Figs. 11 and 12, the storage capacity of the proposed model does not depend on binary or analog pattern. And it does not depend on P in one-to-P relations. It depends on the number of neurons in the Map Layer.

4.4. Robustness for noisy input

4.4.1. Association result for noisy input

Figure 15 shows a part of the association result of the proposed model when the pattern "cat" with 20% noise was given during $t=1\sim 500$. Figure 16 shows a part of the association result of the propsoed model when the pattern "crow" with 20% noise was given $t=501\sim 1000$. As shown in these figures, the proposed model can recall correct patterns even when the noisy input was given.

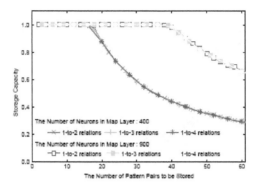

Figure 13. Storage Capacity of Conventional Model [16] (Binary Pattern

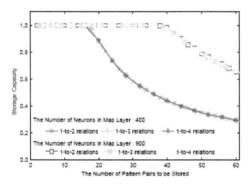

Figure 14. Storage Capacity of Conventional Model [16] (Analog Patterns).

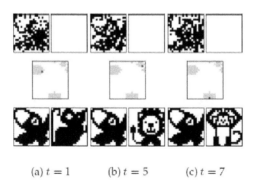

(a) $t = 1$ (b) $t = 5$ (c) $t = 7$

Figure 15. Association Result for Noisy Input (When "crow" was Given.).

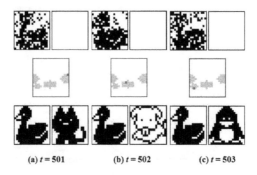

(a) $t = 501$ (b) $t = 502$ (c) $t = 503$

Figure 16. Association Result for Noisy Input (When "duck" was Given.).

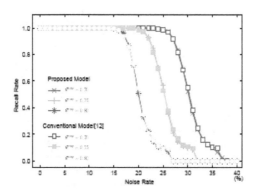

Figure 17. Robustness for Noisy Input (Binary Patterns).

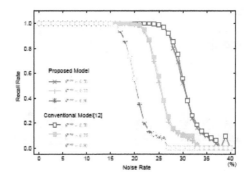

Figure 18. Robustness for Noisy Input (Analog Patterns).

4.4.2. Robustness for noisy input

Figures 17 and 18 show the robustness for noisy input of the proposed model. In this experiment, 10 random patterns in one-to-one relations were memorized in the network composed of 800 neurons in the Input/Output Layer and 900 neurons in the Map Layer. Figures 17 and 18 are the average of 100 trials. As shown in these figures, the proposed model has robustness for noisy input as similar as the conventional model(16).

4.5. Robustness for damaged neurons

4.5.1. Association result when some neurons in map layer are damaged

Figure 19 shows a part of the association result of the proposed model when the pattern "bear" was given during *t*=1~ 500. Figure 20 shows a part of the association result of the proposed model when the pattern "mouse" was given *t*=501~ 1000. In these experiments, the network whose 20% of neurons in the Map Layer are damaged were used. As shown in these figures, the proposed model can recall correct patterns even when the some neurons in the Map Layer are damaged.

4.5.2. Robustness for damaged neurons

Figures 21 and 22 show the robustness when the winner neurons are damaged in the proposed model. In this experiment, 1~ 10 random patterns in one-to-one relations were memorized in the network composed of 800 neurons in the Input/Output Layer and 900 neurons in the Map Layer. Figures 21 and 22 are the average of 100 trials. As shown in these figures, the proposed model has robustness when the winner neurons are damaged as similar as the conventional model [16].

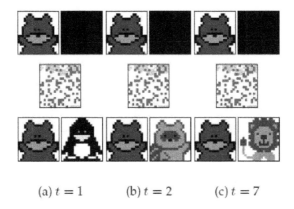

(a) $t = 1$ (b) $t = 2$ (c) $t = 7$

Figure 19. Association Result for Damaged Neurons (When "bear" was Given.).

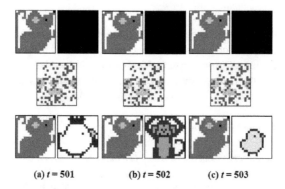

(a) $t = 501$ (b) $t = 502$ (c) $t = 503$

Figure 20. Association Result for Damaged Neurons (When "mouse" was Given.).

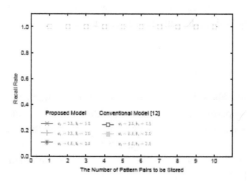

Figure 21. Robustness of Damaged Winner Neurons (Binary Patterns).

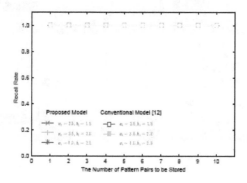

Figure 22. Robustness of Damaged Winner Neurons (Analog Patterns).

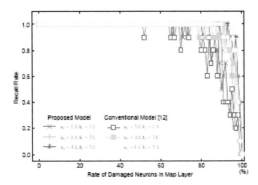

Figure 23: Robustness for Damaged Neurons (Binary Patterns).

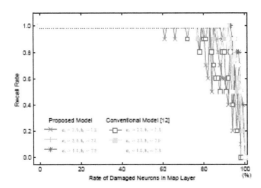

Figure 24. Robustness for Damaged Neurons (Analog Patterns).

Figures 23 and 24 show the robustness for damaged neurons in the proposed model. In this experiment, 10 random patterns in one-to-one relations were memorized in the network composed of 800 neurons in the Input/Output Layer and 900 neurons in the Map Layer. Figures 23 and 24 are the average of 100 trials. As shown in these figures, the proposed model has robustness for damaged neurons as similar as the conventional model [16].

4.6. Learning speed

Here, we examined the learning speed of the proposed model. In this experiment, 10 random patterns were memorized in the network composed of 800 neurons in the Input/Output Layer and 900 neurons in the Map Layer. Table 6 shows the learning time of the proposed model and the conventional model(16). These results are average of 100 trials on the Personal Computer (Intel Pentium 4 (3.2GHz), FreeBSD 4.11, gcc 2.95.3). As shown in Table 6, the learning time of the proposed model is shorter than that of the conventional model.

5. Conclusions

In this paper, we have proposed the Improved Kohonen Feature Map Probabilistic Associative Memory based on Weights Distribution. This model is based on the conventional Kohonen Feature Map Probabilistic Associative Memory based on Weights Distribution. The proposed model can realize probabilistic association for the training set including one-to-many relations. Moreover, this model has enough robustness for noisy input and damaged neurons. We carried out a series of computer experiments and confirmed the effectiveness of the proposed model.

		Learning Time (seconds)
Proposed Model	(Binary Patterns)	0.87
Proposed Model	(Analog Patterns)	0.92
Conventional Model(16)	(Binary Patterns)	1.01
Conventional Model(16)	(Analog Patterns)	1.34

Table 6. Learning Speed.

Author details

Shingo Noguchi and Osana Yuko*

*Address all correspondence to: osana@cs.teu.ac.jp

Tokyo University of Technology, Japan

References

[1] Rumelhart, D. E., McClelland, J. L., & the PDP Research Group. (1986). Parallel Distributed Processing, Exploitations in the Microstructure of Cognition. 11, Foundations, The MIT Press.

[2] Kohonen, T. (1994). Self-Organizing Maps. Springer.

[3] Hopfield, J. J. (1982). Neural networks and physical systems with emergent collective computational abilities. *Proceedings of National Academy Sciences USA*, 79, 2554-2558.

[4] Kosko, B. (1988). Bidirectional associative memories. *IEEE Transactions on Neural Networks*, 18(1), 49-60.

[5] Carpenter, G. A., & Grossberg, S. (1995). Pattern Recognition by Self-organizing Neural Networks. The MIT Press.

[6] Watanabe, M., Aihara, K., & Kondo, S. (1995). Automatic learning in chaotic neural networks. *IEICE-A*, J78-A(6), 686-691, (in Japanese).

[7] Arai, T., & Osana, Y. (2006). Hetero chaotic associative memory for successive learning with give up function -- One-to-many associations --, Proceedings of IASTED Artificial Intelligence and Applications. Innsbruck.

[8] Ando, M., Okuno, Y., & Osana, Y. (2006). Hetero chaotic associative memory for successive learning with multi-winners competition. *Proceedings of IEEE and INNS International Joint Conference on Neural Networks*, Vancouver.

[9] Ichiki, H., Hagiwara, M., & Nakagawa, M. (1993). Kohonen feature maps as a supervised learning machine. *Proceedings of IEEE International Conference on Neural Networks*, 1944-1948.

[10] Yamada, T., Hattori, M., Morisawa, M., & Ito, H. (1999). Sequential learning for associative memory using Kohonen feature map. *Proceedings of IEEE and INNS International Joint Conference on Neural Networks*, 555, Washington D.C.

[11] Hattori, M., Arisumi, H., & Ito, H. (2001). Sequential learning for SOM associative memory with map reconstruction. *Proceedings of International Conference on Artificial Neural Networks*, Vienna.

[12] Sakurai, N., Hattori, M., & Ito, H. (2002). SOM associative memory for temporal sequences. *Proceedings of IEEE and INNS International Joint Conference on Neural Networks*, 950-955, Honolulu.

[13] Abe, H., & Osana, Y. (2006). Kohonen feature map associative memory with area representation. *Proceedings of IASTED Artificial Intelligence and Applications*, Innsbruck.

[14] Ikeda, N., & Hagiwara, M. (1997). A proposal of novel knowledge representation (Area representation) and the implementation by neural network. *International Conference on Computational Intelligence and Neuroscience*, III, 430-433.

[15] Imabayashi, T., & Osana, Y. (2008). Implementation of association of one-to-many associations and the analog pattern in Kohonen feature map associative memory with area representation. *Proceedings of IASTED Artificial Intelligence and Applications*, Innsbruck.

[16] Koike, M., & Osana, Y. (2010). Kohonen feature map probabilistic associative memory based on weights distribution. *Proceedings of IASTED Artificial Intelligence and Applications*, Innsbruck.

Applications

MLP and ANFIS Applied to the Prediction of Hole Diameters in the Drilling Process

Thiago M. Geronimo, Carlos E. D. Cruz,
Fernando de Souza Campos, Paulo R. Aguiar and
Eduardo C. Bianchi

Additional information is available at the end of the chapter

1. Introduction

The control of industrial machining manufacturing processes is of great economic importance due to the ongoing search to reduce raw materials and labor wastage. Indirect manufacturing operations such as dimensional quality control generate indirect costs that can be avoided or reduced through the use of control systems [1]. The use of intelligent manufacturing systems (IMS), which is the next step in the monitoring of manufacturing processes, has been researched through the application of artificial neural networks (ANN) since the 1980s [2].

The machining drilling process ranks among the most widely used manufacturing processes in industry in general [3, 4]. In the quest for higher quality in drilling operations, ANNs have been employed to monitor drill wear using sensors. Among the types of signals employed is that of machining loads measured with a dynamometer [5, 6], electric current measured by applying Hall Effect sensors on electric motors [7], vibrations [8], as well as a combination of the above with other devices such as accelerometers and acoustic emission sensors [9].

This article contributes to the use of MLP [10-12] and ANFIS type [13-16] artificial intelligence systems programmed in MATLAB to estimate the diameter of drilled holes. The two types of network use the backpropagation method, which is the most popular model for manufacturing applications [2]. In the experiment, which consisted of drilling single-layer test specimens of 2024-T3 alloy and of Ti6Al4V alloy, an acoustic emission sensor, a three-dimensional dynamometer, an accelerometer, and a Hall Effect sensor were used to collect information about noise frequency and intensity, table vibrations, loads on the x, y and z ax-es, and electric current in the motor, respectively.

2. Drilling Process

The three drilling processes most frequently employed in industry today are turning, mill-ing and boring [3], and the latter is the least studied process. However, it is estimated that today, boring with helical drill bits accounts for 20% to 25% of all machining processes.

The quality of a hole depends on geometric and dimensional errors, as well as burrs and surface integrity. Moreover, the type of drilling process, the tool, cutting parameters and machine stiffness also affect the precision of the hole [19].

It is very difficult to generate a reliable analytical model to predict and control hole diame-ters, since these holes are usually affected by several parameters. Figure 1 illustrates the loads involved in the drilling process, the most representative of which is the feed force F_Z, since it affects chip formation and surface roughness.

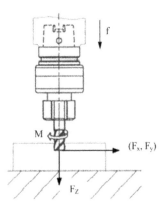

Figure 1. Loads involved in drilling processes.

3. Artificial Intelligent Systems

3.1. Artificial multilayer perceptron (MLP) neural network

Artificial neural networks are gaining ground as a new information processing paradigm for intelligent systems, which can learn from examples and, based on training, generalize to process a new set of information [14].

Artificial neurons have synaptic connections that receive information from sensors and have an attributed weight. The sum of the values of the inputs adjusted by the weight of each synapse is processed and an output is generated. The training error is calculated in each iteration, based on the calculated output and desired output, and is used to adjust the synaptic weights according to the generalized delta rule:

$$w_{ij}^{(l)}(n+1) = w_{ij}^{(l)}(n) + \alpha \left[w_{ij}^{(l)}(n-1) \right] + \eta \delta_j^{(l)}(n) y_i^{(l-1)}(n) \tag{1}$$

where η is the learning rate and α is the moment, which are parameters that influence the learning rate and its stability, respectively; $w_{ij}^{(l)}$ is the weight of each connection; and $\delta_j^{(l)}$ is the local gradient calculated from the error signal.

A neural network artificial (ANN) learns by continuously adjusting the synaptic weights at the connections between layers of neurons until a satisfactory response is produced [9].

In the present work, the MLP network was applied to estimate drilled hole diameters based on an analysis of the data captured by the sensors. The weight readjustment method employed was backpropagation, which consists of propagating the mean squared error generated in the diameter estimation by each layer of neurons, readjusting the weights of the connections so as to reduce the error in the next iteration.

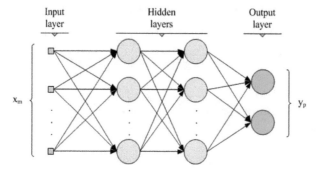

Figure 2. Typical architecture of an MLP with two hidden layers.

Figure 2 shows a typical MLP ANN, with m inputs and p outputs, with each circle representing a neuron. The outputs of a neuron are used as inputs for a neuron in the next layer.

3.2. Adaptive neuro-fuzzy inference system (ANFIS)

The ANFIS system is based on functional equivalence, under certain constraints, between RBF (radial basis function) neural networks and TSK-type fuzzy systems [15]. A single existing output is calculated directly by weighting the inputs according to fuzzy rules. These rules, which are the knowledge base, are determined by a computational algorithm based on neural networks. Figure 3 exemplifies the ANFIS model with two input variables (x and y) and two rules [11].

Obtaining an ANFIS model that performs well requires taking into consideration the initial number of parameters and the number of inputs and rules of the system [16]. These parameters are determined empirically, and an initial model is usually created with equally spaced pertinence functions.

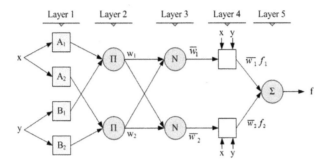

Figure 3. ANFIS architecture for two inputs and two rules based on the first-order Sugeno model.

However, this method is not always efficient because it does not show how many relevant input groups there are. To this end, there are algorithms that help determine the number of pertinence functions, thus enabling one to calculate the maximum number of fuzzy rules.

The subtractive clustering algorithm is used to identify data distribution centers [17], in which are centered the pertinence curves with pertinence values equal to 1. The number of clusters, the radius of influence of each cluster center, and the number of training iterations to be employed should be defined as parameters for the configuration of the inference system. At each pass, the algorithm seeks a point that minimizes the sum of the potential and the neighboring points. The potential is calculated by equation (2):

$$P_i = \sum_{j=i}^{n} \exp\left(-\frac{4}{r_a^2}\|x_i - x_j\|^2\right) \tag{2}$$

where P_i is the potential of the possible cluster, x_i is the possible cluster center, x_j is each point in the neighborhood of the cluster that will be grouped in it, and n is the number of points in the neighborhood.

ANFIS is a fuzzy inference system introduced in the work structure of an adaptive neural network. Using a hybrid learning scheme, the ANFIS system is able to map inputs and outputs based on human knowledge and on input and output data pairs [18]. The ANFIS method is superior to other modeling methods such as autoregressive models, cascade correlation neural networks, backpropagation algorithm neural networks, sixth-order polynomials, and linear prediction methods [10].

4. Methodology

4.1. Signal collection and drilling process

The tests were performed on test specimens composed of a package of sheets of Ti6Al4V titanium alloy and 2024-T3 aluminum alloy, which were arranged in this order to mimic their use in the aerospace industry. The tool employed here was a helical drill made of hard metal.

A total of nine test specimens were prepared, and 162 holes were drilled in each one. Thus, a considerable number of data were made available to train the artificial intelligence systems. The data set consisted of the signals collected during drilling and the diameters measured at the end of the process.

The drilling process was monitored using an acoustic emission sensor, a three-dimensional dynamometer, an accelerometer, and a Hall Effect sensor, which were arranged as illustrated in Figure 4.

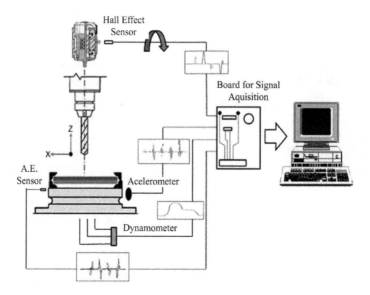

Figure 4. Sensor assembly scheme for testing.

The acoustic emission signal was collected using a Sensis model DM-42 sensor. The electric power was measured by applying a transducer to monitor the electric current and voltage in the terminals of the electric motor that activates the tool holder. The six signals were sent to a National Instruments PCI-6035E data acquisition board installed in a computer. LabView software was used to acquire the signals and store them in binary format for subsequent analysis and processing.

To simulate diverse machining conditions, different cutting parameters were selected for each machined test specimen. This method is useful to evaluate the performance of artificial intelligence systems in response to changes in the process. Each test specimen was dubbed as listed in Table 1.

Condition	ID	Spindle [rpm]	Feed Speed [mm/min]
1	1A	1000	90.0
2	1B	1000	22.4
3	1C	1000	250.0
4	2A	500	90.0
5	2B	500	22.4
6	2C	500	250.0
7	3A	2000	90.0
8	3B	2000	22.4
9	3C	2000	250.0

Table 1. Machining conditions used in the tests.

Each pass consisted of a single drilling movement along the workpiece in a given condition. The signals of acoustic emission, loads, cutting power and acceleration shown in Figure 5 were measured in real time at a rate of 2000 samples per second.

4.2. Diameter measurements

Because the roundness of machined holes is not perfect, two measurements were taken of each hole, one of the maximum and the other of the minimum diameter. Moreover, the diameter of the hole in each machined material will also be different due to the material's particular characteristics.

A MAHR MarCator 1087 B comparator gauge with a precision of ±0.005mm was used to record the measured dimensions and the dimensional control results were employed to train the artificial intelligence systems.

4.3. Definition of the architecture of the artificial intelligence systems

The architecture of the systems was defined using all the collected signals, i.e., those of acoustic emission; loads in the x, y and z directions; electrical power and acceleration. An MLP network and an ANFIS system were created for each test specimen material, due to the differences in the behavior of the signals (see Figure 5) and in the ranges of values found in the measurement of the diameters.

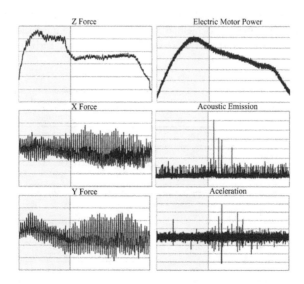

Figure 5. Signals collected during the drilling process of Ti6Al4V alloy (left) and 2024-T3 alloy (right).

4.3.1. Multilayer Perceptron

In this study, the signals from the sensors, together with the maximum and minimum measured diameters, were organized into two matrices, one for each test specimen material. These data were utilized to train the neural network. The entire data set of the tests resulted in 1337 samples, considering tool breakage during testing under condition 2C.

Parameters	Ti6Al4V	2024-T3
Neurons in each layer	[5 20 15]	[20 10 5]
Learning rate	0.15	0.3
Moment	0.2	0.8
Transfer function	tansig	poslin

Table 2. Architecture of the MLP networks.

The MLP network architecture is defined by establishing the number of hidden layers to be used, the number of neurons contained in each layer, the learning rate and the moment. An algorithm was created to test combinations of these parameters. The final choice was the combination that appeared among the five smallest errors in the estimate of the maximum and minimum diameters. Parameters such as the number of training iterations and the desired error are used as criteria to complete the training and were established at 200 training iterations and 1×10^{-7} mm, respectively. This procedure was performed for each material, generating two MLP networks whose configuration is described in Table 2. The remaining parameters were kept according to the MATLAB default.

4.3.2. ANFIS

The same data matrix employed to train the MLP neural network was used to train the ANFIS system. This system consists of a fuzzy inference system (FIS) that collects the available data, converts them into If-Then type rules by means of pertinence functions, and processes them to generate the desired output. The FIS is influenced by the organization of the training data set, whose task is performed with the help of MATLAB's Fuzzy toolbox. The subtractive clustering algorithm (subclust) is used to search for similar data clusters in the training set, optimizing the FIS through the definition of points with the highest potential for the cluster center. Parameters such as the radius of influence, inclusion rate and rejection rate help define the number of clusters, and hence, the number of rules of the FIS. Table 3 lists the parameters used in the ANFIS systems. The desired error was set at 1x10-7mm. The training method consists of a hybrid algorithm with the method of backpropagation and least-squares estimate.

Parameters	Ti6Al4V	2024-T3
Radius of influence	1.25	1.25
Inclusion rate	0.6	0.6
Rejection rate	0.4	0.1

Table 3. ANFIS parameters.

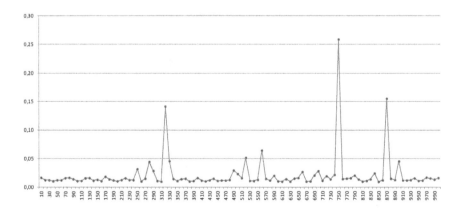

Figure 6. Mean error of hole diameters estimated by the ANFIS system for several training iterations.

Because training in the ANFIS system is performed in batch mode, with the entire training set presented at once, the appropriate number of training iterations was investigated. Thus, an algorithm was created to test several numbers of training iterations ranging from 10 up to 1000. Figure 6 illustrates the result of this test.

The larger the number of training iterations, the greater the computational effort. Thus, avoiding the peaks (Figure 6), the number de training iterations was set at 75, which requires low computational capacity.

5. Influence of inputs on the performance of diameter estimation

5.1. Use of all the collected signals

Initially, the systems were trained using all the collected signals. Given the data set of the sensors and the desired outputs, which Consist of the measured diameters, the performance of the neural network is evaluated based on the error between the estimated diameter and the measured diameter, which are shown on graphs.

5.1.1. MLP

For the Ti6Al4V titanium alloy, the estimate of the minimum diameter resulted in a mean error of 0.0067mm, with a maximum error of 0.0676mm.

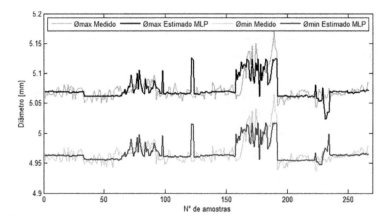

Figure 7. Minimum and maximum diameters (actual vs. estimated by the MLP) for the Ti6Al4V alloy.

For the maximum diameter, the resulting mean error was 0.0066mm, with a maximum error of 0.0668mm. Figure 7 depicts the results of these estimates.

Figure 8 shows the result of the estimation of the hole diameters machined in the 2024-T3 aluminum alloy. The mean error for the minimum diameter was 0.0080mm, with a maximum error of 0.0649mm. For the maximum diameter, the mean error was 0.0086mm, with a maximum error of 0.0655mm.

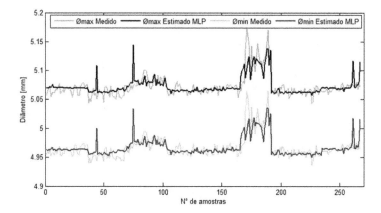

Figure 8. Minimum and maximum diameters (actual vs. estimated by the MLP) for the 2024-T3 alloy.

5.1.2. ANFIS

Figure 9 shows the diameters estimated by ANFIS. The mean error in the estimate of the minimum diameter was 0.01102mm, with a maximum error of 0.0704mm. For the maximum diameter, the resulting mean error was 0.01188mm, and the highest error was 0.0718mm.

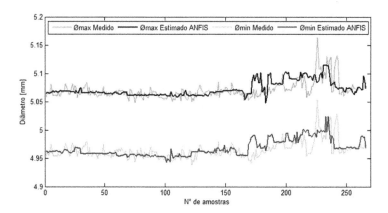

Figure 9. Minimum and maximum diameters (actual vs. estimated by ANFIS) for the Ti6Al4V alloy.

Figure 10 illustrates the result of the machined hole diameter estimated for the 2024-T3 alloy, using the same network configuration. The mean error for the minimum diameter was 0.0980mm, with a maximum error of 0.0739mm. The maximum diameter presented a mean error of 0.00990mm, and a maximum error of 0.0791mm.

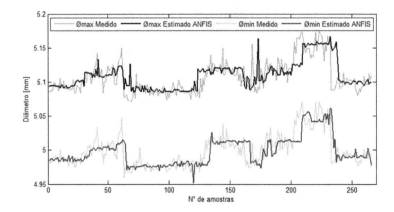

Figure 10. Minimum and maximum diameters (actual vs. estimated by the MLP) for the 2024-T3 alloy.

5.2. Isolated and combined use of signals

To optimize the computational effort, an algorithm was created to test the performance of each type of system in response to each of the signals separately or to a combination of two or more signals. This procedure was adopted in order to identify a less invasive estimation method.

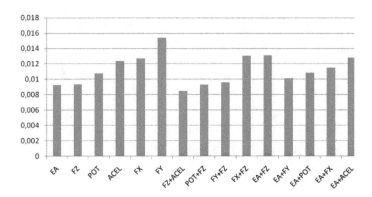

Figure 11. Performance of individual and combined signals in the estimation of hole diameters in Ti6Al4V alloy by the MLP network

Individual signals and a combination of two distinct signals were tested for the MLP network. The best individual inputs for the Ti6Al4V alloy were the acoustic emission and Z force signals. Combined, the Z force and acceleration signals presented the lowest error. The classified signals are illustrated in Figure 11.

For the 2024-T3 alloy, the best individual input was the Z force. When combined, the Z force and acceleration signals presented the lowest error. Figure 11 depicts the classified signals.

In the ANFIS system, the Z force provided the best individual signal for the estimate of the drilled hole diameter in Ti6Al4V alloy. The acoustic emission signal combined with the Z force presented the best result with two combinations, as indicated in Figure 12.

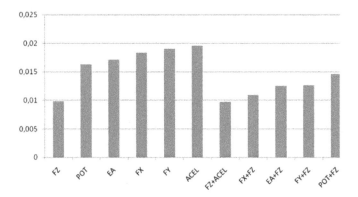

Figure 12. Performance of individual and combined signals in the estimation of hole diameters in 2024-T3 alloy by the MLP system.

For the aluminum alloy, the ANFIS system presented the best performance with the individual Z force signal and with a combination of the Z force and acoustic emission signals, as indicated in Figure 14.

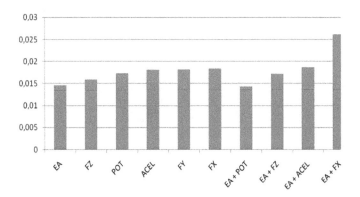

Figure 13. Performance of individual and combined signals in the estimation of hole diameters in Ti6Al4V alloy by the ANFIS system.

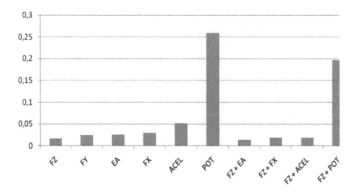

Figure 14. Performance of individual and combined signals in the estimation of hole diameters in 2024-T3 alloy by the ANFIS system.

6. Performance using the Z force

Because the performance of the artificial intelligence systems in the tests was the highest when using the Z force signal, new tests were carried out with only this signal. The errors were divided into four classes, according to the following criteria: precision of the instrument (≤5μm), tolerance required for precision drilling processes (≤ 12μm), tolerance normally employed in industrial settings (≤ 25μm), and the errors that would lead to a non-conformity (> 25μm). The configurations used in the previous tests were maintained in this test.

6.1. MLP

The multilayer perceptron ANN was trained with the information of the Z force and the minimum and maximum measured diameters.

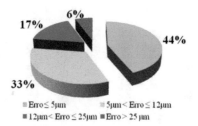

Figure 15. Classification of estimation errors for the 2024-T3 alloy obtained by the MLP network.

The simulation of the MLP network for the aluminum alloy presented lower precision errors than the measurement instrument used in 44% of the attempts. Thirty-three percent of the estimates presented errors within the range stipulated for precision holes and 17% for the tolerances normally applied in industry in general. Only 6% of the estimates performed by the artificial neural network would result in a product conformity rejection.

The simulation of the MLP network for the titanium alloy presented lower precision errors than the measurement instrument used in 45% of the attempts. Thirty-seven percent of the estimates presented errors within the range stipulated for precision holes and 15% for the tolerances normally applied in industry in general. Only 3% of the estimates performed by the artificial neural network would result in a product conformity rejection.

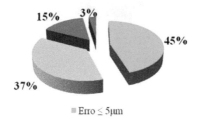

Figure 16. Classification of estimation errors for the Ti6Al4V alloy obtained by the MLP network.

6.2. ANFIS

The ANFIS system was simulated in the same way as was done with the MLP network, but this time using only one input, the Z force. This procedure resulted in changes in the FIS structure due to the use of only one input.

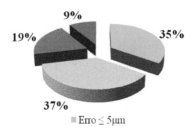

Figure 17. Classification of estimation errors for the 2024-T3 alloy obtained by the ANFIS system.

For the aluminum alloy, ANFIS presented lower precision errors than the measurement instrument employed in 35% of the attempts. Thirty-seven percent of the estimates presented errors within the range stipulated for precision holes and 19% for the tolerances normally used in industry in general. Only 9% of the estimates performed by the artificial neural network would result in a product conformity rejection, as indicated in Figure 17.

For the titanium alloy, ANFIS presented lower precision errors than the measurement instrument employed in 40% of the attempts. Thirty-four percent of the estimates presented errors within the range stipulated for precision holes and 15% for the tolerances normally used in industry. Only 11% of the estimates performed by the artificial neural network would lead to a product conformity rejection, as indicated in Figure 18.

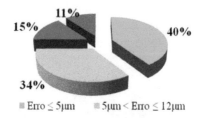

Figure 18. Classification of estimation errors for the Ti6Al4V alloy obtained by the ANFIS system.

7. Conclusions

Artificial intelligence systems today are employed in mechanical manufacturing processes to monitor tool wear and control cutting parameters. This article presented a study of the application of two systems used in the dimensional control of a precision drilling process.

The first system used here consisted of a multiple layer perceptron (MLP) artificial neural network. Its performance was marked by the large number of signals used in its training and for its estimation precision, which produced 52% of correct responses (errors below 5 μm) for the titanium alloy and 42% for the aluminum alloy. As for its unacceptable error rates, the MLP system generated only 4% and 8% for the titanium and aluminum alloys, respectively.

The second approach, which involved the application of an adaptive neuro-fuzzy inference system (ANFIS), generated a large number of correct responses using the six available signals, i.e., 45% for the titanium alloy and 33% for the aluminum alloy. A total of 11% of errors for the titanium alloy and 20% for the aluminum alloy were classified above the admissible tolerances (> 25μm).

The results described herein demonstrate the applicability of the two systems in industrial contexts. However, to evaluate the economic feasibility of their application, another method was employed using the signal from only one sensor, whose simulations generated the lowest error among the available signals. Two signals stood out: the Z force and acoustic emission signals, with the former presenting a better result for the two alloys of the test specimen and the latter presenting good results only in the hole diameter estimation for the titanium alloy. Therefore, the Z force was selected for the continuation of the tests.

The results obtained here are very encouraging in that fewer estimates fell within the range considered inadmissible, i.e., only 6% for the aluminum alloy and 3% for the titanium alloy, using the MLP network.

The results produced by the ANFIS system also demonstrated a drop in the number of errors outside the expected range, i.e., 9% for the aluminum alloy and 11% for the titanium alloy.

Based on the approaches used in this work, it can be stated that the use of artificial intelligence systems in industry, particularly multilayer perceptron neural networks and the adaptive neuro-fuzzy inference systems, is feasible. These systems showed high accuracy and low computational effort, as well as a low implementation cost with the use of only one sensor, which implies few physical changes in the equipment to be monitored.

Acknowledgements

The authors gratefully acknowledge the Brazilian research funding agencies FAPESP (São Paulo Research Foundation), for supporting this research work under Process # 2009/50504-0; and CNPq (National Council for Scientific and Technological Development) and CAPES (Federal Agency for the Support and Evaluation of Postgraduate Education) for providing scholarships. We are also indebted to the company OSG Sulamericana de Ferramentas Ltda. for manufacturing and donating the tools used in this research.

Author details

Thiago M. Geronimo, Carlos E. D. Cruz, Fernando de Souza Campos, Paulo R. Aguiar and Eduardo C. Bianchi*

*Address all correspondence to: bianchi@feb.unesp.br

Universidade Estadual Paulista "Júlio de Mesquita Filho" (UNESP), Bauru campus, Brazil

References

[1] Kamen, W. (1999). *Industrial Controls and Manufacturing*, San Diego, Academic Press, 230.

[2] Huang, S. H., & Zhang, H.-C. (1994, June). Artificial Neural Networks in Manufacturing: Concepts, Applications, and Perspectives. *IEEE Trans. Comp. Pack. Manuf. Tech.-Part A*, 17(2).

[3] Konig, W., & Klocke, F. (2002). *Fertigungsverfahren: drehen, frasen, bohren* (7 ed.), Berlin, Springer-Verlag, 409.

[4] Rivero, A., Aramendi, G., Herranz, S., & López de Lacalle, L. N. (2006). An experimental investigation of the effect of coatings and cutting parameters on the dry drilling performance of aluminium alloys. *Int J Adv Manuf Technol*, 28, 1-11.

[5]   Panda, S. S., Chakraborty, D., & Pal, S. K. (2007). Monitoring of drill flank wear using fuzzy back-propagation neural network. *Int. J. Adv. Manuf. Technol*, 34, 227-235.

[6]   Yang, X., Kumehara, H., & Zhang, W. August(2009). Back-propagation Wavelet Neural Network Based Prediction of Drill Wear from Thrust Force and Cutting Torque Signals. Computer and Information Science, , 2(3)

[7]   Li, X., & Tso, S. K. (1999). Drill wear monitoring based on current signals. *Wear*, 231, 172-178.

[8]   Abu-Mahfouz, I. (2003). Drilling wear detection and classification using vibration signals and artificial neural nerwork. *International Journal of Machine Tools & Manufacture*, 43, 707-720.

[9]   Kandilli, I., Sönmez, M., Ertunc, H. M., & Çakir, B. (2007, August). Online Monitoring of Tool Wear In Drilling and Milling By Multi-Sensor Neural Network Fusion. Harbin. *Proceedings of 2007 IEEE International Conference on Mechatronics and Automation*, 1388-1394.

[10] Haykin, S. (2001). Neural Networks: A Compreensive Foundation. Patparganj, Pearson Prentice Hall, 2 ed., 823.

[11] Sanjay, C., & Jyothi, C. (2006). A study of surface roughness in drilling Technol using mathematical analysis and neural networks. *Int J Adv Manuf*, 29, 846-852.

[12] Huang, B. P., Chenb, J. C., & Li, Y. (2008). Artificial-neural-networksbased surface roughness: pokayoke system for end-milling operations. *Neurocomputing*, 71, 544-549.

[13] J.-S. R., Jang. (1993). ANFIS: Adaptive-Network-Based Fuzzy Inference System. *IEEE Transactions on Systems, Man and Cybernetics*, 23(3), 665-685.

[14] Resende, S. O. (2003). *Sistemas Inteligentes: Fundamentos e Aplicações*, Manole, Barueri, 1 ed., 525.

[15] Lezanski, P. (2001). An Intelligent System for Grinding Wheel Condition Monitoring. *Journal of Materials Processing Technology*, 109, 258-263.

[16] Lee, K. C., Ho, S. J., & Ho, S. Y. (2005). Accurate Estimation of Surface Roughness from Texture Features of The Surface Image Using an Adaptive Neuro-Fuzzy Inference System. *Precision Engineering*, 29, 95-100.

[17] Johnson, J., & Picton, P. (2001). *Concepts in Artificial Intelligence: Designing Intelligent Machines*, 2, Oxford, Butterworth-Heinemann, 376.

[18] Sugeno, M., & Kang, G. T. (1988). Structure Identification of Fuzzy Model. *Fuzzy Sets and Systems*, 28, 15-33.

[19] Lezanski, P. (2001). An Intelligent System for Grinding Wheel Condition Monitoring. *Journal of Materials Processing Technology*, 109, 258-263.

[20] Chiu, S. L. (1994). Fuzzy Model Identification Based on Cluster Estimation. *Journal of Intelligent and Fuzzy Systems*, 2, 267-278.

[21] Lee, K. C., Ho, S. J., & Ho, S. Y. (2005). Accurate Estimation of Surface Roughness from Texture Features of The Surface Image Using an Adaptive Neuro-Fuzzy Inference System. *Precision Engineering*, 29, 95-100.

[22] Drozda, T. J., & Wick, C. (1983). *Tool and Manufacturing Engineers Handbook*, 1, Machining, SME, Dearborn.

Chapter 6

Comparison Between an Artificial Neural Network and Logistic Regression in Predicting Long Term Kidney Transplantation Outcome

Giovanni Caocci, Roberto Baccoli, Roberto Littera, Sandro Orrù, Carlo Carcassi and Giorgio La Nasa

Additional information is available at the end of the chapter

1. Introduction

Predicting clinical outcome following a specific treatment is a challenge that sees physicians and researchers alike sharing the dream of a crystal ball to read into the future. In Medicine, several tools have been developed for the prediction of outcomes following drug treatment and other medical interventions. The standard approach for a binary outcome is to use logistic regression (LR) [1,2] but over the past few years artificial neural networks (ANNs) have become an increasingly popular alternative to LR analysis for prognostic and diagnostic classification in clinical medicine [3]. The growing interest in ANNs has mainly been triggered by their ability to mimic the learning processes of the human brain. The network operates in a feed-forward mode from the input layer through the hidden layers to the output layer. Exactly what interactions are modeled in the hidden layers is still under study. Each layer within the network is made up of computing nodes with remarkable data processing abilities. Each node is connected to other nodes of a previous layer through adaptable inter-neuron connection strengths known as synaptic weights. ANNs are trained for specific applications through a learning process and knowledge is usually retained as a set of connection weights [4]. The backpropagation algorithm and its variants are learning algorithms that are widely used in neural networks. With backpropagation, the input data is repeatedly presented to the network. Each time, the output is compared to the desired output and an error is computed. The error is then fed back through the network and used to adjust the weights in such a way that with each iteration it gradually declines until the neural model produces the desired output.

ANNs have been successfully applied in the fields of mathematics, engineering, medicine, economics, meteorology, psychology, neurology, and many others. Indeed, in medicine, they offer a tantalizing alternative to multivariate analysis, although their role remains advisory since no convincing evidence of any real progress in clinical prognosis has yet been produced [5].

In the field of nephrology, there are very few reports on the use of ANNs [6-10], most of which describe their ability to individuate predictive factors of technique survival in peritoneal dialysis patients as well as their application to prescription and monitoring of hemodialysis therapy, analyis of factors influencing therapeutic efficacy in idiopathic membranous nephropathy, prediction of survival after radical cystectomy for invasive bladder carcinoma and individual risk for progression to end-stage renal failure in chronic nephropathies.

This all led up to the intriguing challenge of discovering whether ANNs were capable of predicting the outcome of kidney transplantation after analyzing a series of clinical and immunogenetic variables.

Figure 1. The prediction of kidney allograft outcome.... a dream about to come true?

2. The complex setting of kidney transplantation

Predicting the outcome of kidney transplantation is important in optimizing transplantation parameters and modifying factors related to the recipient, donor and transplant procedure [8]. The biggest obstacles to be overcome in organ transplantation are the risks of acute and chronic immunologic rejection, especially when they entail loss of graft function despite adjustment of immunosuppressive therapy. Acute renal allograft rejection requires a rapid increase in immunosuppression, but unfortunately, diagnosis in the early stages is often difficult [11]. Blood tests may reveal an increase in serum creatinine but which cannot be considered a specific sign of acute rejection since there are several causes of impaired renal function that can lead to creatinine increase, including excessive levels of some immunosuppressive drugs. Also during ischemic damage, serum creatinine levels are elevated and so provide no indication of rejection. Alternative approaches to the diagnosis of rejection are fine needle aspiration and urine cytology, but the main approach remains histological assessment of needle biopsy.[10] However, because the histological changes of acute rejection develop gradually, the diagnosis can be extremely difficult or late [12]. Although allograft biopsy is considered the gold standard, pathologists working in centres where this approach is used early in the investigation of graft dysfunction, are often faced with a certain degree of uncertainty about the diagnosis. In the past, the Banff classification of renal transplant pathology provided a rational basis for grading of the severity of a variety of histological features, including acute rejection. Unfortunately, the reproducibility of this system has been questioned [13]. What we need is a simple prognostic tool capable of analyzing the most relevant predictive variables of rejection in the setting of kidney transplantation.

3. The role of HLA-G in kidney transplantation outcome

Human Leukocyte Antigen G (HLA-G) represents a "non classic" HLA class I molecule, highly expressed in trophoblast cells. [14] HLA-G plays a key role in embryo implantation and pregnancy by contributing to maternal immune tolerance of the fetus and, more specifically, by protecting trophoblast cells from maternal natural killer (NK) cells through interaction with their inhibitory KIR receptors. It has also been shown that HLA-G expression by tumoral cells can contribute to an "escape" mechanism, inducing NK tolerance toward cancer cells in ovarian and breast carcinomas, melanoma, acute myeloid leukemia, acute lymphoblastic leukemia and B-cell chronic lymphocytic leukemia. [15] Additionally it would seem that HLA-G molecules have a role in graft tolerance following hematopoietic stem cell transplantation. These molecules exert their immunotolerogenic function towards the main effector cells involved in graft rejection through inhibition of NK and cytotoxic T lymphocyte (CTL)-mediated cytolysis and CD4+T-cell alloproliferation. [16]

HLA-G transcript generates 7 alternative messenger ribonucleic acids (mRNAs) that encode 4 membrane-bound (HLA-G1, G2, G3, G4) and 3 soluble protein isoforms (HLA-G5, G6, G7). Moreover, HLA-G allelic variants are characterized by a 14-basepair (bp) deletion-insertion polymorphism located in the 3′-untranslated region (3′UTR) of HLA-G. The presence of the 14-bp insertion is known to generate an additional splice whereby 92 bases are removed from the 3′UTR [28]. HLA-G mRNAs having the 92-base deletion are more stable than the complete mRNA forms, and thus determine an increment in HLA-G expression. Therefore, the 14-bp polymorphism is involved in the mechanisms controlling post-transcriptional regulation of HLA-G molecules

A crucial role has been attributed to the ability of these molecules to preserve graft function from the insults caused by recipient alloreactive NK cells and cytotoxic T lymphocytes (CTL). [17] This is well supported by the numerous studies demonstrating that high HLA-G plasma concentrations in heart, liver or kidney transplant patients is associated with better graft survival [18-20].

Recent studies of association between the HLA-G +14-bp /−14-bp polymorphism and the outcome of kidney transplantation have provided interesting, though not always concordant results [21-22].

4. Kydney transplantation outcome

In one cohort, a total of 64 patients (20,4%) lost graft function. The patients were divided into 2 groups according to the presence or absence of HLA-G alleles exhibiting the 14-bp insertion polymorphism. The first group included 210 patients (66.9%) with either HLA-G +14-bp/+14-bp or HLA-G −14/+14-bp whereas the second group included 104 homozygotes (33.1%) for the HLA-G −14-bp polymorphism. The patients had a median age of 49 years (range 18-77) and were prevalently males (66.6%). The donors had a median age of 47 years (range 15-75). Nearly all patients (94,9%) had been given a cadaver donor kidney transplant and for most of them (91.7%) it was their first transplant. The average (±SD) number of mismatches was 3 ± 1 antigens for HLA Class I and 1 ± 0.7 antigens for HLA Class II. Average ±SD cold ischemia time (CIT) was 16 ± 5.6 hours. The percentage of patients hyperimmunized against HLA Class I and II antigens (PRA > 50%) was higher in the group of homozygotes for the HLA-G 14-bp deletion. Pre-transplantation serum levels of interleukin-10 (IL-10) were lower in the group of homozygotes for the 14-bp deletion.

Kidney transplant outcome was evaluated by glomerular filtration rate (GFR), serum creatinine and graft function tests. At one year after transplantation, a stronger progressive decline of the estimated GFR, using the abbreviated Modification of Diet in Renal Disease (MDRD) study equation, was observed in the group of homozygotes for the HLA-G 14-bp deletion in comparison with the group of heterozygotes for the 14-bp insertion. This difference between the 2 groups became statistically significant at two years (5.3 ml/min/1.73 m2; P<0.01; 95% CI 1.2 -9.3) and continued to rise at 3 (10.4 ml/min/1.73m2; P<0.0001; 95% CI 6.4-14.3) and 6 years (11.4 ml/min/1.73m2; P<0.0001; 95% CI 7.7 − 15.1) after transplantation.

5. Logistic regression and neural network training

We compared the prognostic performance of ANNs versus LR for predicting rejection in a group of 353 patients who underwent kidney transplantation. The following clinical and immunogenetic parameters were considered: recipient gender, recipient age, donor gender, donor age, patient/donor compatibility: class I (HLA-A, -B) mismatch (0-4), class II (HLA-DRB1 mismatch; positivity for anti-HLA Class I antibodies >50%; positivity for anti-HLA Class II antibodies >50%; IL-10 pg/mL; first versus second transplant, antithymocyte globulin (ATG) induction therapy; type of immunosoppressive therapy (rapamycin, cyclosporine, corticosteroids, mycophenolate mophetyl, everolimus, tacrolimus); time of cold ischemia, recipients homozygous/heterozygous for the 14-bp insertion (+14-bp/+14-bp and +14-bp/−14-bp) and homozygous for the 14-bp deletion (−14-bp/−14-bp). Graft survival was calculated from the date of transplantation to the date of irreversible graft failure or graft loss or the date of the last follow up or death with a functioning graft.

ANNs have different architectures, which consequently require different types of algorithms. The multilayer perceptron is the most popular network architecture in use today (Figure 2). This type of network requires a desired output in order to learn. The network is trained with historical data so that it can produce the correct output when the output is unknown. Until the network is appropriately trained its responses will be random. Finding appropriate architecture needs trial and error method and this is where backpropagation steps in. Each single neuron is connected to the neurons of the previous layer through adaptable synaptic weights. By adjusting the strengths of these connections, ANNs can approximate a function that computes the proper output for a given input pattern. The training data set includes a number of cases, each containing values for a range of well-matched input and output variables. Once the input is propagated to the output neuron, this neuron compares its activation with the expected training output. The difference is treated as the error of the network which is then backpropagated through the layers, from the output to the input layer, and the weights of each layer are adjusted such that with each backpropagation cycle the network gets closer and closer to producing the desired output [4]. We used the Neural Network Toolbox™ 6 of the software Matlab® 2008, version 7.6 (MathWorks, inc.) to develop a three layer feed forward neural network. [23]. The input layer of 15 neurons was represented by the 15 previously listed clinical and immunogenetic parameters. These input data were then processed in the hidden layer (30 neurons). The output neuron predicted a number between 1 and 0 (goal), representing the event "Kidney rejection yes" [1] or "Kidney rejection no" (0), respectively. For the training procedure, we applied the 'on-line back-propagation' method on 10 data sets of 300 patients previously analyzed by LR. The 10 test phases utilized 63 patients randomly extracted from the entire cohort and not used in the training phase. Mean sensitivity (the ability of predicting rejection) and specificity (the ability of predicting no-rejection) of data sets were determined and compared to LR. (Table 1)

		Rejection	Observed Cases	LR Expected cases (%)	ANN Expected cases (%)
Extraction_1	Test N=63	No	55	40 (73)	48 (87)
		Yes	8	2 (25)	4 (50)
Extraction_2	Test N=63	No	55	38 (69)	48 (87)
		Yes	8	3 (38)	4 (50)
Extraction_3	Test N=63	No	55	30 (55)	48(87)
		Yes	8	3 (38)	5 (63)
Extraction_4	Test N=63	No	55	40 (73)	49 (89)
		Yes	8	3 (38)	5 (63)
Extraction_5	Test N=63	No	7	40 (73)	46 (84)
		Yes	8	4 (50)	6 (75)
Extraction_6	Test N=63	No	55	30 (55)	34 (62)
		Yes	8	4 (50)	6 (75)
Extraction_7	Test N=63	No	55	40 (73)	47 (85)
		Yes	8	3 (38)	5 (63)
Extraction_8	Test N=63	No	55	38 (69)	46 (84)
		Yes	8	4 (50)	5 (63)
Extraction_9	Test N=63	No	55	44 (80)	51 (93)
		Yes	8	2 (25)	4 (50)
Extraction_10	Test N=63	No	55	32 (58)	52 (95)
		Yes	8	2 (25)	5 (63)
Specificity % (mean)	No Rejection			68%	85%
Sensitivity % (mean)	YES Rejection			38%	62%

Table 1. Sensitivity and specificity of Logistic Regression and an Artificial Neural Network in the prediction of Kidney rejection in 10 training and validating datasets of kidney transplant recipients

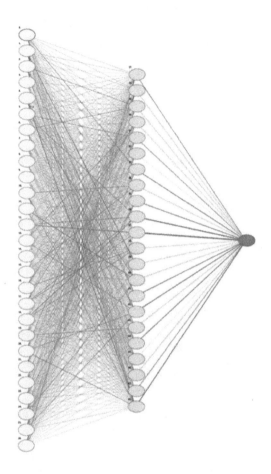

Figure 2. Structure of a three-layered ANN

6. Results and perspectives

ANNs can be considered a useful supportive tool in the prediction of kidney rejection following transplantation. The decision to perform analyses in this particular clinical setting
was motivated by the importance of optimizing transplantation parameters and modifying
factors related to the recipient, donor and transplant procedure. Another motivation was the
need for a simple prognostic tool capable of analyzing the relatively large number of immunogenetic and other variables that have been shown to influence the outcome of transplanta-

tion. When comparing the prognostic performance of LR to ANN, the ability of predicting kidney rejection (sensitivity) was 38% for LR versus 62% for ANN. The ability of predicting no-rejection (specificity) was 68% for LR compared to 85% of ANN.

The advantage of ANNs over LR can theoretically be explained by their ability to evaluate complex nonlinear relations among variables. By contrast, ANNs have been faulted for being unable to assess the relative importance of the single variables while LR determines a relative risk for each variable. In many ways, these two approaches are complementary and their combined use should considerably improve the clinical decision-making process and prognosis of kidney transplantation.

Acknowledgement

We wish to thank Anna Maria Koopmans (affiliations [1,3]) for her precious assistance in preparing the manuscript

Author details

Giovanni Caocci[1], Roberto Baccoli[2], Roberto Littera[3], Sandro Orrù[3], Carlo Carcassi[3] and Giorgio La Nasa[1]

1 Division of Hematology and Hematopoietic Stem Cell Transplantation, Department of Internal Medical Sciences, University of Cagliari, Cagliari, Italy

2 Technical Physics Division, Faculty of Engineering, Department of Engineering of the Territory, University of Cagliari, Cagliari, Italy

3 Medical Genetics, Department of Internal Medical Sciences, University of Cagliari, Cagliari, Italy

References

[1] Royston P. A strategy for modelling the effect of a continuous covariate in medicine and epidemiology. Stat Med. 2000;19:1831-1847.

[2] Harrell FE, Lee KL, Mark DB. Multivariable prognostic models: issues in developing models, evaluating assumptions and adequacy, and measuring and reducing errors. Stat Med.1996;15:361-387.

[3] Schwarzer G, Vach W, Schumacher M. On the misuses of artificial neural networks for prognostic and diagnostic classification in oncology. Stat Med. 2000;19:541-561.

[4] Soteris A. Kalogirou. Artificial neural networks in renewable energy systems applications: a review. Renewable and Sustainable Energy Review. 2001;5:373–401.

[5] 5. Linder R, König IR, Weimar C, Diener HC, Pöppl SJ, Ziegler A. Two models for outcome prediction - a comparison of logistic regression and neural networks. Methods Inf Med. 2006;45:536-540.

[6] Simic-Ogrizovic S, Furuncic D, Lezaic V, Radivojevic D, Blagojevic R, Djukanovic L. Using ANN in selection of the most important variables in prediction of chronic renal allograft rejection progression. Transplant Proc. 1999; 31:368.

[7] Brier ME, Ray PC, Klein JB. Prediction of delayed renal allograft function using an artificial neural network. Nephrol Dial Transplant. 2003; 18:2655-9.

[8] Tang H, Poynton MR, Hurdle JF, Baird BC, Koford JK, Goldfarb-Rumyantzev AS. Predicting three-year kidney graft survival in recipients with systemic lupus erythematosus. ASAIO J. 2011; 57:300-9.

[9] Kazi JI, Furness PN, Nicholson M. Diagnosis of early acute renal allograft rejection by evaluation of multiple histological features using a Bayesian belief network. J Clin Pathol. 1998; 51:108-13.

[10] Furness PN, Kazi J, Levesley J, Taub N, Nicholson M. A neural network approach to the diagnosis of early acute allograft rejection. Transplant Proc. 1999; 31:3151

[11] Furness PN. Advances in the diagnosis of renal transplant rejection. Curr. Diag. Pathol. 1996; 3:81-90.

[12] Rush DN, Henry SF, Jeffery JR, Schroeder TJ, Gough J. Histological findings in early routine biopsies of stable renal allograft recipients. Transplantation 1994; 57:208-211.

[13] Solez K, Axelsen RA, Benediktsson H, et al. International standardization of criteria for the histologic diagnosis of renal allograft rejection: the Banff working classification of kidney transplant pathology. Kidney Int 1993; 44:411-22.

[14] Kovats S, Main EK, Librach C, Dtubblebine M, Fisher SJ, DeMars R. A class I antigen, HLA-G, expressed in human trophoblasts. Science, 1990; 248:220-223

[15] Carosella ED, Favier B, Rouas-Freiss N, Moreau P, LeMaoult P. Beyond the increasing complexity of the immunomodulatory HLA-G molecule. Blood 2008; 11:4862-4870

[16] Le Rond S, Aze´ma C, Krawice-Radanne I, Durrbach A, Guettier C, Carosella ED, Rouas-Freiss N. Evidence to support the role of HLA-G5 in allograft acceptance through induction of immunosuppressive/ regulatory T cells. Journal of Immunology, 2006; 176:3266–3276.17.

[17] Rouas-Freiss N, Gonçalves RM, Menier C, Dausset J, Carosella ED. Direct evidence to support the role of HLA-G in protecting the fetus from maternal uterine natural killer cytolysis. Proc Natl Acad Sci U S A. 1997; 94:11520-5.

[18] Lila N, Amrein C, Guillemain R, Chevalier P, Fabiani JN, Carpentier A. Soluble human leukocyte antigen-G: a new strategy for monitoring acute and chronic rejections
after heart transplantation. J Heart Lung Transplant. 2007; 26:421-2.

[19] Baştürk B, Karakayali F, Emiroğlu R, Sözer O, Haberal A, Bal D, Haberal M. Human
leukocyte antigen-G, a new parameter in the follow-up of liver transplantation.
Transplant Proc. 2006; 38:571-4.

[20] Qiu J, Terasaki PI, Miller J, Mizutani K, Cai J, Carosella ED. Soluble HLA-G expression and renal graft acceptance. Am J Transplant. 2006; 6:2152-6.

[21] Crispim JC, Duarte RA, Soares CP, Costa R, Silva JS, Mendes-Júnior CT, Wastowski
IJ, Faggioni LP, Saber LT, Donadi EA. Human leukocyte antigen-G expression after
kidney transplantation is associated with a reduced incidence of rejection. Transpl
Immunol. 2008; 18:361-7.

[22] Piancatelli D, Maccarone D, Liberatore G, Parzanese I, Clemente K, Azzarone R, Pisa-
ni F, Famulari A, Papola F. HLA-G 14-bp insertion/deletion polymorphism in kidney
transplant patients with metabolic complications. Transplant Proc. 2009; 41:1187-8.

[23] Demuth H, Beale M, Hagan M. Neural Network Toolbox™ 6. User's Guide. The
MathWorks, Inc. 2008; Natick, MA.

Chapter 7

Applying Artificial Neural Network Hadron - Hadron Collisions at LHC

Amr Radi and Samy K. Hindawi

Additional information is available at the end of the chapter

1. Introduction

High Energy Physics (HEP) targeting on particle physics, searches for the fundamental particles and forces which construct the world surrounding us and understands how our universe works at its most fundamental level. Elementary particles of the Standard Model are gauge Bosons (force carriers) and Fermions which are classified into two groups: Leptons (i.e. Muons, Electrons, etc) and Quarks (Protons, Neutrons, etc).

The study of the interactions between those elementary particles requests enormously high energy collisions as in LHC [1-8], up to the highest energy hadrons collider in the world $\sqrt{s}$ =14 Tev. Experimental results provide excellent opportunities to discover the missing particles of the Standard Model. As well as, LHC possibly will yield the way in the direction of our awareness of particle physics beyond the Standard Model.

The proton-proton (p-p) interaction is one of the fundamental interactions in high-energy physics. In order to fully exploit the enormous physics potential, it is important to have a complete understanding of the reaction mechanism. The particle multiplicity distributions, as one of the first measurements made at LHC, used to test various particle production models. It is based on different physics mechanisms and also provide constrains on model features. Some of these models are based on string fragmentation mechanism [9-11] and some are based on Pomeron exchange [12].

Recently, different modeling methods, based on soft computing systems, include the application of Artificial Intelligence (AI) Techniques. Those Evolution Algorithms have a physical powerful existence in that field [13-17]. The behavior of the p-p interactions is complicated due to the nonlinear relationship between the interaction parameters and the output. To understand the interactions of fundamental particles, multipart data analysis are needed and AI techniques are vital. Those techniques are becoming useful as alternate approaches to conventional ones [18]. In this sense, AI techniques, such as Artificial Neural Network (ANN) [19], Genetic Algorithm (GA) [20], Genetic Programming (GP) [21 and Gene Expression Programming (GEP) [22], can be used as alternative tools for the simulation of these interactions [13-17, 21-23].

The motivation of using a NN approach is its learning algorithm that learns the relationships between variables in sets of data and then builds models to explain these relationships (mathematically dependant).

In this chapter, we have discovered the functions that describe the multiplicity distribution of the charged shower particles of p-p interactions at different values of high energies using the GA-ANN technique. This chapter is organized on five sections. Section 2, gives a review to the basics of the NN & GA technique. Section 3 explains how NN & GA is used to model the p-p interaction. Finally, the results and conclusions are provided in sections 4 and 5 respectively.

2. An overview of Artificial Neural Networks (ANN)

An ANN is a network of artificial neurons which can store, gain and utilize knowledge. Some researchers in ANNs decided that the name ``neuron'' was inappropriate and used other terms, such as ``node''. However, the use of the term neuron is now so deeply established that its continued general use seems assured. A way to encompass the NNs studied in the literature is to regard them as dynamical systems controlled by synaptic matrixes (i.e. Parallel Distributed Processes (PDPs)) [24].

In the following sub-sections we introduce some of the concepts and the basic components of NNs:

2.1. Neuron-like Processing Units

A processing neuron based on neural functionality which equals to the summation of the products of the input patterns element $\{x_1, x_2,..., x_p\}$ and its corresponding weights $\{w_1, w_2,..., w_p\}$ plus the bias θ. Some important concepts associated with this simplified neuron are defined below.

A single-layer network is an area of neurons while a multilayer network consists of more than one area of neurons.

Let $u_i{}^\ell$ be the ith neuron in ℓ^{th} layer. The input layer is called the xth layer and the output layer is called the Oth layer. Let $n\ell$ be the number of neurons in the ℓth layer. The weight of the link between neuron $u_i{}^\ell$ in layer ℓ and neuron $u_i{}^{\ell+1}$ in layer $\ell+1$ is denoted by $w_{ij}{}^\ell$. Let $\{x_1, x_2,..., x_p\}$ be the set of input patterns that the network is supposed to learn its classification and let $\{d_1, d_2,..., d_p\}$be the corresponding desired output patterns. It should be noted that x_p is an n dimension vector $\{x_{1p}, x_{2p},..., x_{np}\}$ and d_p is an n dimension vector $\{d_{1p}, d_{2p},..., d_{np}\}$. The pair (x_p, d_p) is called a training pattern.

The output of a neuron $u_i{}^0$ is the input x_{ip} (for input pattern p). For the other layers, the network input $net_{pi}{}^{\ell+1}$ to a neuron $u_i{}^{\ell+1}$ for the input $x_{pi}{}^{\ell+1}$ is usually computed as follows:

$$net_{pi}^{t+1} = \sum_{j=1}^{n_i} w_{ij}^t o_{pj}^t - \theta_i^{t+1} \tag{1}$$

where $O_{pj}{}^\ell = x_{pi}{}^{\ell+1}$ is the output of the neuron $u_j{}^\ell$ of layer ℓ and $\theta_i{}^{\ell+1}$ is the neuron's bias value of neuron $u_i{}^{\ell+1}$ of layer $\ell+1$. For the sake of a homogeneous representation, θ_i is often substituted by a ``bias neuron'' with a constant output 1. This means that biases can be treated like weights, which is done throughout the remainder of the text.

2.2. Activation Functions

The activation function converts the neuron input to its activation (i.e. a new state of activation) by f (net_p). This allows the variation of input conditions to affect the output, usually included as O_p.

The sigmoid function, as a non-linear function, is also often used as an activation function. The logistic function is an example of a sigmoid function of the following form:

$$o_{pj}^t = f(net_{pi}^t) = \frac{1}{1+e^{-\beta net_{pi}^t}} \tag{2}$$

where β determines the steepness of the activation function. In the rest of this chapter we assume that $\beta=1$.

2.3. Network Architectures

Network architectures have different types (single-layer feedforward, multi-layer feedforward, and recurrent networks) [25]. In this chapter the Multi-layer Feedforward Networks are considered, these contain one or more hidden layers. Hidden layers are placed between input and output layers. Those hidden layers enable extraction of higher-order features.

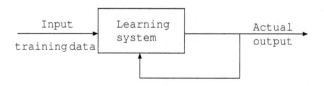

Figure 1. the three layers (input, hidden and output) of neurons are fully interconnected.

The input layer receives an external activation vector, and passes it via weighted connections to the neurons in the first hidden layer [25]. An example of this arrangement, a three layer NN, is shown in Fig 1. This is a common form of NN.

2.4. Neural Networks Learning

To use a NN, it is essential to have some form of training, through which the values of the weights in the network are adjusted to reflect the characteristics of the input data. When the network is trained sufficiently, it will obtain the most nearest correct output for a presented set of input data.

A set of well-defined rules for the solution of a learning problem is called a learning algorithm. No unique learning algorithm exists for the design of NN. Learning algorithms differ from each other in the way in which the adjustment of Δw_{ij} to the synaptic weight w_{ij} is formulated. In other words, the objective of the learning process is to tune the weights in the network so that the network performs the desired mapping of input to output activation.

NNs are claimed to have the feature of generalization, through which a trained NN is able to provide correct output data to a set of previously (unseen) input data. Training determines the generalization capability in the network structure.

Supervised learning is a class of learning rules for NNs. In which a teaching is provided by telling the network output required for a given input. Weights are adjusted in the learning system so as to minimize the difference between the desired and actual outputs for each input training data. An example of a supervised learning rule is the delta rule which aims to minimize the error function. This means that the actual response of each output neuron, in the network, approaches the desired response for that neuron. This is illustrated in Fig 2.

The error ε_{pi} for the ith neuron $u_i{}^o$ of the output layer o for the training pair (x_p, t_p) is computed as:

$$\varepsilon_{pi} = t_{pi} - o_{pi}{}^o \tag{3}$$

This error is used to adjust the weights in such a way that the error is gradually reduced. The training process stops when the error for every training pair is reduced to an acceptable level, or when no further improvement is obtained.

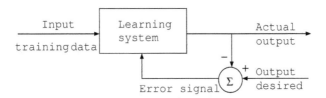

Figure 2. Example of Supervised Learning.

A method, known as "learning by epoch", first sums gradient information for the whole pattern set and then updates the weights. This method is also known as "batch learning" and most researchers use it for its good performance [25]. Each weight-update tries to minimize the summed error of the pattern set. The error function can be defined for one training pattern pair (x_p, d_p) as:

$$E_p = 1/2 \sum_{i=1}^{n_o} \varepsilon_{pi} \qquad (4)$$

Then, the error function can be defined for all the patterns (Known as the Total Sum of Squared, (TSS) errors as:

$$E = \frac{1}{2} \sum_{p=1}^{m} \sum_{i=1}^{n} \varepsilon_{pi} \qquad (5)$$

The most desirable condition that we could achieve in any learning algorithm training is $\varepsilon_{pi} \geq 0$. Obviously, if this condition holds for all patterns in the training set, we can say that the algorithm found a global minimum.

The weights in the network are changed along a search direction, to drive the weights in the direction of the estimated minimum. The weight updating rule for the batch mode is given by:

$$w_{ij}^{s+1} = \Delta w_{ij}^{\ell}(s) + w_{ij}^{\ell}(s) \qquad (6)$$

where w_{ij}^{s+1} is the update weight of w_{ij}^{ℓ} of layer ℓ in the sth learning step, and s is the step number in the learning process.

In training a network, the available input data set consists of many facts and is normally divided into two groups. One group of facts is used as the training data set and the second group is retained for checking and testing the accuracy of the performance of the network after training. The proposed ANN model was trained using Levenberg- Marquardt optimization technique [26].

Data collected from experiments are divided into two sets, namely, training set and testing set. The training set is used to train the ANN model by adjusting the link weights of network model, which should include the data covering the entire experimental space. This means that the training data set has to be fairly large to contain all the required information and must include a wide variety of data from different experimental conditions, including different formulation composition and process parameters.

Linearly, the training error keeps dropping. If the error stops decreasing, or alternatively starts to rise, the ANN model starts to over-fit the data, and at this point, the training must be stopped. In case over-fitting or over-learning occurs during the training process, it is usually advisable to decrease the number of hidden units and/or hidden layers. In contrast, if the network is not sufficiently powerful to model the underlying function, over-learning is not likely to occur, and the training errors will drop to a satisfactory level.

3. An overview of Genetic Algorithm

3.1. Introduction

Evolutionary Computation (EC) uses computational models of evolutionary processes based on concepts in biological theory. Varieties of these evolutionary computational models have been proposed and used in many applications, including optimization of NN parameters and searching for new NN learning rules. We will refer to them as Evolutionary Algorithms (EAs) [27-29]

EAs are based on the evolution of a population which evolves according to rules of selection and other operators such as crossover and mutation. Each individual in the population is given a measure of its fitness in the environment. Selection favors individual with high fitness. These individuals are perturbed using the operators. This provides general heuristics for exploration in the environment. This cycle of evaluation, selection, crossover, mutation and survival continues until some termination criterion is met. Although, it is very simple from a biological point of view, these algorithms are sufficiently complex to provide strong and powerful adaptive search mechanisms.

Genetic Algorithms (GAs) were developed in the 70s by John Holland [30], who strongly stressed recombination as the energetic potential of evolution [32]. The notion of using abstract syntax trees to represent programs in GAs, Genetic Programming (GP), was suggested in [33], first implemented in [34] and popularised in [35-37]. The term Genetic Programming is used to refer to both tree-based GAs and the evolutionary generation of programs [38,39]. Although similar at the highest level, each of the two varieties implements genetic operators in a different manner. This thesis concentrates on the tree-based variety. We will discuss GP further in Section 3.4. In the following two sections, whose descriptions are mainly based on [30,32,33,35,36,37], we give more background information about natural and artificial evolution in general, and on GAs in particular.

3.2. Natural and Artificial Evolution

As described by Darwin [40], evolution is the process by which a population of organisms gradually adapt over time to enhance their chances of surviving. This is achieved by ensuring that the stronger individuals in the population have a higher chance of reproducing and creating children (offspring).

In artificial evolution, the members of the population represent possible solutions to a particular optimization problem. The problem itself represents the environment. We must apply each potential solution to the problem and assign it a fitness value, indicating its performance on the problem. The two essential features of natural evolution which we need to maintain are propagation of more adaptive features to future generations (by applying a selective pressure which gives better solutions a greater opportunity to reproduce) and the heritability of features from parent to children (we need to ensure that the process of reproduction keeps most of the features of the parent solution and yet allows for variety so that new features can be explored) [30].

3.3. The Genetic Algorithm

GAs is powerful search and optimization techniques, based on the mechanics of natural selection [31]. Some basic terms used are:

- A *phenotype* is a possible solution to the problem;
- A *chromosome* is an encoding representation of a phenotype in a form that can be used;
- A *population* is the variety of chromosomes that evolves from generation to generation;
- A *generation* (a population set) represents a single step toward the solution;
- *Fitness* is the measure of the performance of an individual on the problem;
- *Evaluation* is the interpretation of the genotype into the phenotype and the computation of its fitness;
- *Genes* are the parts of data which make up a chromosome.

The advantage of GAs is that they have a consistent structure for different problems. Accordingly, one GA can be used for a variety of optimization problems. GAs are used for a number of different application areas [30]. GA is capable of finding good solutions quickly [32]. Also, the GA is inherently parallel, since a population of potential solutions is maintained.

To solve an optimization problem, a GA requires four components and a termination criterion for the search. The components are: a representation (encoding) of the problem, a fitness evaluation function, a population initialization procedure and a set of genetic operators.

In addition, there are a set of GA control parameters, predefined to guide the GA, such as the size of the population, the method by which genetic operators are chosen, the probabilities of each genetic operator being chosen, the choice of methods for implementing probability in selection, the probability of mutation of a gene in a selected individual, the method used to select a crossover point for the recombination operator and the seed value used for the random number generator.

The structure of a typical GA can be described as follows [41]

In the algorithm, an initial population is generated in line 2. Then, the algorithm computes the fitness for each member of the initial population in line 3. Subsequently, a loop is entered based on whether or not the algorithm's termination criteria are met in line 4. Line 6 contains the control code for the inner loop in which a new generation is created. Lines 7 through 10 contain the part of the algorithm in which new individuals are generated. First, a genetic operator is selected. The particular numbers of parents for that operator are then selected. The operator is then applied to generate one or more new children. Finally, the new children are added to the new generation.

```
(1)                     0→t;
(2)                     population(s) → P(t);
(3)                     evaluate(P(t));
(4)                     REPEAT until solution is found
(5)                             {
(6)                                 t+1 → t;
(7)                                 selection(P(t)) → B(t);
(8)                                 breeding(B(t)) → R(t);
(9)                                 mutation(R(t)) → M(t);
(10)                                evaluate(M(t));
(11)                                survival(M(t),P(t-1)) → P(t);
(12)                            }
(13)                    END REPEAT;
```

where:

s is a random generator seed;
t represents the generation;
P(t) is the population in generation t;
B(t) is the buffer of parents in generation t;
R(t) are the children generated by recombining or cloning B(t);
M(t) are the children created by mutating R(t).

Lines 11 and 12 serve to close the outer loop of the algorithm. Fitness values are computed for each individual in the new generation. These values are used to guide simulated natural selection in the new generation. The termination criterion is tested and the algorithm is either repeated or terminated.

The most significant differences in GAs are:

- GAs search a population of points in parallel, not a single point

- GAs do not require derivative information (unlike gradient descending methods, e.g. SBP) or other additional knowledge - only the objective function and corresponding fitness levels affect the directions of search

- GAs use probabilistic transition rules, not deterministic ones

- GA can provide a number of potential solutions to a given problem

- GAs operate on fixed length representations.

4. The Proposed Hybrid GA - ANN Modeling

Genetic connectionism combines genetic search and connectionist computation. GAs have been applied successfully to the problem of designing NNs with supervised learning processes, for evolving the architecture suitable for the problem [42-47]. However, these applications do not address the problem of training neural networks, since they still depend on other training methods to adjust the weights.

4.1. GAs for Training NNs

GAs have been used for training NNs either with fixed architectures or in combination with constructive/destructive methods. This can be made by replacing traditional learning algorithms such as gradient-based methods [48]. Not only have GAs been used to perform weight training for supervised learning and for reinforcement learning applications, but they have also been used to select training data and to translate the output behavior of NNs [49-51]. GAs have been applied to the problem of finding NN architectures [52-57], where an architecture specification indicates how many hidden units a network should have and how these units should be connected.

The process key in the evolutionary design of neural architectures is shown in Fig. The topologies of the network have to be distinct before any training process. The definition of the architecture has great weight on the network performance, the effectiveness and efficiency of the learning process. As discussed in [58], the alternative provided by destructive and constructive techniques is not satisfactory.

The network architecture designing can be explained as a search in the architecture space that each point represents a different topology. The search space is huge, even with a limited number of neurons, and a controlled connectivity. Additionally, the search space makes things even more difficult in some cases. For instance when networks with different topologies may show similar learning and generalization abilities, alternatively, networks with similar structures may have different performances. In addition, the performance evaluation depends on the training method and on the initial conditions (weight initialization) [59]. Building the architectures by means of GAs is strongly reliant on how the features of the network are encoded in the genotype. Using a bitstring is not essentially the best approach to evolve the architecture. Therefore, a determination has to be made concerning how the information about the architecture should be encoded in the genotype.

To find good NN architectures using GAs, we should know how to encode architectures (neurons, layers, and connections) in the chromosomes that can be manipulated by the GA. Encoding of NNs onto a chromosome can take many different forms.

4.2. Modeling by Using ANN and GA

This study proposed a hybrid model combined of ANN and GA (We called it "GA–ANN hybrid model") for optimization of the weights of feed-forward neural networks to improve the effectiveness of the ANN model. Assuming that the structure of these networks has been decided. Genetic algorithm is run to have the optimal parameters of the architectures, weights and biases of all the neurons which are joined to create vectors.We construct a genetic algorithm, which can search for the global optimum of the number of hidden units and the connection structure between the inputs and the output layers. During the weight training and adjusting process, the fitness functions of a neural network can be defined by considering two important factors: the error is the different between target and actual outputs. In this work, we defined the fitness function as the mean square error (SSE).The approach is to use the GA-ANN model that is enough intelligent to discover functions for p-p interactions (mean multiplicity distribution of charged particles with respects of the total center of mass energy). The model is trained/predicated by using experimental data to simulate the p-p interaction. GA-ANN has the potential to discover a new model, to show that the data sets are subdivided into two sets (training and predication). GA-ANN discovers a new model by using the training set while the predicated set is used to examine their generalization capabilities.To measure the error between the experimental data and the simulated data we used the statistic measures. The total deviation of the response values from the fit to the response values. It is also called the summed square of residuals and is usually labeled as *SSE*. The statistical measures of sum squared error (SSE),

$$SSE = \sum_{i=1}^{n} (y_i - \hat{y}_i)^2 \tag{7}$$

where $\hat{y}_i = b_0 + b_1 x_i$ is the *predicted value* for x_i and y_i is the observed data value occurring at x_i.

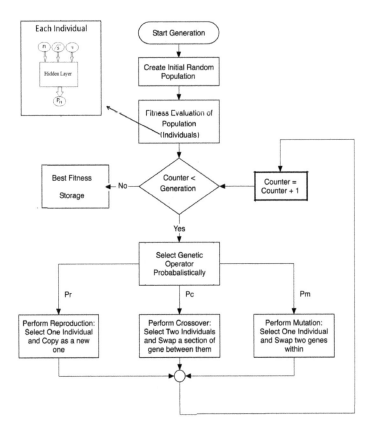

Figure 3. Overview of GA-ANN hybrid model.

The proposed GA-ANN hybrid model has been used to model the multiplicity distribution of the charged shower particles. The proposed model was trained using Levenberg-Marquardt optimization technique [26]. The architecture of GA-ANN has three inputs and one output. The inputs are the charged particles multiplicity (n), the total center of mass energy ($\sqrt{s}$), and the pseudo rapidity (η).The output is the charged particles multiplicity distribution (P_n). Figure 1 shows the schematic of GA-ANN model.

Data collected from experiments are divided into two sets, namely, training set and testing set. The training set is used to train the GA- ANN hybrid model. The testing data set is used to confirm the accuracy of the proposed model. It ensures that the relationship between inputs and outputs, based on the training and test sets are real. The data set is divided into two groups 80% for training and 20% for testing. For work completeness, the final weights and biases after training are given in Appendix A.

5. Results and discussion

The input patterns of the designed GA-ANN hybrid have been trained to produce target patterns that modeling the pseudo-rapidity distribution. The fast Levenberg-Marquardt algorithm (LMA) has been employed to train the ANN. In order to obtain the optimal structure of ANN, we have used GA as hybrid model.

Simulation results based on both ANN and GA-ANN hybrid model, to model the distribution of shower charged particle produced for P-P at different the total center of mass energy, $\sqrt{s}$ 0.9 TeV, 2.36 Tev and 7 TeV, are given in Figure 2-a, b, and c respectively. We notice that the curves obtained by the trained GA-ANN hybrid model show an exact fitting to the experimental data in the three cases.

Then, the GA-ANN Hybrid model is able to exactly model for the charge particle multiplicity distribution. The total sum of squared error SSE, the weights and biases which used for the designed network are provided in the Appendix A.

Structure	Number of connections	Error values	Learning rule
ANN: 3 x15x15x1	285	0.01	LMA
GA optimization structure	229	0.0001	GA

Table 1. Comparison between the different training algorithms (ANN and GA-ANN) for the for charge particle Multiplicity distribution.

In this model we have obtained the minimum error (=0.0001) by using GA. Table 1 shows a comparison between the ANN model and the GA-ANN model for the prediction of the pseudo-rapidity distribution. In the 3x15x15x1 ANN structure, we have used 285 connections and obtained an error equal to 0.0001, while the connection in GA-ANN model is 225. Therefore, we noticed in the ANN model that by increasing the number of connections to 285 the error decreases to 0.01, but this needs more calculations. By using GA optimization search, we have obtained the structure which minimizes the number of connections equals to 229 only and the error (= 0.0001). This indicates that the GA-ANN hybrid model is more efficient than the ANN model.

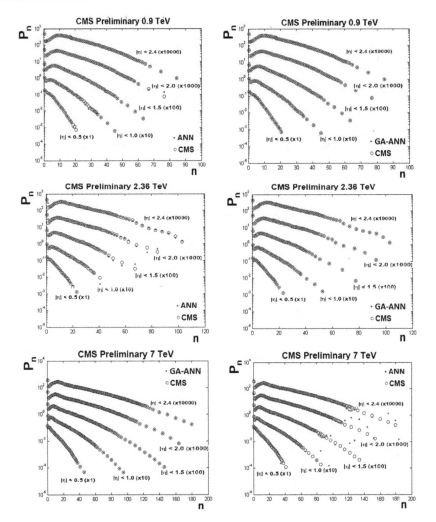

Figure 4. ANN and GA-ANN simulation results for charge particle Multiplicity distribution of shower p-p.

6. Conclusions

The chapter presents the GA-ANN as a new technique for constructing the functions of the multiplicity distribution of charged particles, P_n (n, η, $\sqrt{s}$) of p-p interaction. The discovered models show good match to the experimental data. Moreover, they are capable of testing experimental data for P_n (n, η, $\sqrt{s}$) that are not used in the training session.

Consequence, the testing values of P_n (n, η, $\sqrt{s}$) in terms of the same parameters are in good agreement with the experimental data from Particle Data Group. Finally, we conclude that GA-ANN has become one of important research areas in the field of high Energy physics.

Appendices

The efficient ANN structure is given as follows: [3x15x15x1] or [ixjxkxm].

Weights coefficient after training are:

Wji =	[3.5001	-1.0299	1.6118
	0.7565	-2.2408	3.2605
	-1.4374	1.1033	-3.1349
	2.0116	2.8137	-1.7322
	-3.6012	-1.5717	-0.2805
	-1.6741	-2.5844	2.7109
	-2.0600	-3.1519	1.2488
	-0.1986	1.0028	-4.0855
	2.6272	0.8254	3.6292
	-2.3420	3.0259	-1.9551
	-3.2561	0.4683	3.0896
	1.2442	-0.8996	-3.4896
	-3.2589	-1.1887	2.0875
	-1.0889	-1.2080	4.3688
	-2.7820	-1.4291	2.3577
	3.1861	-0.6309	2.0691
	3.4979	0.2456	-2.6633
	-0.4889	2.4145	-2.8041
	2.1091	-0.1359	-3.4762
	-0.1010	4.1758	-0.2120
	3.5538	-1.5615	-1.4795
	-3.4153	1.2517	2.1415
	2.6232	-3.0757	0.0831
	1.7632	1.9749	-2.5519
	7.6987	0.0526	0.4267].

Wkj =	[0.3294	0.5006	0.0421	0.3603	0.5147
	0.5506	0.2498	0.2678	0.2670	0.3568
	0.3951	0.2529	0.2169	0.4323	0.0683
	0.1875	0.2948	0.2705	0.2209	0.1928
	0.2207	0.6121	0.0693	0.0125	0.4214
	0.4698	0.0697	0.4795	0.0425	0.2387
	0.1975	0.1441	0.2947	0.1347	0.0403
	0.0745	0.2345	0.1572	0.2792	0.3784
	0.1043	0.4784	0.2899	0.2012	0.4270
	0.5578	0.7176	0.3619	0.2601	0.2738
	0.1081	0.2412	0.0074	0.3967	0.2235
	0.0466	0.0407	0.0592	0.3128	0.1570
	0.4321	0.4505	0.0313	0.5976	0.0851
	0.4295	0.4887	0.0694	0.3939	0.0354
	0.1972	0.1416	0.1706	0.1719	0.0761

Columns 6 through 10

0.2102	0.0185	-0.1658	-0.1943	-0.4253
0.2685	0.4724	0.4946	-0.3538	0.1559
0.3198	0.1207	0.5657	-0.3894	0.1497
-0.5528	0.4031	0.5570	0.4562	-0.5802
0.3498	-0.3870	0.2453	0.4581	0.2430
0.2047	-0.0802	0.1584	0.2806	-0.2790
0.0981	-0.5055	0.2559	-0.0297	-0.2058
-0.3498	-0.5513	0.0022	-0.3034	0.2156
-0.6226	-0.4085	0.4338	-0.0441	-0.4801
-0.0093	0.0875	0.0815	0.3935	0.1840
0.0063	0.2790	0.7558	0.3383	0.5882
-0.5506	-0.0518	0.5625	0.2459	-0.0612
0.0036	0.4404	-0.3268	-0.5626	-0.2253
0.5591	-0.2797	-0.0408	0.1302	-0.4361

Columns 11 through 15				
-0.6123	0.4833	-0.0457	0.3927	-0.3694
-0.0746	-0.0978	0.0710	-0.7610	0.1412
-0.3373	0.4167	0.3421	-0.0577	0.2109
0.2422	0.2013	-0.1384	-0.3700	-0.4464
0.0868	-0.5964	-0.0837	-0.7971	-0.4299
-0.6500	-1.1315	-0.4557	1.6169	-0.3205
0.2205	1.0185	0.4752	-0.4155	0.1614
1.2311	0.0061	-0.0539	0.6813	0.9395
-0.4295	-0.3083	0.2768	-0.1151	0.0802
-0.6988	0.2346	-0.3455	0.0432	0.1663
-0.0601	0.0527	0.3519	0.3520	-0.7821
-0.6241	-0.1201	-0.4317	0.7441	0.7305
0.5433	-0.6909	0.4848	-0.3888	0.3710
-0.6920	-0.0190	-0.4892	0.1678	0.0808
-0.3752	-0.1745	-0.7304	0.0462	-0.3883].

Wmk = [0.9283 1.6321 0.0356 -0.4147 -0.8312 -3.0722 -1.9368 1.7113 0.0100 -0.4066 0.0721 0.1362 0.4692 -0.9749 1.7950].

bi = [-4.7175 -2.2157 3.6932].

bj = [-4.1756 -3.8559 3.9766 -3.3430 2.7598 2.5040 2.1326 1.9297

-0.6547 0.7272 0.5859 -1.1575 0.3029 0.3486 -0.4088].

bk = [1.7214 -1.7100 1.5000 -1.2915 1.1448 1.0033 -0.6584 -0.4397

-0.4963 -0.3211 0.2594 -0.1649 0.0603 -0.1078].

bm = [-0.2071].

The optimized GA-ANN:

The standard GA has been used. The parameters are given as follows: Generation = 1000, Population = 4000, probability of crossover = 0.9, probability of mutation = 0.001, Fitness function is SSE. A neural network had been optimized as 229 of neurons.

Acknowledgements

The authors highly acknowledge and deeply appreciate the supports of the Egyptian Academy of Scientific Research and Technology (ASRT) and the Egyptian Network for High Energy Physics (ENHEP).

Author details

Amr Radi[1*] and Samy K. Hindawi[2]

*Address all correspondence to: Amr.radi@cern.ch

1 Department of Physics, Faculty of Sciences, Ain Shams University, Abbassia, Cairo, Egypt / Center of Theoretical Physics at the British University in Egypt (BUE), Egypt

2 Department of Physics, Faculty of Sciences, Ain Shams University, Abbassia, Cairo, Egypt

References

[1] CMS Collaboration. (2011). *J. High Energy Phys.*, 01, 079.

[2] CMS Collaboration. (2011). *J. High Energy Phys.*, 08, 141.

[3] CMS Collaboration. (2010). *Phys. Rev. Lett.*, 105, 022002.

[4] ATLAS Collaboration. (2012). *Phys. Lett. B*, 707, 330-348.

[5] ATLAS Collaboration,. (2011). *Phys. Lett. B*.

[6] ALICE Collaboration,. (2010). *Phys. Lett. B*, 693, 53-68.

[7] ALICE Collaboration,. (2010). *Eur. Phys. J. C*, 68345-354.

[8] TOTEM Collaboration,. (2011). *EPL*, 96, 21002.

[9] Jacob, M., & Slansky, R. (1972). *Phys. Rev.*, D5, 1847.

[10] Hwa, R. (1970). *Phys. Rev.*, D1, 1790.

[11] Hwa, R. (1971). *Phys. Rev. Lett.*, 26, 1143.

[12] Engel, R., Phys, Z., & , C. (1995). *R. Engel, J. Ranft and S. Roesler, Phys. Rev.*, D52.

[13] Teodorescu, L., & Sherwood, D. (2008). *Comput. Phys. Commun.*, 178, 409.

[14] Teodorescu, L. (2006). *IEEE T. Nucl. Sci.*, 53, 2221.

[15] Link, J. M. (2005). *Nucl. Instrum. Meth. A*, 551, 504.

[16] El-Bakry, S. Yaseen, & Radi, Amr. (2007). *Int. J. Mod. Phys. C*, 18, 351.

[17] El-dahshan, E., Radi, A., & El-Bakry, M. Y. (2009). *Int. J. Mod. Phys. C*, 20, 1817.

[18] Whiteson, S., & Whiteson, D. (2009). *Eng. Appl. Artif. Intel.*, 22, 1203.

[19] Haykin, S. (1999). *Neural networks a comprehensive foundation* (2nd ed.), Prentice Hall.

[20] Holland, J. H. (1975). *Adaptation in Natural and Artificial Systems*, University of Michigan Press, Ann Arbor.

[21] Koza, J. R. (1992). Genetic Programming: On the Programming of Computers by means of Natural Selection. The MIT Press, Cambridge, MA.

[22] Ferreira, C. (2006). Gene Expression Programming: Mathematical Modeling by an Artificial Intelligence. 2nd Edition, Springer-Verlag, Germany.

[23] Eiben, A. E., & Smith, J. E. (2003). Introduction to Evolutionary Algorithms. Springer, Berlin.

[24] Radi, Amr. (2000). Discovery of Neural network learning rules using genetic programming. *PHD, the School of computers Sciences*, Birmingham University.

[25] Teodorescu, L. (2005). High energy physics data analysis with gene expression programming. *In 2005 IEEE Nuclear Science Symposium Conference Record*, 1, 143-147.

[26] Hagan, M. T., & Menhaj, M. B. (1994). Training feedforward networks with the Marquardt algorithm. *IEEE Transactions on Neural Networks*, 6, 861-867.

[27] Back, T. (1996). *Evolutionary Algorithms in Theory and Practice*, Oxford University Press, New York.

[28] Fogel, D. B. (1994). An Introduction to Simulated Evolutionary Optimization. *IEEE Trans. Neural Networks*, 5(1), 3-14.

[29] Back, T., Hammel, U., & Schwefel, H. P. (1997). Evolutionary Computation: Comments on the History and Current State. *IEEE Trans. Evolutionary Computation*, 1(1), 3-17.

[30] Holland, . H. ((1975).) Adaptation in Natural and Artificial Systems The University of Michigan Press Ann Arbor, Michigan

[31] Fogel, D. B. (1995). Evolutionary Computation: Toward a New Philosophy of Machine Intelligence. *IEEE Press*, Piscataway, NJ.

[32] Goldberg, D. E. (1989). *Genetic Algorithm in Search Optimization and Machine Learning*, Addison-Wesley, New York.

[33] Richard. Forsyth (1981). BEAGLE A Darwinian Approach to Pattern Recognition. Kybernetes , 10(3), 159-166.

[34] Cramer, Nichael Lynn. (1985). A representation for the Adaptive Generation of Simple Sequential Programs. *in Proceedings of an International Conference on Genetic Algorithms and the Applications*, Grefenstette, John J. (ed.), CMU.

[35] Koza, J. R. (1992). Genetic Programming: On the Programming of Computers by Means of Natural Selection. MIT Press.

[36] Koza, J. R. (1994). Genetic Programming II: Automatic Discovery of Reusable Programs. MIT Press.

[37] Koza, J. R., Bennett, F. H., Andre, D., & Keane, M. A. (1999). *Genetic Programming III: Darwinian Invention and Problem Solving*, Morgan Kaufmann.

[38] Banzhaf, W., Nordin, P., Keller, R. E., & Francone, F. D. (1998). *Genetic Programming: An Introduction: On the Automatic Evolution of Computer Programs and its Applications*, Morgan Kaufmann.

[39] Mitchell, M. (1996). *An Introduction to Genetic Algorithms*, MIT Press.

[40] Darwin, C. (1959). *The Autobiography of Charles Darwin: With original omissions restored, edited with appendix and notes by his grand-daughter*, Nora Barlow, Norton.

[41] Whitley, Darrel. (1994). A genetic algorithm tutorial. *Statistics and Computing*, 4, 65-85.

[42] A new algorithm for developing dynamic radial basis function neural network models based on genetic algorithms

[43] Sarimveis, H., Alexandridis, A., Mazarkakis, S., & Bafas, G. (2004). *in Computers & Chemical Engineering*.

[44] An optimizing BP neural network algorithm based on genetic algorithm

[45] Ding, Shifei., & Su, Chunyang. (2010). *in Artificial Intelligence Review*.

[46] Hierarchical genetic algorithm based neural network design

[47] Yen, G. G., & Lu, H. (2000). *in IEEE Symposium on Combinations of Evolutionary Computation and Neural Networks*.

[48] Genetic Algorithm based Selective Neural Network Ensemble

[49] Zhou, Z. H., Wu, J. X., Jiang, Y., & Chen, S. F. (2001). *in Proceedings of the 17th International Joint Conference on Artificial Intelligence*.

[50] Modified backpropagation algorithms for training the multilayer feedforward neural networks with hard-limiting neurons

[51] Yu, Xiangui, Loh, N. K., Jullien, G. A., & Miller, W. C. (1993). *in Proceedings of Canadian Conference on Electrical and Computer Engineering*.

[52] Training Feedforward Neural Networks Using Genetic Algorithms

[53] Montana, David J., & Davis, Lawrence. (1989). *in Machine Learning*.

[54] van Rooij, A. J. F., Jain, L. C., & Johnson, R. P. (1996). *Neural network training using genetic algorithms*, Singapore, World Scientific.

[55] Maniezzo, Vittorio. (1994). Genetic Evolution of the Topology and Weight Distribution of Neural Networks. *in: IEEE Transactions of Neural Networks*, 5(1), 39-53.

[56] Bornholdt, Stefan., & Graudenz, Dirk. (1992). General Asymmetric Neural Networks and Structure Design by Genetic Algorithms. *in: Neural Networks*, 5, 327-334, Pergamon Press.

[57] Kitano, Hiroaki. (1990a). Designing Neural Networks Using Genetic Algorithms with Graph Generation Systems. *in: Complex Systems* [4], 461-476.

[58] Nolfi, S., & Parisi, D. (1994). Desired answers do not correspond to good teaching inputs in ecological neural networks. *Neural processing letters*, 1, 1-4.

[59] Nolfi, S., & Parisi, D. (1996). Learning to adapt to changing environments in evolving neural networks. *Adaptive Behavior*, 5, 75-97.

[60] Nolfi, S., Parisi, D., & Elman, J. L. (1994). Learning and evolution in neural networks. *Adaptive Behavior*, 3(1), 5-28.

[61] Pujol, J. C. F., & Poli, R. (1998). Efficient evolution of asymmetric recurrent neural networks using a two-dimensional representation. *Proceedings of the first European workshop on genetic programming (EUROGP)*, 130-141.

[62] Miller, G. F., Todd, P. M., & Hedge, S. U. (1989). Designing neural networks using genetic algorithms. *Proceedings of the third international conference on genetic algorithms and their applications*, 379-384.

[63] Mandischer, M. (1993). Representation and evolution of neural networks. Paper presented at Artificial neural nets and genetic algorithms proceedings of the international conference at Innsbruck, Austria. 643-649, Wien and New York, Springer.

[64] Figueira Pujol, Joao Carlos. (1999). Evolution of Artificial Neural Networks Using a Two-dimensional Representation. *PhD thesis*, School of Computer Science, University of Birmingham, UK.

[65] Yao, X. (1995f). Evolutionary artificial neural networks. *In Encyclopedia of Computer Science and Technology, ed. A. Kent and J. G. Williams, Marcel Dekker Inc., New York*, 33, 137-170, Also appearing in Encyclopedia of Library and Information Science.

Chapter 8

Edge Detection in
Biomedical Images Using Self-Organizing Maps

Lucie Gráfová, Jan Mareš, Aleš Procházka and
Pavel Konopásek

Additional information is available at the end of the chapter

1. Introduction

The application of self-organizing maps (SOMs) to the edge detection in biomedical images is discussed. The SOM algorithm has been implemented in MATLAB program suite with various optional parameters enabling the adjustment of the model according to the user's requirements. For easier application of SOM the graphical user interface has been developed. The edge detection procedure is a critical step in the analysis of biomedical images, enabling for instance the detection of the abnormal structure or the recognition of different types of tissue. The self-organizing map provides a quick and easy approach for edge detection tasks with satisfying quality of outputs, which has been verified using the high-resolution computed tomography images capturing the expressions of the Granulomatosis with polyangiitis. The obtained results have been discussed with an expert as well.

2. Self-organizing map

2.1. Self-organizing map in edge detection performance

The self-organizing map (SOM) [5, 9] is widely applied approach for clustering and pattern recognition that can be used in many stages of the image processing, e. g. in color image segmentation [18], generation of a global ordering of spectral vectors [26], image compression [25], binarisation document [4] etc.

The edge detection approaches based on SOMs are not extensively used. Nevertheless there are some examples of SOM utilization in edge detection, e. g. texture edge detection [27], edge detection by contours [13] or edge detection performed in combination with conventional edge detector [24] and methods of image de-noising [8] .

In our case, the SOM has been utilized in edge detection process in order to reduce the image intensity levels.

2.2. Structure of self-organizing map

A SOM has two layers of neurons, see Figure 1.

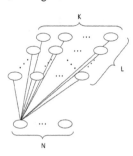

Figure 1. Structure of SOM

The input layer (size $Nx1$) represents input data x_1, x_2, $\ldots$, x_M (M inputs, each input is N dimensional). The output layer (size KxL), that may have a linear or 2D arrangement, represents clusters in which the input data will be grouped. Each neuron of the input layer is connected with all neurons of the output layer through the weights W (size of the weight matrix is $KxLxN$).

2.3. Training of self-organizing map

A SOM is neural network with *unsupervised* type of learning, i. e. no cluster values denoting an a priori grouping of the data instances are provided.

The learning process is divided in *epochs*, during which the entire batch of input vectors is processed. The epoch involves the following steps:

1. Consecutive submission of an input data vector to the network.

2. Calculation of a distances between the input vector and the weight vectors of the neurons of the output layer.

3. Selection of the nearest (the most similar) neuron of the output layer to the presented input data vector.

4. An adjustment of the weights.

SOM can be trained in either *recursive* or *batch mode*. In recursive mode, the weights of the winning neurons are updated after each submission of an input vector, whereas in batch mode, the weight adjustment for each neuron is made after the entire batch of inputs has been processed, i. e. at the end of an epoch.

The weights adapt during the learning process based on a competition, i. e. the nearest (the most similar) neuron of the output layer to the submitted input vector becomes a winner and its weight vector and the weight vectors of its neighbouring neurons are adjusted according to

$$W = W + \lambda \, \phi_s \, (x_i - W), \tag{1}$$

where **W** is the weight matrix, $\mathbf{x_i}$ the submitted input vector, λ the learning parameter determining the strength of the learning and ϕ_s the neighbourhood strength parameter determining how the weight adjustment decays with distance from the winner neuron (it depends on s, the value of the neighbourhood size parameter).

The learning process can be divided into two phases: *ordering* and *convergence*. In the ordering phase, the topological ordering of the weight vectors is established using reduction of learning rate and neighbourhood size with iterations. In the convergence phase, the SOM is fine tuned with the shrunk neighbourhood and constant learning rate. [23]

2.3.1. Learning Parameter

The *learning parameter*, corresponding to the strength of the learning, is usually reduced during the learning process. It decays from the *initial value* to the *final value*, which can be reached already during the learning process, not only at the end of the learning. There are several common forms of the decay function (see Figure 2):

1. No decay

$$\lambda_t = \lambda_0, \tag{2}$$

2. Linear decay

$$\lambda_t = \lambda_0 \left(1 - \frac{t}{\tau}\right), \tag{3}$$

3. Gaussian decay

$$\lambda_t = \lambda_0 e^{-\frac{t^2}{2\tau^2}}, \tag{4}$$

4. Exponential decay

$$\lambda_t = \lambda_0 e^{-\frac{t}{\tau}}, \tag{5}$$

where T is the total number of iterations, λ_0 and λ_t are the initial learning rate and that at iteration t, respectively. The learning parameter should be in the interval $\langle 0.01, 1\rangle$.

2.3.2. Neighbourhood

In the learning process not only the *winner* but also the *neighbouring* neurons of the winner neuron learn, i. e. adjust their weights. All neighbour weight vectors are shifted towards the submitted input vector, however, the winning neuron update is the most pronounced and the farther away the neighbouring neuron is, the less its weight is updated. This procedure of the weight adjustment produces *topology preservation*.

There are several ways how to define a neighbourhood (some of them are depicted in Figure 3).

The initial value of the *neighbourhood size* can be up to the size of the output layer, the final value of the neighbourhood size must not be less than 1. The *neighbourhood strength parameter*, determining how the weight adjustment of the neighbouring neurons decays with distance from the winner, is usually reduced during the learning process (as well as the learning parameter, analogue of Equations 2–5 and Figure 2). It decays from the *initial value* to the *final value*, which can be reached already during the learning process, not only at the end of the learning process. The neighbourhood strength parameter should be in the interval $\langle 0.01, 1 \rangle$. The Figure 4 depicts one of the possible development of neighbourhood size and strength parameters during the learning process.

2.3.3. Weights

The resulting weight vectors of the neurons of the output layer, obtained at the end of the learning process, represent the centers of the clusters. The resulting patterns of the weight vectors may depend on the type of the *weights initialization*. There are several ways how to initialize the weight vector, some of them are depicted in Figure 5.

2.3.4. Distance Measures

The criterion for victory in the competition of the neurons of the output layer, i. e. the measure of the distance between the presented input vector and its weight vectors, may have many forms. The most commonly used are:

1. Euclidean distance

$$d_j = \sqrt{\sum_{i=1}^{N} \left(x_i - w_{ji} \right)^2}, \tag{6}$$

2. Correlation

$$d_j = \sum_{i=1}^{N} \frac{(x_i - \bar{x})(w_{ji} - \overline{w_j})}{\sigma_x \sigma_{w_j}}, \tag{7}$$

3. Direction cosine

$$d_j = \frac{\sum_{i=1}^{N} x_i w_{ji}}{\|x_i\| \|w_{ji}\|}, \tag{8}$$

4. Block distance

$$d_j = \sum_{i=1}^{N} |x_i - w_{ji}|, \tag{9}$$

where x_i is i-th component of the input vector, w_{ji} i-th component of the j-th weight vector, N dimension of the input and weight vectors, $\bar{x}$ mean value of the input vector x, $\overline{w_j}$ mean value of the weight vector w_j, σ_x standard deviation of the input vector x, σ_{w_j} standard deviation of the weight vector w_j, $\|x_i\|$ length of the input vector x and $\|w_{ji}\|$ length of the weight vector w_j.

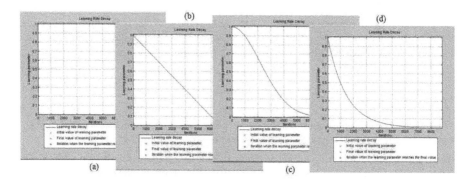

Figure 2. Learning rate decay function (dependence of the value of the learning parameter on the number of iterations): (a) No decay, (b) Linear decay, (c) Gaussian decay, (d) Exponential decay

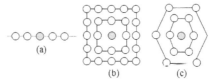

Figure 3. Types of neighbourhood: (a) Linear arrangements, (b) Square arrangements, (c) Hexagonal arrangements

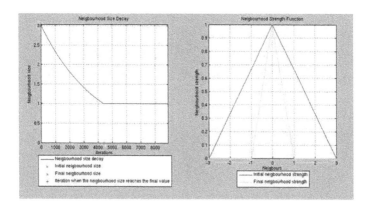

Figure 4. Neighbourhood size decay function (dependence of the neighbourhood size on the number of iterations) and neighbourhood strength decay function (dependence of the value of the neighbourhood strength on the distance from the winner)

2.3.5. Learning Progress Criterion

The *learning progress criterion*, minimized over the learning process, is the sum of distances between all input vectors and their respective winning neuron weights, calculated after the end of each epoch, according to

$$D = \sum_{i=1}^{k} \sum_{n \in c_i} (\mathbf{x_n} - \mathbf{w_i})^2, \tag{10}$$

where $\mathbf{x_n}$ is the n-th input vector belonging to cluster c_i whose center is represented by $\mathbf{w_i}$ (e. i. the weight vector of the winning neuron representing cluster c_i).

The weight adjustment corresponding to the smallest learning progress criterion is the result of the SOM learning process, see Figure 6. These weights represent the cluster centers.

For the best result, the SOM should be run several times with various settings of SOM parameters to avoid detection of local minima and to find the global optimum on the error surface plot.

2.3.6. Errors

The errors of trained SOM can be evaluated according to

1. Learning progress criterion (see Equation 10),
2. Normalized learning progress criterion

$$E = \frac{1}{M} \sum_{i=1}^{k} \sum_{n \in c_i} (\mathbf{x_n} - \mathbf{w_i})^2, \tag{11}$$

3. Normalized error in the cluster

$$E = \frac{1}{k} \sum_{i=1}^{k} \frac{1}{M_i} \sum_{n \in c_i} (\mathbf{x_n} - \mathbf{w_i})^2, \tag{12}$$

4. Error in the i-th cluster

$$E_i = \sum_{n \in c_i} (\mathbf{x_n} - \mathbf{w_i})^2, \tag{13}$$

5. Normalized error in the i-th cluster

$$E_i = \frac{1}{M_i} \sum_{n \in c_i} (\mathbf{x_n} - \mathbf{w_i})^2, \tag{14}$$

where $\mathbf{x_n}$ is the n-th input vector belonging to cluster c_i whose center is represented by w_i (e. i. the weight vector of the winning neuron representing cluster c_i), M is number of input vectors, M_i is number of input vectors belonging to i-th cluster and k is number of clusters.

For more information about the trained SOM, the distribution of the input vectors in the clusters and the errors of the clusters can be visualized, see Figure 7.

2.3.7. Forming Clusters

The *U-matrix* (the matrix of average distance between weights vectors of neighbouring neurons) can be used for finding of realistic and distinct clusters. The other approach for forming clusters on the map can be to utilize any established clustering method (e. g. K-means clustering). [23, 28]

2.3.8. Validation of Trained Self-organizing Map

The validation of the trained SOM can be done so, a portion of the input data is used for map training and another portion for validation (e. g. in proportion 70:30). Different approach for SOM validation is *n*-fold cross validation with the leave-one out method. [16, 23]

2.4. Using of trained self-organizing map

A trained SOM can be used according the following steps for clustering:

1. Consecutive submission of an input data vector to the network.
2. Calculation of a distances between the input vector and the weight vectors of the neurons of the output layer.
3. Selection of the nearest (the most similar) neuron of the output layer (e. i. the cluster) to the presented input data vector.

2.5. Implementation of self-organizing map

The SOM algorithm has been implemented in MATLAB program suite [17] with various optional parameters enabling the adjustment of the model according to the user's requirements. For easier application of SOM the graphical user interface has been developed facilitating above all the setting of the neural network, see Figure 8.

3. Edge detection

Edge detection techniques are commonly used in image processing, above all for feature detection, feature extraction and segmentation.

The aim of the edge detection process is to detect the object boundaries based on the abrupt changes in the image tones, i. e. to detect discontinuities in either the image intensity or the derivatives of the image intensity.

3.1. Conventional edge detector

The image edge is a property attached to a single pixel. However it is calculated from the image intensity function of the adjacent pixels.

Many commonly used edge detection methods (*Roberts* [22], *Prewitt* [20], *Sobel* [19], *Canny* [6], *Marr-Hildreth* [15] etc), employ derivatives (the first or the second one) to measure the rate of change in the‘image intensity function. The large value of the first derivative and zero-crossings in the second derivative of the image intensity represent necessary condition for the location of the edge. The differential operations are usually approximated discretely by proper convolution mask. Moreover, for simplification of derivative calculation, the edges are usually detected only in two or four directions.

The essential step in edge detection process is *thresholding*, i. e. determination of the threshold limit corresponding to a dividing value for the evaluation of the edge detector response either as the edge or non-edge. Due to the thresholding, the result image of the edge detection process is comprised only of the edge (white) and non-edge (black) pixels. The quality of thresholding setting has an impact on the quality of the whole edge detection process, i. e. exceedingly small value of the threshold leads to assignment of the noise as the edge, on the other hand exceedingly large value of the threshold leads to omission of some significant edges.

3.2. Self-organizing map

A SOM may facilitate the edge detection task, for instance by reducing the dimensionality of an input data or by segmentation of an input data.

In our case, the SOM has been utilized for the reduction of image intensity levels, from 256 to 2 levels. Each image has been transformed to mask (3x3), see Table 1, that forms the set of input vectors (9-dimensional). The input vectors have been then classified into 2 classes according to the weights of the beforehand trained SOM. The output set of the classified vectors has been reversely transformed into the binary (black and white) image.

Due to this image preprocessing using SOM, the following edge detection process has been strongly simplified, i. e. only the *numerical gradient* has been calculated

$$G = \sqrt{G_x^2 + G_y^2},\tag{15}$$

where G is the edge gradient, G_x and G_y are values of the first derivative in the horizontal and in the vertical direction, respectively.

The ability of SOM for edge detection in biomedical images has been tested using the high-resolution computed tomography (CT) images capturing the expressions of the Granulomatosis with polyangiitis disease.

4. Granulomatosis with polyangiitis

4.1. Diagnosis of granulomatosis with polyangiitis

Granulomatosis with polyangiitis (GPA), in the past also known as Wegener's granulomatosis is a disease belonging to the group of vasculitic diseases affecting mainly small caliber blood vessels [7].

They can be distinguished from other vasculitides by the presence of *ANCA* antibodies (ANCA - Anti- Neutrophil Cytoplasmic Antibodies). GPA is quite a rare disease, its yearly incidence is around 10 cases per million inhabitants. The course of the disease is extremely variable on the one hand there are cases of organ limited disease that affects only single organ, on the other hand there is a possibility of generalized disease affecting multiple organs and threatening the patients life. Diagnostics of this disease has been improved

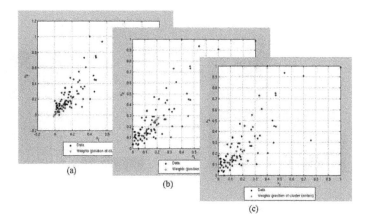

Figure 5. Weight vectors initialization: (a) Random small numbers, (b) Vectors near the center of mass of inputs, (c) Some of the input vectors are randomly chosen as the initial weight vectors

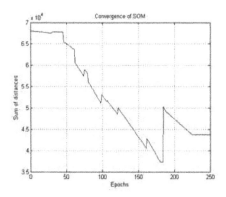

Figure 6. The training criterion of the learning process.
The figure shows the example of the evolution of the training criterion (sum of the distances between all input vectors and their respective winning neuron weights) as the function of the number of epochs. In this case, the smallest sum of distances was achieved in the 189th epoch

P1	P2	P3
P4	P5	P6
P7	P8	P9

Table 1. The image mask used for the preparation of the set of the input vectors.
The mask (9 adjacent pixels) was moved over the whole image pixel by pixel row-wise and the process continued until the whole image was scanned. From each location of the scanning mask in the image the single input vector has been formed, i. e. $\mathbf{x} = (P1, P2, P3, P4, P5, P6, P7, P8, P9)$, where $P1$–$P9$ denote the intensity values of the image pixel. The (binary) output value of SOM for each input vector replaced the intensity value in the position of the pixel with original intensity value $P5$

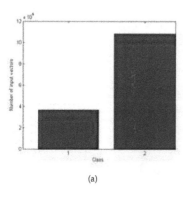
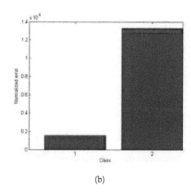

(a)   (b)

Figure 7. The additional information about the SOM result.
(a) The distribution of the input vectors in the clusters, (b) The errors of the clusters (the mean value of the distance between the respective input vectors and the cluster center with respect to the maximum value of the distance)

by the discovery of ANCA antibodies and their routine investigation since the nineties of the past century. The onset of GPA may occur at any age, although patients typically present at age 35–55 years [11].

A classic form of GPA is characterized by necrotizing granulomatous vasculitis of the upper and lower respiratory tract, glomerulonefritis, and small-vessel vasculitis of variable degree. Because of the respiratory tract involvement nearly all the patients have some respiratory symptoms including cough, dyspnea or hemoptysis. Due to this, nearly all of them have a chest X-ray at the admission to the hospital, usually followed by a high-resolution computed CT scan. The major value of CT scanning is in the further characterization of lesions found on chest radiography.

The spectrum of high-resolution CT findings of GPA is broad, ranging from nodules and masses to ground glass opacity and lung consolidation. All of the findings may mimic other conditions such as pneumonia, neoplasm, and noninfectious inflammatory diseases [2].

The prognosis of GPA depends on the activity of the disease and disease-caused damage and response to therapy. There are several drugs used to induce remission, including cyclophosphamide, glucocorticoids or monoclonal anti CD 20 antibody rituximab. Once the remission is induced, mainly azathioprin or mycophenolate mofetil are used for its maintenance.

Unfortunately, relapses are common in GPA. Typically, up to half of patients experience relapse within 5 years [21].

4.2. Analysis of granulomatosis with polyangiitis

Up to now, all analysis of CT images with GPA expressions have been done using manual measurements and subsequent statistical evaluation [1, 3, 10, 12, 14]. It has been based on the experience of a radiologist who can find abnormalities in the CT scan and who is able to classify types of the finding. The standard software [1] used for CT image visualization usually includes some interactive tools (zoom, rotation, distance or angle measurements, etc.) but no analysis is done (e. g. detection of the abnormal structure or recognition of different types of tissue). Moreover, there is no software customized specifically for requirements of GPA analysis.

Therefore, there is a place to introduce a new approach for analysis based on SOM. CT finding analysis is then less time consuming and more precise.

5. Results and discussion

The aim of the work has been to detect all three expression forms of the GPA disease in high-resolution CT images (provided by Department of Nephrology, First Faculty of Medicine and General Faculty Hospital, Prague, Czech Republic) using the SOM, i. e. to detect *granulomatosin*, *mass* and *ground-glass*, see Figure 10a, 11a, 12a. The particular expression forms occur often together, therefore there has been the requirement to distinguish the particular expression forms from each other.

Firstly, the SOM has been trained using the test image, see Figure 9 (For detailed information about the training process, please see Table 2).

Secondly, the edge detection of the validating images has been done using the result weights from the SOM training process, see Figure 10b, 11b, 12b (For detailed information about the edge detection process, please see Table 3).

Setting description	Value
Size of the output layer	(1,2)
Type of the weights initialization	Some of the input vectors are randomly chosen as the initial weight vectors.
Initial value of the'learning parameter	1
Final value of the learning parameter	0.1
A point in the learning process in which the learning parameter reaches the final value	0.9
Initial value of the cneighbourhood size parameter	2
Final value of the cneighbourhood size parameter	1
A point in the learning process in which the neighbourhood size parameter reaches the final value	0.75
Type of the distance measure	1
Type of the learning rate decay function	Exponential
Type of neighbourhood size strength function	Linear
Type of the neighbourhood size rate decay function	Exponential
Number of the epochs	500

Table 2. Setting of the SOM training process

[1] Syngo Imaging XS-VA60B, Siemens AG Medical Solutions, Health Services, 91052 Erlangen, Germany

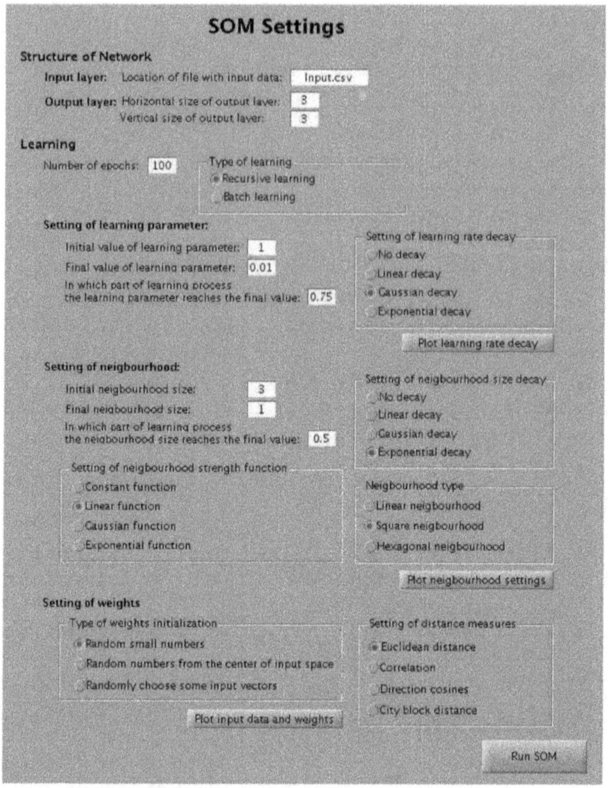

Figure 8. The graphical user interface of the software using SOM for clustering

Stages	Description
Image preprocessing	Histogram matching of the input image to the test image.
Image transformation	The image is transformed to M masks (3x3) that form the set of M input vectors (9 dimensional).
Clustering using SOM	The set of the input vectors is classified into 2 classes according to the obtained weights from the SOM training process.
Reverse image transformation	The set of classified input vectors is reversely transformed into the image. The intensity values are replaced by the values of the class membership.
Edge detection	Computation of image gradient.

Table 3. Stages of the edge detection process

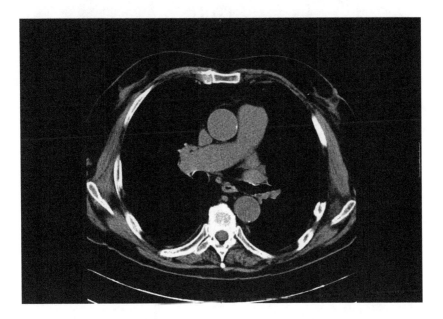

Figure 9. Test image (transverse high-resolution CT image of both lungs)

The obtained results have been discussed with an expert from Department of Nephrology of the First Faculty of Medicine and General Teaching Hospital in Prague.

In the first case, a high-resolution CT image capturing a granuloma in the left lung has been processed, see Figure 10a. The expert has been satisfied with the quality of the GPA detection (see Figure 10b) provided by the SOM, since the granuloma has been detected without any artifacts.

In the second case, the expert has pointed out that the high-resolution CT image, capturing both masses and ground-glass (see Figure 11a, 12a), was problematic to be evaluated. The possibility of the detection of the masses was aggravated by the ground-glass surrounding the lower part of the first mass and the upper part of the second mass. The artifacts, which originated in the coughing movements of the patient ('wavy' lower part of the image), made the detection process of the masses and the ground-glass difficult as well. Despite these inconveniences, the expert has confirmed, that the presented software has been able to distinguish between the particular expression forms of GPA with satisfying accuracy and it has detected the mass and ground-glass correctly (see Figure 11b, 12b, 12c).

In conclusion, the presented SOM approach represents a new helpful approach for GPA disease diagnostics.

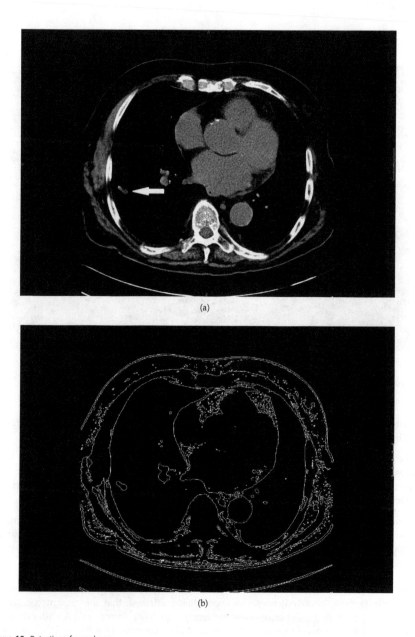

(a)

(b)

Figure 10. Detection of granuloma.
(a) Transverse high-resolution CT image of both lungs with active granulomatosis (white arrow).
b) The edge detection result obtained by the SOM. The granulomatosin is detected with sufficient accuracy

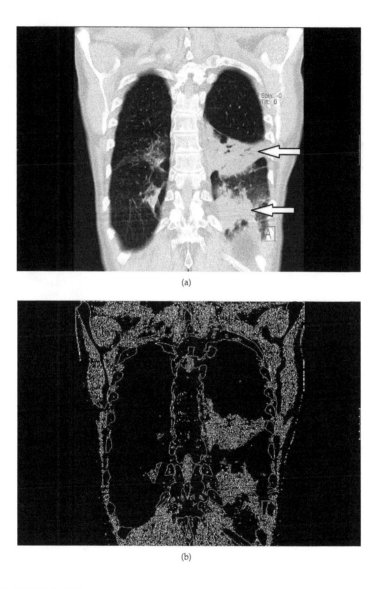

(a)

(b)

Figure 11. Detection of masses.
(a) Coronal high-resolution CT image of both lungs with masses (white arrows). Possibility of the detection of the masses is aggravated by the'ground-glass surrounding the lower part of the first mass and the upper part of the second mass. The artifacts originated by coughing movements of the patient makes the detection process difficult as well.
(b) The edge detection result obtained by the SOM. The'masses are detected and distinguished from the ground-glass with sufficient accuracy

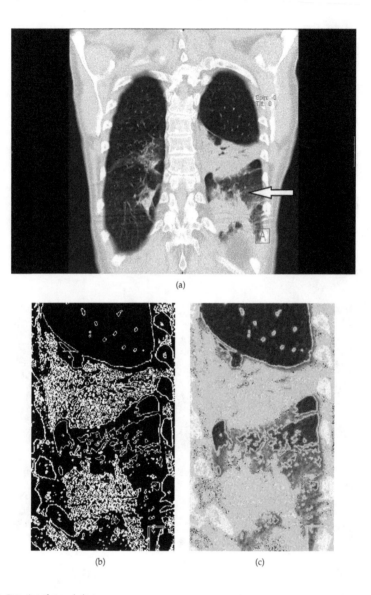

(a)

(b)   (c)

Figure 12. Detection of ground-glass.
(a) Coronal high-resolution CT image of both lungs with ground-glasses (white arrows). Possibility of the detection of the ground-glasses is complicated by the masses in close proximity to the ground-glasses. The artifacts originated by coughing movements of the patient makes the detection process hard as well.
(b) The edge detection result obtained by the SOM. The ground-glasses are detected and distinguished from the masses.
(c) The overlap of the original CT image and the edge detection result (cyan color)

6. Conclusions

The edge detection procedure is a'critical step in the analysis of biomedical images, enabling above all the detection of the abnormal structure or the'recognition of different types of tissue.

The application of SOM for edge detection in biomedical images has been discussed and its contribution to the solution of the edge detection task has been confirmed. The'ability of SOM has been verified using the'high-resolution CT images capturing all three forms of the expressions of the GPA disease (granulomatosin, mass, ground-glass). Using SOM, particular expression forms of the GPA disease have been detected and distinguished from each other. The obtained results have been discussed by the expert who has confirmed that the SOM provides a quick and easy approach for edge detection tasks with satisfying quality of output.

Future plans are based on the problem extension to three-dimensional space to enable CT image analysis involving (i) pathological finding 3D visualization and (ii) 3D reconstruction of the whole region (using the whole set of CT images).

Acknowledgements

The work was supported by specific university research MSMT No. 21/2012, the reaserch grant MSM No. 6046137306 and PRVOUK-P25/LF1/2.

Author details

Lucie Gráfová[1], Jan Mareš[1], Aleš Procházka[1] and Pavel Konopásek[2]

[1]Department of Computing and Control Engineering, Institute of Chemical Technology, Prague, Czech Republic
[2]Department of Nephrology, First Faculty of Medicine and General Faculty Hospital, Prague, Czech Republic

7. References

[1] Ananthakrishnan, L., Sharma, N. & Kanne, J. P. [2009]. Wegener?s granulomatosis in the chest: High-resolution ct findings, *Am J Roentgenol* 192(3): 676–82.

[2] Annanthakrishan, L., Sharma, N. & Kanne, J. P. [2009]. Wegener's granulomatosis in the chest: High-resolution ct findings, *Am J Roentgenol* 192(3): 676–82.

[3] Attali, P., Begum, R., Romdhane, H. B., Valeyre, D., Guillevin, L. & Brauner, M. W. [1998]. Pulmonary wegener?s granulomatosis: changes at follow-up ct, *European Radiology* 8: 1009–1113.

[4] Badekas, E. & Papamarkos, N. [2007]. Document binarisation using kohonen som, *IET Image Processing* 1: 67–84.

[5] Baez, P. G., Araujo, C. S., Fernandez, V. & Procházka, A. [2011]. *Differential Diagnosis of Dementia Using HUMANN-S Based Ensembles*, Springer, Berlin, Germany, chapter 14, pp. 305–324.

[6] Canny, J. [1986]. A computational approach to edge detection, *IEEE Transactions on Pattern Analysis and Machine Intelligence* PAMI-8(6): 679–698.

[7] Jennette, J. C. [2011]. Nomenclature and classification of vasculitis: lessons learned from granulomatosis with polyangiitis (wegener's granulomatosis), *Clin Exp Immunol* 164: 7–10.

[8] Jerhotová, E., Švihlík, J. & Procházka, A. [2011]. *A. Biomedical Image Volumes Denoising via the Wavelet Transform*, InTech, chapter 14.

[9] Kohonen, T. [1989]. *Self-Organization and Associative Memory*, Springer-Verlag.

[10] Komócsi, A., Reuter, M., Heller, M., Muraközi, H., Gross, W. L. & Schnabel, A. [2003]. Active disease and residual damage in treated wegener?s granulomatosis: an observational study using pulmonary high-resolution computed tomography, *European Radiology* 13: 36–42.

[11] Lane, S. E., Watts, R. & Scott, D. G. I. [2005]. Epidemiology of systemic vasculitis, *Curr Rheumatol Rep* 7: 270–275.

[12] Lee, K. S., Kim, T. S., Fujimoto, K., Moriya, H., Watanabe, H., Tateishi, U., Ashizawa, K., Johkoh, T., Kim, E. A. & Kwon, O. J. [2003]. Thoracic manifestation of wegener?s granulomatosis: Ct findings in 30 patients, *European Radiology* 13: 43–51.

[13] Liu, J.-C. & Pok, G. [1999]. Texture edge detection by feature encoding and predictive model, *Proceedings of the IEEE International Conference on Acoustics, Speech, and Signal Processing*, pp. 1105–1108.

[14] Lohrmann, C., Uhl, M., Schaefer, O., Ghanem, N., Kotter, E. & Langer:, M. [2005]. Serial high-resolution computed tomography imaging in patients with wegener granulomatosis: Differentiation between active inflammatory and chronic fibrotic lesions, *Acta Radiologica* 46: 484–491.

[15] Marr, D. & Hildreth, E. [1980]. Theory of edge detection, *Proc. Roy. Soc. Landon*, Vol. B.207, pp. 187–217.

[16] Mitchell, T. [1997]. *Machine Learning*, McGraw-Hill.

[17] Moore, H. [2007]. *Matlab for Engineers*, Pearson, Prentice Hall.

[18] Moreira, J. & Fontuora, L. D. [1996]. Neural-based color image segmentation and classification, *Anais do IX SIBGRAPI*: 47–54.

[19] Pingle, K. K. [1969]. *Visual perception by computer. Automatic Interpretation and Classification of Images*, Academic Press, New York.

[20] Prewitt, J. M. S. [1970]. *Object enhancement and extraction. Picture Processing and Psychophysics*, Academic Press, New York.

[21] Renaudineau, Y. & Meur, Y. L. [2008]. Renal involvement in wegener's granulomatosis, *Clinic Rev Allerg Immunol* 35: 22–29.

[22] Roberts, L. G. [1963]. *Machine Perception of Three Dimensional Solids*, PhD thesis, Massachusetts Institute of Technology, Electrical Engineering Department.

[23] Samarasinghe, S. [2006]. *Neural Networks for Applied Sciences and Engineering: From Fundamentals to Complex Pattern Recognition*.

[24] Sampaziotis, P. & Papamarko, N. [2005]. Automatic edge detection by combining kohonen som and the canny operator, *Proceedings of the 10th Iberoamerican Congress conference on Progress in Pattern Recognition, Image Analysis and Applications*, pp. 954–965.

[25] Sharma, D. K., Gaur, L. & Okunbor, D. [2007]. Image compression and feature extraction using kohonen's self-organizing map neural network, *Journal of Strategic E-Commerce* 5(No. 0): 25–38.

[26] Toivanen, P. J., Ansamäki, J., Parkkinen, J. P. S. & Mielikäinen, J. [2003]. Edge detection in multispectral images using the self-organizing map, *Pattern Recognition Letters* 24: 2987–2994.

[27] Venkatesh, Y. V., K.Raja, S. & Ramya, N. [2006]. Multiple contour extraction from graylevel images using an artificial neural network, *IEEE Transactions on Image Processing* 15: 892–899.

[28] Wilson, C. L. [2010]. *Mathematical Modeling, Clustering Algorithms and Applications*.

Chapter 9

Applications of Artificial Neural Networks in Chemical Problems

Vinícius Gonçalves Maltarollo,
Káthia Maria Honório and
Albérico Borges Ferreira da Silva

Additional information is available at the end of the chapter

1. Introduction

In general, chemical problems are composed by complex systems. There are several chemical processes that can be described by different mathematical functions (linear, quadratic, exponential, hyperbolic, logarithmic functions, etc.). There are also thousands of calculated and experimental descriptors/molecular properties that are able to describe the chemical behavior of substances. In several experiments, many variables can influence the chemical desired response [1,2]. Usually, chemometrics (scientific area that employs statistical and mathematical methods to understand chemical problems) is largely used as valuable tool to treat chemical data and to solve complex problems [3-8].

Initially, the use of chemometrics was growing along with the computational capacity. In the 80's, when small computers with relatively high capacity of calculation became popular, the chemometric algorithms and softwares started to be developed and applied [8,9]. Nowadays, there are several softwares and complex algorithms available to commercial and academic use as a result of the technological development. In fact, the interest for robust statistical methodologies for chemical studies also increased. One of the most employed statistical methods is partial least squares (PLS) analysis [10,11]. This technique does not perform a simple regression as multiple linear regression (MLR). PLS method can be employed to a large number of variables because it treats the colinearity of descriptors. Due the complexity of this technique, when compared to other statistical methods, PLS analysis is largely employed to solve chemical problems [10,11].

We can cite some examples of computational packages employed in chemometrics and containing several statistical tools (PLS, MLR, etc.): MATLAB [12], R-Studio [13], Statistica [14] and Pirouette [15]. There are some molecular modeling methodologies as HQSAR [16], CoMFA [17-18], CoMSIA [19] and LTQA-QSAR [20] that also use the PLS analysis to treat their generated descriptors. In general, the PLS method is used to analyse only linear problems. However, when a large number of phenomena and noise are present in the calibration problem, the relationship becomes non-linear [21]. Therefore, artificial neural networks (ANNs) may provide accurate results for very complex and non-linear problems that demand high computational costs [22,23]. One of the most employed learning algorithm is the back-propagation and its main advantage is the use of output information and expected pattern to error corrections [24]. The main advantages of ANN techniques include learning and generalization ability of data, fault tolerance and inherent contextual information processing in addition to fast computation capacity [25]. It is important to mention that since 90's many studies have related advantages of applying ANN techniques when compared to other statistical methods [23,26-31].

Due to the popularization, there is a large interest in ANN techniques, in special in their applications in various chemical fields such as medicinal chemistry, pharmaceutical, theoretical chemistry, analytical chemistry, biochemistry, food research, etc [32-33]. The theory of some ANN methodologies and their applications will be presented as follows.

2. Artificial Neural Networks (ANNs)

The first studies describing ANNs (also called perceptron network) were performed by McCulloch and Pitts [34,35] and Hebb [36]. The initial idea of neural networks was developed as a model for neurons, their biological counterparts. The first applications of ANNs did not present good results and showed several limitations (such as the treatment of linear correlated data). However, these events stimulated the extension of initial perceptron architecture (a single-layer neural network) to multilayer networks [37,38]. In 1982, Hopfield [39] described a new approach with the introduction of nonlinearity between input and output data and this new architecture of perceptrons yielded a good improvement in the ANN results. In addition to Holpfield's study, Werbos [40] proposed the back-propagation learning algorithm, which helps the ANN popularization.

In few years (1988), one of the first applications of ANNs in chemistry was performed by Hoskins et al. [41] that reported the employing of a multilayer feed-forward neural network (described in Session 2.1) to study chemical engineering processes. In the same year, two studies employing ANNs were published with the aim to predict the secondary structure of proteins [42,43].

In general, ANN techniques are a family of mathematical models that are based on the human brain functioning. All ANN methodologies share the concept of "neurons" (also called "hidden units") in their architecture. Each neuron represents a synapse as its biological counterpart. Therefore, each hidden unity is constituted of activation functions that control the propagation of neuron signal to the next layer (e.g. positive weights simulate the excita-tory stimulus and negative weights simulate the inhibitory ones). A hidden unit is com-posed by a regression equation that processes the input information into a non-linear output data. Therefore, if more than one neuron is used to compose an ANN, non-linear correla-tions can be treated. Due to the non-linearity between input and output, some authors com-pare the hidden unities of ANNs like a "black box" [44-47]. Figure 1 shows a comparison between a human neuron and an ANN neuron.

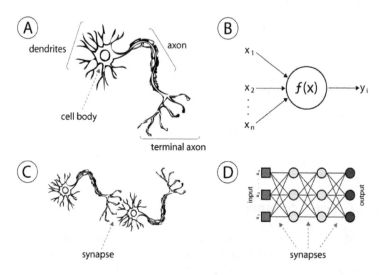

Figure 1. (A) Human neuron; (B) artificial neuron or hidden unity; (C) biological synapse; (D) ANN synapses.

The general purpose of ANN techniques is based on stimulus–response activation functions that accept some input (parameters) and yield some output (response). The difference be-tween the neurons of distinct artificial neural networks consists in the nature of activation function of each neuron. There are several typical activation function used to compose ANNs, as threshold function, linear, sigmoid (e.g. hyperbolic tangent), radial basis function (e.g. gaussian) [25,44-48]. Table 1 illustrates some examples of activation functions.

Different ANN techniques can be classified based on their architecture or neuron connec-tion pattern. The feed-forward networks are composed by unidirectional connections be-tween network layers. In other words, there is a connection flow from the input to output direction. The feedback or recurrent networks are the ANNs where the connections among layers occur in both directions. In this kind of neural network, the connection pat-tern is characterized by loops due to the feedback behavior. In recurrent networks, when the output signal of a neuron enter in a previous neuron (the feedback connection), the new input data is modified [25,44-47].

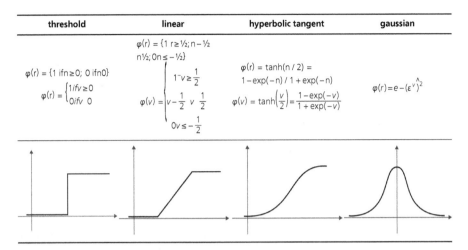

threshold	linear	hyperbolic tangent	gaussian
$\varphi(r) = \{1 \text{ if } n \geq 0;\ 0 \text{ if } n 0\}$ $\varphi(r) = \begin{cases} 1/\textit{if}\ v \geq 0 \\ 0\textit{if}\ 0 \end{cases}$	$\varphi(r) = \{1 \ r \geq \tfrac{1}{2};\ n - \tfrac{1}{2}$ $n\tfrac{1}{2};\ 0\ n \leq -\tfrac{1}{2}\}$ $\varphi(v) = \begin{vmatrix} 1^- v \geq \dfrac{1}{2} \\ v - \dfrac{1}{2} \quad v \quad \dfrac{1}{2} \\ 0 v \leq -\dfrac{1}{2} \end{vmatrix}$	$\varphi(r) = \tanh(n/2) =$ $1 - \exp(-n)\,/\,1 + \exp(-n)$ $\varphi(v) = \tanh\!\left(\dfrac{v}{2}\right) = \dfrac{1 - \exp(-v)}{1 + \exp(-v)}$	$\varphi(r) = e - (\varepsilon^v)^{\hat{}2}$

Table 1. Some activation functions used in ANN studies.

Each ANN architecture has an intrinsic behavior. Therefore, the neural networks can be classified according to their connections pattern, the number of hidden unities, the nature of activation functions and the learning algorithm [44-47]. There are an extensive number of ANN types and Figure 2 exemplifies the general classification of neural networks showing the most common ANN techniques employed in chemistry.

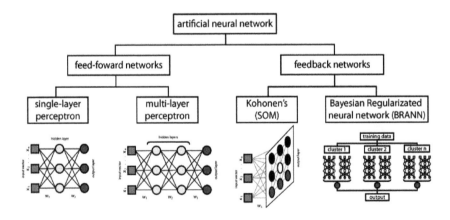

Figure 2. The most common neural networks employed in chemistry (adapted from Jain & Mao, 1996 [25]).

According to the previous brief explanation, ANN techniques can be classified based on some features. The next topics explain the most common types of ANN employed in chemical problems.

2.1. Multilayer perceptrons

Multilayer perceptrons (MLP) is one of the most employed ANN algorithms in chemistry. The term "multilayer" is used because this methodology is composed by several neurons arranged in different layers. Each connection between the input and hidden layers (or two hidden layers) is similar to a synapse (biological counterpart) and the input data is modified by a determined weight. Therefore, a three layer feed-forward network is composed by an input layer, two hidden layers and the output layer [38,48-50].

MLP is also called feed-forward neural networks because the data information flows only in the forward direction. In other words, the produced output of a layer is only used as input for the next layer. An important characteristic of feed-forward networks is the supervised learning [38,48-50].

The crucial task in the MLP methodology is the training step. The training or learning step is a search process for a set of weight values with the objective of reducing/minimizing the squared errors of prediction (experimental x estimated data). This phase is the slowest one and there is no guarantee of minimum global achievement. There are several learning algorithms for MLP such as conjugate gradient descent, quasi-Newton, Levenberg-Marquardt, etc., but the most employed one is the back-propagation algorithm. This algorithm uses the error values of the output layer (prediction) to adjust the weight of layer connections. Therefore, this algorithm provides a guarantee of minimum (local or global) convergence [38,48-50].

The main challenge of MLP is the choice of the most suitable architecture. The speed and the performance of the MLP learning are strongly affected by the number of layers and the number of hidden unities in each layer [38,48-50]. Figure 3 displays the influence of number of layers on the pattern recognition ability of neural network.

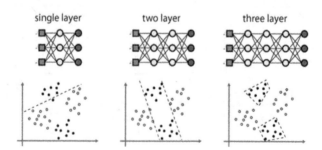

Figure 3. Influence of the number of layers on the pattern recognition ability of MLP (adapted from Jain & Mao, 1996 [25]).

The increase in the number of layers in a MLP algorithm is proportional to the increase of complexity of the problem to be solved. The higher the number of hidden layers, the higher the complexity of the pattern recognition of the neural network.

2.2. Self-organizing map or Kohonen neural network

Self-organizing map (SOM), also called Kohonen neural network (KNN), is an unsupervised neural network designed to perform a non-linear mapping of a high-dimensionality data space transforming it in a low-dimensional space, usually a bidimensional space. The visualization of the output data is performed from the distance/proximity of neurons in the output 2D-layer. In other words, the SOM technique is employed to cluster and extrapolate the data set keeping the original topology. The SOM output neurons are only connected to its nearest neighbors. The neighborhood represents a similar pattern represented by an output neuron. In general, the neighborhood of an output neuron is defined as square or hexagonal and this means that each neuron has 4 or 6 nearest neighbors, respectively [51-53]. Figure 4 exemplifies the output layers of a SOM model using square and hexagonal neurons for a combinatorial design of purinergic receptor antagonists [54] and cannabinoid compounds [30], respectively.

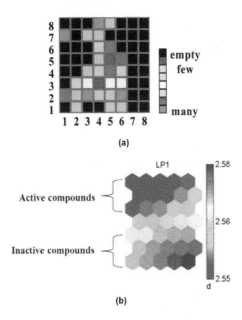

Figure 4. Example of output layers of SOM models using square and hexagonal neurons for the combinatorial design of (a) purinergic receptor antagonists [54] and (b) cannabinoid compounds [30], respectively.

The SOM technique could be considered a competitive neural network due to its learning algorithm. The competitive learning means that only the neuron in the output layer is selected if its weight is the most similar to the input pattern than the other input neurons. Finally, the learning rate for the neighborhood is scaled down proportional to the distance of the winner output neuron [51-53].

2.3. Bayesian regularized artificial neural networks

Different from the usual back-propagation learning algorithm, the Bayesian method considers all possible values of weights of a neural network weighted by the probability of each set of weights. This kind of neural network is called Bayesian regularized artificial neural (BRANN) networks because the probability of distribution of each neural network, which provides the weights, can be determined by Bayes's theorem [55]. Therefore, the Bayesian method can estimate the number of effective parameters to predict an output data, practically independent from the ANN architecture. As well as the MLP technique, the choice of the network architecture is a very important step for the learning of BRANN. A complete review of the BRANN technique can be found in other studies [56-59].

2.4. Other important neural networks

Adaptative resonance theory (ART) neural networks [60,61] constitute other mathematical models designed to describe the biological brain behavior. One of the most important characteristic of this technique is the capacity of knowledge without disturbing or destroying the stored knowledge. A simple variation of this technique, the ART-2a model, has a simple learning algorithm and it is practically inexpensive compared to other ART models [60-63]. The ART-2a method consists in constructing a weight matrix that describes the centroid nature of a predicted class [62,63]. In the literature, there are several chemical studies that employ the ART-based neural networks [64-73].

The neural network known as radial basis function (RBF) [74] typically has the input layer, a hidden layer with a RBF as the activation function and the output layer. This network was developed to treat irregular topographic contours of geographical data [75-76] but due to its capacity of solving complex problems (non-linear specially), the RBF networks have been successfully employed to chemical problems. There are several studies comparing the robustness of prediction (prediction coefficients, r^2, pattern recognition rates and errors) of RBF-based networks and other methods [77-80].

The Hopfield neural network [81-82] is a model that uses a binary $n \times n$ matrix (presented as $n \times n$ pixel image) as a weight matrix for n input signals. The activation function treats the activation signal only as 1 or -1. Besides, the algorithm treats black and white pixels as 0 and 1 binary digits, respectively, and there is a transformation of the matrix data to enlarge the interval from $0 - 1$ to $(-1) - (+1)$. The complete description of this technique can be found in reference [47]. In chemistry research, we can found some studies employing the Hopfield model to obtain molecular alignments [83], to calculate the intermolecular potential energy function from the second virial coefficient [84] and other purposes [85-86].

3. Applications

Following, we will present a brief description of some studies that apply ANN techniques as important tools to solve chemical problems.

3.1. Medicinal Chemistry and Pharmaceutical Research

The drug design research involves the use of several experimental and computational strategies with different purposes, such as biological affinity, pharmacokinetic and toxicological studies, as well as quantitative structure-activity relationship (QSAR) models [87-95]. Another important approach to design new potential drugs is virtual screening (VS), which can maximize the effectiveness of rational drug development employing computational assays to classify or filter a compound database as potent drug candidates [96-100]. Besides, various ANN methodologies have been largely applied to control the process of the pharmaceutical production [101-104].

Fanny et al. [105] constructed a SOM model to perform VS experiments and tested an external database of 160,000 compounds. The use of SOM methodology accelerated the similarity searches by using several pharmacophore descriptors. The best result indicated a map that retrieves 90% of relevant neighbors (output neurons) in the similarity search for virtual hits.

3.2. Theoretical and Computational Chemistry

In theoretical/computational chemistry, we can obtain some applications of ANN techniques such as the prediction of ionization potential [106], lipophilicity of chemicals [107, 108], chemical/physical/mechanical properties of polymer employing topological indices [109] and relative permittivity and oxygen diffusion of ceramic materials [110].

Stojković et al. [111] also constructed a quantitative structure-property relationship (QSPR) model to predict pK_{BH^+} for 92 amines. To construct the regression model, the authors calculated some topological and quantum chemical descriptors. The counter-propagation neural network was employed as a modeling tool and the Kohonen self-organizing map was employed to graphically visualize the results. The authors could clearly explain how the input descriptors influenced the pK_{BH^+} behavior, in special the presence of halogens atoms in the amines structure.

3.3. Analytical Chemistry

There are several studies in analytical chemistry employing ANN techniques with the aim to obtain multivariate calibration and analysis of spectroscopy data [112-117], as well as to model the HPLC retention behavior [118] and reaction kinetics [119].

Fatemi [120] constructed a QSPR model employing the ANN technique with back-propagation algorithm to predict the ozone tropospheric degradation rate constant of organic compounds. The data set was composed of 137 organic compounds divided into training, test and validation sets. The author also compared the ANN results with those obtained from the MLR method. The correlation coefficients obtained with ANN/MLR were 0.99/0.88, 0.96/0.86 and 0.96/0.74 for the training, test and validation sets, respectively. These results showed the best efficacy of the ANN methodology in this case.

3.4. Biochemistry

Neural networks have been largely employed in biochemistry and correlated research fields such as protein, DNA/RNA and molecular biology sciences [121-127].

Petritis *et al.* [128] employed a three layer neural network with back-propagation algorithm to predict the reverse-phase liquid chromatography retention time of peptides enzymatically digested from proteomes. In the training set, the authors used 7000 known peptides from D. radiodurans. The constructed ANN model was employed to predict a set with 5200 peptides from S. oneidensis. The used neural network generated some weights for the chromatographic retention time for each aminoacid in agreement to results obtained by other authors. The obtained ANN model could predict a peptide sequence containing 41 aminoacids with an error less than 0.03. Half of the test set was predicted with less than 3% of error and more than 95% of this set was predicted with an error around 10%. These results showed that the ANN methodology is a good tool to predict the peptide retention time from liquid chromatography.

Huang *et al.* [129] introduced a novel ANN approach combining aspects of QSAR and ANN and they called this approach of physics and chemistry-driven ANN (Phys-Chem ANN). This methodology has the parameters and coefficients clearly based on physicochemical insights. In this study, the authors employed the Phys-Chem ANN methodology to predict the stability of human lysozyme. The data set was composed by 50 types of mutated lysozymes (including the wild type) and the experimental property used in the modeling was the change in the unfolding Gibbs free energy (kJ^{-1} mol). This study resulted in significant coefficients of calibration and validation (r^2=0.95 and q^2=0.92, respectively). The proposed methodology provided good prediction of biological activity, as well as structural information and physical explanations to understand the stability of human lysozyme.

3.5. Food Research

ANNs have also been widely employed in food research. Some examples of application of ANNs in this area include vegetable oil studies [130-138], beers [139], wines [140], honeys [141-142] and water [143-144].

Bos *et al.* [145] employed several ANN techniques to predict the water percentage in cheese samples. The authors tested several different architecture of neurons (some functions were employed to simulate different learning behaviors) and analyzed the prediction errors to assess the ANN performance. The best result was obtained employing a radial basis function neural network.

Cimpoiu *et al.* [146] used the multi-layer perceptron with the back-propagation algorithm to model the antioxidant activity of some classes of tea such as black, express black and green teas. The authors obtained a correlation of 99.9% between experimental and predicted antioxidant activity. A classification of samples was also performed using an ANN technique with a radial basis layer followed by a competitive layer with a perfect match between real and predicted classes.

4. Conclusions

Artificial Neural Networks (ANNs) were originally developed to mimic the learning process of human brain and the knowledge storage functions. The basic unities of ANNs are called neurons and are designed to transform the input data as well as propagating the signal with the aim to perform a non-linear correlation between experimental and predicted data. As the human brain is not completely understood, there are several different architectures of artificial neural networks presenting different performances. The most common ANNs applied to chemistry are MLP, SOM, BRANN, ART, Hopfield and RBF neural networks. There are several studies in the literature that compare ANN approaches with other chemometric tools (e.g. MLR and PLS), and these studies have shown that ANNs have the best performance in many cases. Due to the robustness and efficacy of ANNs to solve complex problems, these methods have been widely employed in several research fields such as medicinal chemistry, pharmaceutical research, theoretical and computational chemistry, analytical chemistry, biochemistry, food research, etc. Therefore, ANN techniques can be considered valuable tools to understand the main mechanisms involved in chemical problems.

Notes

Techniques related to artificial neural networks (ANNs) have been increasingly used in chemical studies for data analysis in the last decades. Some areas of ANN applications involve pattern identification, modeling of relationships between structure and biological activity, classification of compound classes, identification of drug targets, prediction of several physicochemical properties and others. Actually, the main purpose of ANN techniques in chemical problems is to create models for complex input–output relationships based on learning from examples and, consequently, these models can be used in prediction studies. It is interesting to note that ANN methodologies have shown their power and robustness in the creation of useful models to help chemists in research projects in academy and industry. Nowadays, the evolution of computer science (software and hardware) has allowed the development of many computational methods used to understand and simulate the behavior of complex systems. In this way, the integration of technological and scientific innovation has helped the treatment of large databases of chemical compounds in order to identify possible patterns. However, people that can use computational techniques must be prepared to understand the limits of applicability of any computational method and to distinguish between those opportunities which are appropriate to apply ANN methodologies to solve chemical problems. The evolution of ANN theory has resulted in an increase in the number of successful applications. So, the main contribution of this book chapter will be briefly outline our view on the present scope and future advances of ANNs based on some applications from recent research projects with emphasis in the generation of predictive ANN models.

Author details

Vinícius Gonçalves Maltarollo[1], Káthia Maria Honório[1,2] and
Albérico Borges Ferreira da Silva[3*]

*Address all correspondence to: alberico@iqsc.usp.br

1 Centro de Ciências Naturais e Humanas – UFABC – Santo André – SP

2 Escola de Artes, Ciências e Humanidades – USP – São Paulo – SP

3 Departamento de Química e Física Molecular – Instituto de Química de São Carlos – USP –
São Carlos – SP

References

[1] Teófilo, R. F., & Ferreira, M. M. C. (2006). Quimiometria II: Planilhas Eletrônicas para
     Cálculos de Planejamento Experimental um Tutorial. *Quim. Nova*, 29, 338-350.

[2] Lundstedt, T., Seifert, E., Abramo, L., Theilin, B., Nyström, A., Pettersen, J., & Berg-
     man, R. (1998). Experimental design and optimization. *Chemom. Intell. Lab.*, 42, 3-40.

[3] Kowalski, B. R. J. (1957). Chemometrics: Views and Propositions. *J. Chem. Inf. Comp.
     Sci.*, 15, 201-203.

[4] Wold, S. (1976). Pattern recognition by means of disjoint principal component mod-
     els. *Pattern Recognition*, 8, 127-139.

[5] Vandeginste, B. G. M. (1987). Chemometrics- General Introduction and Historical
     Development. *Top. Curr. Chem.*, 141, 1-42.

[6] Wold, S., & Sjöström, M. (1998). Chemometrics present and future success. *Chemom.
     Intell. Lab.*, 44, 3-14.

[7] Ferreira, M. M. C., Antunes, A. M., Melgo, M. S., & Volpe, P. L. O. (1999). Quimiome-
     tria I: calibração multivariada um tutorial. *Quím. Nova*, 22, 724-731.

[8] Neto, B. B., Scarminio, I. S., & Bruns, R. E. (2006). Anos de Quimiometria no Brasil.
     Quim. Nova, 29, 1401-1406.

[9] Hopke, P. K. (2003). The evolution of chemometrics. *Anal. Chim. Acta*, 500, 365-377.

[10] Wold, S., Ruhe, A., Wold, H., & Dunn, W. (1984). The collinearity problem in linear
     regression: The partial least squares approach to generalized inverses. *SIAM J. Sci.
     Stat. Comput.*, 5, 753-743.

[11] Wold, S., Sjöströma, M., & Eriksson, L. (2001). PLS-regression: a basic tool of chemo-
     metrics. *Chemom. Intell. Lab.*, 58, 109-130.

[12] MATLAB r. (2011). *MathWorks Inc.*

[13] RStudioTM 3. (2012). *RStudio Inc.*

[14] Statistica. (2011). *Data Analysis Software System.*

[15] Pirouette. (2001). *Infometrix Inc.*

[16] HQSAR™ . (2007). *Manual Release in Sybyl 7.3. Tripos Inc.*

[17] Cramer, R. D., Patterson, D. E., & Bunce, J. D. (1988). Comparative molecular field analysis (CoMFA). 1. Effect of shape on binding of steroids to carrier proteins. *J. Am. Chem. Soc.,* 110, 5959-5967.

[18] Cramer, R. D., Patterson, D. E., & Bunce, J. D. (1989). *Recent advances in comparative molecular field analysis (CoMFA), Prog. Clin. Biol. Res.,* 291, 161-165.

[19] Klebe, G., Abraham, U., & Mietzner, T. (1994). Molecular Similarity Indices in a Comparative Analysis (CoMSIA) of Drug Molecules to Correlate and Predict Their Biological Activity. *J. Med. Chem.,* 37, 4130-4146.

[20] Martins, J. P. A., Barbosa, E. G., Pasqualoto, K. F. M., & Ferreira, M. M. C. (2009). LQTA-QSAR: A New 4D-QSAR Methodology. *J. Chem. Inf. Model.,* 49, 1428-1436.

[21] Long, J. R., Gregoriou, V. G., & Gemperline, P. J. (1990). Spectroscopic calibration and quantitation using artificial neural networks. *Anal. Chem.,* 62, 1791-1797.

[22] Cerqueira, E. O., Andrade, J. C., & Poppi, R. J. (2001). Redes neurais e suas aplicações em calibração multivariada. *Quím. Nova,* 24, 864-873.

[23] Sigman, M. E., & Rives, S. S. (1994). Prediction of Atomic Ionization Potentials I-III Using an Artificial Neural Network. *J. Chem. Inf. Comput. Sci.,* 34, 617-620.

[24] Hsiao, T., Lin, C., Zeng, M., & Chiang, H. K. (1998). The Implementation of Partial Least Squares with Artificial Neural Network Architecture. *Proceedings of the 20th Annual International Conference of the IEEE Engineering in Medicine and Biology Society,* 20, 1341-1343.

[25] Jain, A. K., Mao, J., & Mohiuddin, K. M. (1996). Artificial Neural Networks: A Tutorial. *IEEE Computer,* 29, 31-44.

[26] Borggaard, C., & Thodberg, H. H. (1992). Optimal minimal neural interpretation of spectra. *Anal. Chem.,* 64, 545-551.

[27] Zheng, F., Zheng, G., Deaciuc, A. G., Zhan, C. G., Dwoskin, L. P., & Crooks, P. A. (2007). Computational neural network analysis of the affinity of lobeline and tetrabenazine analogs for the vesicular monoamine transporter-2. *Bioorg. Med. Chem.,* 15, 2975-2992.

[28] Louis, B., Agrawal, V. K., & Khadikar, P. V. (2010). Prediction of intrinsic solubility of generic drugs using mlr, ann and svm analyses. *Eur. J. Med. Chem.,* 45, 4018-4025.

[29] Fatemi, M. H., Heidari, A., & Ghorbanzade, M. (2010). Prediction of aqueous solubility of drug-like compounds by using an artificial neural network and least-squares support vector machine. *Bull. Chem. Soc. Jpn.*, 83, 1338-1345.

[30] Honório, K. M., de Lima, E. F., Quiles, M. G., Romero, R. A. F., Molfetta, F. A., & da, Silva. A. B. F. (2010). Artificial Neural Networks and the Study of the Psychoactivity of Cannabinoid Compounds. *Chem. Biol. Drug. Des.*, 75, 632-640.

[31] Qin, Y., Deng, H., Yan, H., & Zhong, R. (2011). An accurate nonlinear QSAR model for the antitumor activities of chloroethylnitrosoureas using neural networks. *J. Mol. Graph. Model.*, 29, 826-833.

[32] Himmelblau, D. M. (2000). Applications of artificial neural networks in chemical engineering. *Korean J. Chem. Eng.*, 17, 373-392.

[33] Marini, F., Bucci, R., Magri, A. L., & Magri, A. D. (2008). Artificial neural networks in chemometrics: History examples and perspectives. *Microchem. J.*, 88, 178-185.

[34] Mc Cutloch, W. S., & Pttts, W. (1943). A logical calculus of the Ideas imminent in nervous activity. *Bull. Math. Biophys.*, 5, 115-133.

[35] Pitts, W., & Mc Culloch, W. S. (1947). How we know universals: the perception of auditory and visual forms. *Bull. Math. Biophys.*, 9, 127-147.

[36] Hebb, D. O. (1949). *The Organization of Behavior*, New York, Wiley.

[37] Zupan, J., & Gasteiger, J. (1991). Neural networks: A new method for solving chemical problems or just a passing phase? *Anal. Chim. Acta*, 248, 1-30.

[38] Smits, J. R. M., Melssen, W. J., Buydens, L. M. C., & Kateman, G. (1994). Using artificial neural networks for solving chemical problems. Part I. Multi-layer feed-forward networks. *Chemom. Intell. Lab.*, 22, 165-189.

[39] Hopfield, J. J. (1982). Neural networks and physical systems with emergent collective computational abilities. *Proc. Nat. Acad. Set.*, 79, 2554-2558.

[40] Werbos, P. (1974). Beyond Regression: New Tools for Prediction and Analysis in the Behavioral Sciences. *PhD thesis*, Harvard University Cambridge.

[41] Hoskins, J. C., & Himmelbau, D. M. (1988). Artificial Neural Network Models of Knowledge Representation in Chemical Engineering. *Comput. Chem. Eng.*, 12, 881-890.

[42] Qian, N., & Sejnowski, T. J. (1988). Predicting the Secondary Structure of Globular Proteins Using Neural Network Models. *J. Mol. Biol.*, 202, 865-884.

[43] Bohr, H., Bohr, J., Brunak, S., Cotterill, R., Lautrup, B., Norskov, L., Olsen, O., & Petersen, S. (1988). Protein Secondary Structure and Homology by Neural Networks. *FEBS Lett.*, 241, 223-228.

[44] Hassoun, M. H. (2003). *Fundamentals of Artificial Neural Networks. A Bradford Book.*

[45] Zurada, J. M. (1992). *Introduction to Artificial Neural Systems*, Boston, PWS Publishing Company.

[46] Zupan, J., & Gasteiger, J. (1999). *Neural Networks in Chemistry and Drug Design* (2 ed.), Wiley-VCH.

[47] Gasteiger, J., & Zupan, J. (1993). Neural Networks in Chemistry. *Angew. Chem. Int. Edit.*, 32, 503-527.

[48] Marini, F. (2009). Artificial neural networks in foodstuff analyses: Trends and perspectives. A review. *Anal. Chim. Acta*, 635, 121-131.

[49] Miller, F. P., Vandome, A. F., & Mc Brewster, J. (2011). *Multilayer Perceptron*, Alphascript Publishing.

[50] Widrow, B., & Lehr, M. A. (1990). 30 years of Adaptive Neural Networks: Perceptron Madaline and Backpropagation. *Proc. IEEE*, 78, 1415-1442.

[51] Kohonen, T. (2001). *Self Organizing Maps* (3 ed.), New York, Springer.

[52] Zupan, J., Noviča, M., & Ruisánchez, I. (1997). Kohonen and counterpropagation artificial neural networks in analytical chemistry. *Chemom. Intell. Lab.*, 38, 1-23.

[53] Smits, J. R. M., Melssen, W. J., Buydens, L. M. C., & Kateman, G. (1994). Using artificial neural networks for solving chemical problems. Part II. Kohonen self-organising feature maps and Hopfield networks. *Chemom. Intell. Lab.*, 23, 267-291.

[54] Schneider, G., & Nettekoven, M. (2003). Ligand-based combinatorial design of selective purinergic receptor (a2a) antagonists using self-organizing maps. *J. Comb. Chem.*, 5-233.

[55] Bayes, T. (1764). An Essay toward solving a problem in the doctrine of chances. *Philosophical Transactions of the Royal Society of London*, 53, 370-418.

[56] Mackay, D. J. C. (1995). Probable Networks and Plausible Predictions- a Review of Practical Bayesian Methods for Supervised Neural Networks. *Comput. Neural Sys.*, 6, 469-505.

[57] Mackay, D. J. C. (1992). Bayesian Interpolation. *Neural Comput.*, 4, 415-447.

[58] Buntine, W. L., & Weigend, A. S. (1991). Bayesian Back-Propagation. *Complex. Sys.*, 5, 603-643.

[59] de Freitas, J. F. G. (2003). Bayesian Methods for Neural Networks. *PhD thesis*, University Engineering Dept Cambridge.

[60] Grossberg, S. (1976). Adaptive pattern classification and universal recoding I. Parallel development and coding of neural feature detectors. *Biol. Cybern.*, 23, 121-134.

[61] Grossberg, S. (1976). Adaptive pattern classification and universal recoding II. Feedback expectation olfaction and illusions. *Biol. Cybern.*, 23, 187-203.

[62] Carpenter, G. A., Grossberg, S., & Rosen, D. B. (1991). ART-2a-an adaptive resonance algorithm for rapid category learning and recognition. *Neural Networks*, 4, 493-504.

[63] Wienke, D., & Buydens, L. (1995). Adaptive resonance theory based neural networks-the'ART' of real-time pattern recognition in chemical process monitoring? *TrAC Trend. Anal. Chem.*, 14, 398-406.

[64] Lin, C. C., & Wang, H. P. (1993). Classification of autoregressive spectral estimated signal patterns using an adaptive resonance theory neural network. *Comput. Ind.*, 22, 143-157.

[65] Whiteley, J. R., & Davis, J. F. (1994). A similarity-based approach to interpretation of sensor data using adaptive resonance theory. *Comput. Chem. Eng.*, 18, 637-661.

[66] Whiteley, J. R., & Davis, J. F. (1993). Qualitative interpretation of sensor patterns. *IEEE Expert*, 4, 54-63.

[67] Wienke, D., & Kateman, G. (1994). Adaptive resonance theory based artificial neural networks for treatment of open-category problems in chemical pattern recognition-application to UV-Vis and IR spectroscopy. *Chemom. Intell. Lab.*, 23, 309-329.

[68] Wienke, D., Xie, Y., & Hopke, P. K. (1994). An adaptive resonance theory based artificial neural network (ART-2a) for rapid identification of airborne particle shapes from their scanning electron microscopy images. *Intell. Lab.*, 26, 367-387.

[69] Xie, Y., Hopke, P. K., & Wienke, D. (1994). Airborne particle classification with a combination of chemical composition and shape index utilizing an adaptive resonance artificial neural network. *Environ. Sci. Technol.*, 28, 1921-1928.

[70] Wienke, D., van den, Broek. W., Melssen, W., Buydens, L., Feldhoff, R., Huth-Fehre, T., Kantimm, T., Quick, L., Winter, F., & Cammann, K. (1995). Comparison of an adaptive resonance theory based neural network (ART-2a) against other classifiers for rapid sorting of post consumer plastics by remote near-infrared spectroscopic sensing using an InGaAs diode array. *Anal. Chim. Acta*, 317, 1-16.

[71] Domine, D., Devillers, J., Wienke, D., & Buydens, L. (1997). ART 2-A for Optimal Test Series Design in QSAR. *J. Chem. Inf. Comput. Sci.*, 37, 10-17.

[72] Wienke, D., & Buydens, L. (1996). Adaptive resonance theory based neural network for supervised chemical pattern recognition (FuzzyARTMAP). Part 1: Theory and network properties. *Chemom. Intell. Lab.*, 32, 151-164.

[73] Wienke, D., van den, Broek. W., Buydens, L., Huth-Fehre, T., Feldhoff, R., Kantimm, T., & Cammann, K. (1996). Adaptive resonance theory based neural network for supervised chemical pattern recognition (FuzzyARTMAP). Part 2: Classification of post-consumer plastics by remote NIR spectroscopy using an InGaAs diode array. *Chemom. Intell. Lab.*, 32, 165-176.

[74] Buhmann, M. D. (2003). *Radial Basis Functions: Theory and Implementations,* Cambridge University.

[75] Lingireddy, S., & Ormsbee, L. E. (1998). Neural Networks in Optimal Calibration of Water Distribution Systems. In: Flood I, Kartam N. (eds.) Artificial Neural Networks for Civil Engineers: Advanced Features and Applications. *Amer. Society of Civil Engineers*, 53-76.

[76] Shahsavand, A., & Ahmadpour, A. (2005). Application of Optimal Rbf Neural Networks for Optimization and Characterization of Porous Materials. *Comput. Chem. Eng.*, 29, 2134-2143.

[77] Regis, R. G., & Shoemaker, C. (2005). A Constrained Global Optimization of Expensive Black Box Functions Using Radial Basis Functions. *J. Global. Optim.*, 31, 153-171.

[78] Han, H., Chen, Q., & Qiao, J. (2011). An efficient self-organizing RBF neural network for water quality prediction. *Neural Networks*, 24, 717-725.

[79] Fidêncio, P. H., Poppi, R. J., Andrade, J. C., & Abreu, M. F. (2008). Use of Radial Basis Function Networks and Near-Infrared Spectroscopy for the Determination of Total Nitrogen Content in Soils from Sao Paulo State. *Anal. Sci.*, 24, 945-948.

[80] Yao, X., Liu, M., Zhang, X., Zhang, R., Hu, Z., & Fan, B. (2002). Radial Basis Function Neural Networks Based QSPR for the Prediction of log P. *Chinese J. Chem.*, 20, 722-730.

[81] Hopfield, J. J. (1982). Neural networks and physical systems with emergent collective computational abilities. *Proc. Natl. Acad. Sci.*, USA, 79, 2554-2558.

[82] Hopfield, J. J. (1984). Neurons with graded response have collective computational properties like those of two-state neurons. *Proc. Natl. Acad. Sci.*, USA, 81, 3088-3092.

[83] Arakawa, M., Hasegawa, K., & Funatsu, K. (2003). Application of the Novel Molecular Alignment Method Using the Hopfield Neural Network to 3D-QSAR. *J. Chem. Inf. Comput. Sci.*, 43, 1396-1402.

[84] Braga, J. P., Almeida, M. B., Braga, A. P., & Belchior, J. C. (2000). Hopfield neural network model for calculating the potential energy function from second virial data. *Chem. Phys.*, 260, 347-352.

[85] Hjelmfelt, A., & Ross, J. (1992). Chemical implementation and thermodynamics of collective neural networks. *PNAS*, 89, 388-391.

[86] Hjelmfelt, A., Schneider, F. W., & Ross, J. (1993). Pattern Recognition in Coupled Chemical Kinetic Systems. *Science*, 260, 335-337.

[87] Vracko, M. (2005). Kohonen Artificial Neural Network and Counter Propagation Neural Network in Molecular Structure-Toxicity Studies. *Curr. Comput-Aid. Drug*, 1, 73-78.

[88] Guha, R., Serra, J. R., & Jurs, P. C. (2004). Generation of QSAR sets with a self-organizing map. *J. Mol. Graph. Model.*, 23, 1-14.

[89] Hoshi, K., Kawakami, J., Kumagai, M., Kasahara, S., Nishimura, N., Nakamura, H., & Sato, K. (2005). An analysis of thyroid function diagnosis using Bayesian-type and SOM-type neural networks. *Chem. Pharm. Bull.*, 53, 1570-1574.

[90] Nandi, S., Vracko, M., & Bagchi, M. C. (2007). Anticancer activity of selected phenolic compounds: QSAR studies using ridge regression and neural networks. *Chem. Biol. Drug Des.*, 70, 424-436.

[91] Xiao, Y. D., Clauset, A., Harris, R., Bayram, E., Santago, P., & Schmitt, . (2005). Supervised self-organizing maps in drug discovery. 1. Robust behavior with overdetermined data sets. *J. Chem. Inf. Model.*, 45, 1749-1758.

[92] Molfetta, F. A., Angelotti, W. F. D., Romero, R. A. F., Montanari, C. A., & da, Silva. A. B. F. (2008). A neural networks study of quinone compounds with trypanocidal activity. *J. Mol. Model.*, 14, 975-985.

[93] Zheng, F., Zheng, G., Deaciuc, A. G., Zhan, C. G., Dwoskin, L. P., & Crooks, P. A. (2007). Computational neural network analysis of the affinity of lobeline and tetrabenazine analogs for the vesicular monoamine transporter-2. Bioorg. *Med. Chem.*, 15, 2975-2992.

[94] Caballero, J., Fernandez, M., & Gonzalez-Nilo, F. D. (2008). Structural requirements of pyrido[23-d]pyrimidin-7-one as CDK4/D inhibitors: 2D autocorrelation CoMFA and CoMSIA analyses. *Bioorg. Med. Chem.*, 16, 6103-6115.

[95] Schneider, G., Coassolo, P., & Lavé, T. (1999). Combining in vitro and in vivo pharmacokinetic data for prediction of hepatic drug clearance in humans by artificial neural networks and multivariate statistical techniques. *J. Med. Chem.*, 42, 5072-5076.

[96] Hu, L., Chen, G., & Chau, R. M. W. (2006). A neural networks-based drug discovery approach and its application for designing aldose reductase inhibitors. *J. Mol. Graph. Model.*, 24, 244-253.

[97] Afantitis, A., Melagraki, G., Koutentis, P. A., Sarimveis, H., & Kollias, G. (2011). Ligand- based virtual screening procedure for the prediction and the identification of novel β-amyloid aggregation inhibitors using Kohonen maps and Counterpropagation Artificial Neural Networks. *Eur. J. Med. Chem.*, 46, 497-508.

[98] Noeske, T., Trifanova, D., Kauss, V., Renner, S., Parsons, C. G., Schneider, G., & Weil, T. (2009). Synergism of virtual screening and medicinal chemistry: Identification and optimization of allosteric antagonists of metabotropic glutamate receptor 1. *Bioorg. Med. Chem.*, 17, 5708-5715.

[99] Karpov, P. V., Osolodkin, D. I., Baskin, I. I., Palyulin, V. A., & Zefirov, N. S. (2011). One-class classification as a novel method of ligand-based virtual screening: The case of glycogen synthase kinase 3β inhibitors. *Bioorg. Med. Chem. Lett.*, 21, 6728-6731.

[100] Molnar, L., & Keseru, G. M. (2002). A neural network based virtual screening of cytochrome p450a4 inhibitors. *Bioorg. Med. Chem. Lett.*, 12, 419-421.

[101] Di Massimo, C., Montague, G. A., Willis, Tham. M. T., & Morris, A. J. (1992). Towards improved penicillin fermentation via artificialneuralnetworks. *Comput. Chem. Eng.*, 16, 283-291.

[102] Palancar, M. C., Aragón, J. M., & Torrecilla, J. S. (1998). pH-Control System Based on Artificial Neural Networks. *Ind. Eng. Chem. Res.*, 37, 2729-2740.

[103] Takayama, K., Fujikawa, M., & Nagai, T. (1999). Artificial Neural Network as a Novel Method to Optimize Pharmaceutical Formulations. *Pharm. Res.*, 16, 1-6.

[104] Takayama, K., Morva, A., Fujikawa, M., Hattori, Y., Obata, Y., & Nagai, T. (2000). Formula optimization of theophylline controlled-release tablet based on artificial neural networks. *J. Control. Release*, 68, 175-186.

[105] Fanny, B., Gilles, M., Natalia, K., Alexandre, V., & Dragos, H. Using Self-Organizing Maps to Accelerate Similarity Search. *Bioorg. Med. Chem.*, In Press, http://dxdoiorg/101016/jbmc201204024.

[106] Sigman, M. E., & Rives, S. S. (1994). Prediction of Atomic Ionization Potentials I-III Using an Artificial Neural Network. *J. Chem. Inf. Comput. Sci.*, 34, 617-620.

[107] Tetko, I. V., & Tanchuk, V. Y. (2002). Application of Associative Neural Networks for Prediction of Lipophilicity in ALOGPS 2.1 Program. *J. Chem. Inf. Comput. Sci.*, 42, 1136-1145.

[108] Tetko, I. V., Tanchuk, V. Y., & Villa, A. E. P. (2001). Prediction of n-Octanol/Water Partition Coefficients from PHYSPROP Database Using Artificial Neural Networks and E-State Indices. *J. Chem. Inf. Comput. Sci.*, 41, 1407-1421.

[109] Sumpter, B. G., & Noid, D. W. (1994). Neural networks and graph theory as computational tools for predicting polymer properties. *Macromol. Theor. Simul.*, 3, 363-378.

[110] Scotta, D. J., Coveneya, P. V., Kilnerb, J. A., Rossinyb, J. C. H., & Alford, N. M. N. (2007). Prediction of the functional properties of ceramic materials from composition using artificialneuralnetworks. *J. Eur. Ceram. Soc.*, 27, 4425-4435.

[111] Stojković, G., Novič, M., & Kuzmanovski, I. (2010). Counter-propagation artificial neural networks as a tool for prediction of pKBH+ for series of amides. *Chemom. Intell. Lab.*, 102, 123-129.

[112] Næs, T., Kvaal, K., Isaksson, T., & Miller, C. (1993). Artificial neural networks in multivariate calibration. *J. Near. Infrared Spectrosc.*, 1, 1-11.

[113] Munk, M. E., Madison, M. S., & Robb, E. W. (1991). Neural-network models for infrared-spectrum interpretation. *Mikrochim. Acta*, 2, 505-524.

[114] Meyer, M., & Weigelt, T. (1992). Interpretation of infrared spectra by artificial neural networks. *Anal. Chim. Acta*, 265, 183-190.

[115] Smits, J. R. M., Schoenmakers, P., Stehmann, A., Sijstermans, F., & Chemom, Kateman G. (1993). Interpretation of infrared spectra with modular neural-network systems. *Intell. Lab.*, 18, 27-39.

[116] Goodacre, R., Neal, M. J., & Kell, D. B. (1994). Rapid and Quantitative Analysis of the Pyrolysis Mass Spectra of Complex Binary and Tertiary Mixtures Using Multivariate Calibration and Artificial Neural Networks. *Anal. Chem.*, 66, 1070-1085.

[117] Cirovic, D. (1997). Feed-forward artificial neural networks: applications to spectroscopy. *TrAC Trend. Anal. Chem.*, 16, 148-155.

[118] Zhao, R. H., Yue, B. F., Ni, J. Y., Zhou, H. F., & Zhang, Y. K. (1999). Application of an artificial neural network in chromatography-retention behavior prediction and pattern recognition. *Chemom. Intell. Lab.*, 45, 163-170.

[119] Blanco, M., Coello, J., Iturriaga, H., Maspoch, S., & Redon, M. (1995). Artificial Neural Networks for Multicomponent Kinetic Determinations. *Anal. Chem.*, 67, 4477-4483.

[120] Fatemi, M. H. (2006). Prediction of ozone tropospheric degradation rate constant of organic compounds by using artificial neural networks. *Anal. Chim. Acta*, 556, 355-363.

[121] Diederichs, K., Freigang, J., Umhau, S., Zeth, K., & Breed, J. (1998). Prediction by a neural network of outer membrane {beta}-strand protein topology. *Protein Sci.*, 7, 2413-2420.

[122] Meiler, J. (2003). PROSHIFT: Protein chemical shift prediction using artificial neural networks. *J. Biomol. NMR*, 26, 25-37.

[123] Lohmann, R., Schneider, G., Behrens, D., & Wrede, P. A. (1994). Neural network model for the prediction of membrane-spanning amino acid sequences. *Protein Sci.*, 3, 1597-1601.

[124] Dombi, G. W., & Lawrence, J. (1994). Analysis of protein transmembrane helical regions by a neural network. *Protein Sci.*, 3, 557-566.

[125] Wang, S. Q., Yang, J., & Chou, K. C. (2006). Using stacked generalization to predict membrane protein types based on pseudo-amino acid composition. *J. Theor. Biol.*, 242, 941-946.

[126] Ma, L., Cheng, C., Liu, X., Zhao, Y., Wang, A., & Herdewijn, P. (2004). A neural network for predicting the stability of RNA/DNA hybrid duplexes. Chemom. *Intell. Lab.*, 70, 123-128.

[127] Ferran, E. A., Pflugfelaer, B., & Ferrara, P. (1994). Self-organized neural maps of human protein sequences. *Protein Sci.*, 3, 507-521.

[128] Petritis, K., Kangas, L. J., Ferguson, P. L., Anderson, G. A., Paša-Tolić, L., Lipton, M. S., Auberry, K. J., Strittmatter, E. F., Shen, Y., Zhao, R., & Smith, R. D. (2003). Use of Artificial Neural Networks for the Accurate Prediction of Peptide Liquid Chromatography Elution Times in Proteome Analyses. *Anal. Chem.*, 75, 1039-1048.

[129] Huang, R., Du, Q., Wei, Y., Pang, Z., Wei, H., & Chou, K. (2009). Physics and chemistry-driven artificial neural network for predicting bioactivity of peptides and proteins and their design. *J. Theor. Biol.*, 256, 428-435.

[130] Martin, Y. G., Oliveros, M. C. C., Pavon, J. L. P., Pinto, C. G., & Cordero, B. M. (2001). Electronic nose based on metal oxide semiconductor sensors and pattern recognition techniques: characterisation of vegetable oils. *Anal. Chim. Acta*, 449, 69-80.

[131] Brodnjak-Voncina, D., Kodba, Z. C., & Novic, M. (2005). Multivariate data analysis in classification of vegetable oils characterized by the content of fatty acids. *Chemom. Intell. Lab.*, 75, 31-43.

[132] Zhang, G. W., Ni, Y. N., Churchill, J., & Kokot, S. (2006). Authentication of vegetable oils on the basis of their physico-chemical properties with the aid of chemometrics. *Talanta*, 70, 293-300.

[133] Goodacre, R., Kell, D. B., & Bianchi, G. (1993). Rapid assessment of the adulteration of virgin olive oils by other seed oils using pyrolysis mass spectrometry and artificial neural networks. *J. Sci. Food Agr.*, 63, 297-307.

[134] Bianchi, G., Giansante, L., Shaw, A., & Kell, D. B. (2001). Chemometric criteria for the characterisation of Italian DOP olive oils from their metabolic profiles. *Eur. J. Lipid. Sci. Tech.*, 103, 141-150.

[135] Bucci, R., Magri, A. D., Magri, A. L., Marini, D., & Marini, F. (2002). Chemical Authentication of Extra Virgin Olive Oil Varieties by Supervised Chemometric Procedures. *J. Agric. Food Chem.*, 50, 413-418.

[136] Marini, F., Balestrieri, F., Bucci, R., Magri, A. D., Magri, A. L., & Marini, D. (2004). Supervised pattern recognition to authenticate Italian extra virgin olive oil varieties. *Chemom. Intell. Lab.*, 73, 85-93.

[137] Marini, F., Balestrieri, F., Bucci, R., Magri, A. L., & Marini, D. (2003). Supervised pattern recognition to discriminate the geographical origin of rice bran oils: a first study. *Microch. J.*, 74, 239-248.

[138] Marini, F., Magri, A. L., Marini, D., & Balestrieri, F. (2003). Characterization of the lipid fraction of Niger seeds (Guizotia abyssinica cass) from different regions of Ethiopia and India and chemometric authentication of their geographical origin. *Eur. J. Lipid. Sci. Tech.*, 105, 697-704.

[139] Alexander, P. W., Di Benedetto, L. T., & Hibbert, D. B. (1998). A field-portable gas analyzer with an array of six semiconductor sensors. Part 2: Identification of beer samples using artificial neural networks. *Field. Anal. Chem. Tech.*, 2, 145-153.

[140] Penza, M., & Cassano, G. (2004). Chemometric characterization of Italian wines by thin-film multisensors array and artificial neural networks. *Food Chem.*, 86, 283-296.

[141] Latorre, Pena. R., Garcia, S., & Herrero, C. (2000). Authentication of Galician (NW Spain) honeys by multivariate techniques based on metal content data. *Analyst.*, 125, 307-312.

[142] Cordella, C. B. Y., Militao, J. S. L. T., & Clement, M. C. (2003). Cabrol-Bass D Honey Characterization and Adulteration Detection by Pattern Recognition Applied on HPAEC-PAD Profiles. 1. Honey Floral Species Characterization. *J. Agric. Food Chem.*, 51, 3234-3242.

[143] Brodnjak-Voncina, D., Dobcnik, D., Novic, M., & Zupan, J. (2002). Chemometrics characterisation of the quality of river water. *Anal. Chim. Acta*, 462, 87-100.

[144] Voncina, E., Brodnjak-Voncina, D., Sovic, N., & Novic, M. (2007). Chemometric characterisation of the Quality of Ground Waters from Different wells in Slovenia. *Acta Chim. Slov.*, 54, 119-125.

[145] Bos, A., Bos, M., & van der Linden, W. E. (1992). Artificial neural networks as a tool for soft-modelling in quantitative analytical chemistry: the prediction of the water content of cheese. *Anal. Chim. Acta*, 256, 133-144.

[146] Cimpoiu, C., Cristea, V., Hosu, A., Sandru, M., & Seserman, L. (2011). Antioxidant activity prediction and classification of some teas using artificial neural networks. *Food Chem.*, 127, 1323-1328.

Chapter 10

Integrating Modularity and Reconfigurability for Perfect Implementation of Neural Networks

Hazem M. El-Bakry

Additional information is available at the end of the chapter

1. Introduction

In this chapter, we introduce a powerful solution for complex problems that are required to be solved by using neural nets. This is done by using modular neural nets (MNNs) that divide the input space into several homogenous regions. Such approach is applied to implement XOR functions, 16 logic function on one bit level, and 2-bit digital multiplier. Compared to previous non- modular designs, a salient reduction in the order of computations and hardware requirements is obtained.

Modular Neural Nets (MNNs) present a new trend in neural network architecture design. Motivated by the highly-modular biological network, artificial neural net designers aim to build architectures which are more scalable and less subjected to interference than the traditional non-modular neural nets [1]. There are now a wide variety of MNN designs for classification. Non-modular classifiers tend to introduce high internal interference because of the strong coupling among their hidden layer weights [2]. As a result of this, slow learning or over fitting can be done during the learning process. Sometime, the network could not be learned for complex tasks. Such tasks tend to introduce a wide range of overlap which, in turn, causes a wide range of deviations from efficient learning in the different regions of input space [3]. Usually there are regions in the class feature space which show high overlap due to the resemblance of two or more input patterns (classes). At the same time, there are other regions which show little or even no overlap, due to the uniqueness of the classes therein. High coupling among hidden nodes will then, result in over and under learning at different regions [8]. Enlarging the network, increasing the number and quality of training samples, and techniques for avoiding local minina, will not stretch the learning capabilities of the NN classifier beyond a certain limit as long as hidden nodes are tightly coupled, and hence cross talking during learning [2]. A MNN classifier attempts to reduce the effect of these problems via a divide and conquer approach. It, generally, decomposes the large size / high complexity task into several sub-tasks, each one is handled by a simple, fast, and efficient module. Then, sub-solutions are integrated via a multi-module decision-making strategy. Hence, MNN classifiers, generally, proved to be more efficient than non-modular alternatives [6]. However, MNNs can not offer a real alternative to non-modular networks unless the MNNs designer balances the simplicity of subtasks and the efficiency of the multi module decision-making strategy. In other words, the task decomposition algorithm should produce sub tasks as they can be, but meanwhile modules have to be able to give the multi module decision making strategy enough information to take accurate global decision [4].

In a previous paper [9], we have shown that this model can be applied to realize non-binary data. In this chapter, we prove that MNNs can solve some problems with a little amount of requirements than non-MNNs. In section 2, XOR function, and 16 logic functions on one bit level are simply implemented using MNN. Comparisons with conventional MNN are given. In section 3, another strategy for the design of MNNS is presented and applied to realize, and 2-bit digital multiplier.

2. Complexity reduction using modular neural networks

In the following subsections, we investigate the usage of MNNs in some binary problems. Here, all MNNs are feedforward type, and learned by using backpropagation algorithm. In comparison with non-MNNs, we take into account the number of neurons and weights in both models as well as the number of computations during the test phase.

2.1. A simple implementation for XOR problem

There are two topologies to realize XOR function whose truth Table is shown in Table 1 using neural nets. The first uses fully connected neural nets with three neurons, two of which are in the hidden layer, and the other is in the output layer. There is no direct connections between the input and output layer as shown in Fig.1. In this case, the neural net is trained to classify all of these four patterns at the same time.

x	y	O/P
0	0	0
0	1	1
1	0	1
1	1	0

Table 1. Truth table of XOR function.

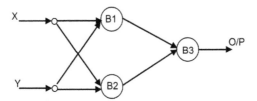

Figure 1. Realization of XOR function using three neurons.

The second approach was presented by Minsky and Papert which was realized using two neurons as shown in Fig. 2. The first representing logic AND and the other logic OR. The value of +1.5 for the threshold of the hidden neuron insures that it will be turned on only when both input units are on. The value of +0.5 for the output neuron insures that it will turn on only when it receives a net positive input greater than +0.5. The weight of -2 from the hidden neuron to the output one insures that the output neuron will not come on when both input neurons are on [7].

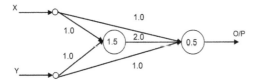

Figure 2. Realization of XOR function using two neurons.

Using MNNs, we may consider the problem of classifying these four patterns as two individual problems. This can be done at two steps:

1. We deal with each bit alone.

2. Consider the second bit Y, Divide the four patterns into two groups.

The first group consists of the first two patterns which realize a buffer, while the second group which contains the other two patterns represents an inverter as shown in Table 2. The first bit (X) may be used to select the function.

X	Y	O/P	New Function
0	0	0	Buffer (Y)
0	1	1	
1	0	1	Inverter ($\bar{Y}$)
1	1	0	

Table 2. Results of dividing XOR Patterns.

So, we may use two neural nets, one to realize the buffer, and the other to represent the inverter. Each one of them may be implemented by using only one neuron. When realizing these two neurons, we implement the weights, and perform only one summing operation. The first input X acts as a detector to select the proper weights as shown in Fig.3. In a special case, for XOR function, there is no need to the buffer and the neural net may be represented by using only one weight corresponding to the inverter as shown in Fig.4. As a result of using cooperative modular neural nets, XOR function is realized by using only one neuron. A comparison between the new model and the two previous approaches is given in Table 3. It is clear that the number of computations and the hardware requirements for the new model is less than that of the other models.

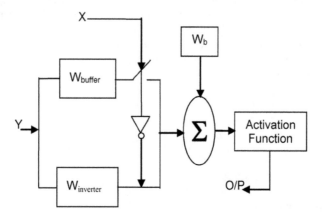

Figure 3. Realization of XOR function using modular neural nets.

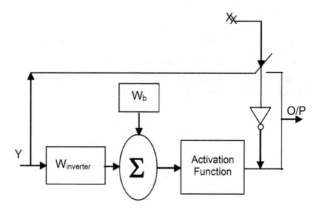

Figure 4. Implementation of XOR function using only one neuron.

Type of Comparison	First model (three neurons)	Second model (two neurons)	New model (one neuron)
No. of computations	O(15)	O(12)	O(3)
Hardware requirements	3 neurons, 9 weights	2 neurons, 7 weights	1 neuron, 2 weights, 2 switches, 1 inverter

Table 3. A comparison between different models used to implement XOR function.

2.2. Implementation of logic functions by using MNNs

Realization of logic functions in one bit level (X,Y) generates 16 functions which are (AND, OR, NAND, NOR, XOR, XNOR, $\overline{X},\overline{Y}$, X, Y, 0, 1, $\overline{X}Y$, $X\overline{Y}$, $\overline{X}+Y$, $X+\overline{Y}$). So, in order to control the selection for each one of these functions, we must have another 4 bits at the input, thereby the total input is 6 bits as shown in Table 4.

Function	C1	C2	C3	C4	X	Y	O/p
AND	0	0	0	0	0	0	0
	0	0	0	0	0	1	0
	0	0	0	0	1	0	0
	0	0	0	0	1	1	1
....	....	....	....	....	....	....	....
$X+\overline{Y}$	1	1	1	1	0	0	1
	1	1	1	1	0	1	0
	1	1	1	1	1	0	1
	1	1	1	1	1	1	1

Table 4. Truth table of Logic function (one bit level) with their control selection.

Non-MNNs can classify these 64 patterns using a network of three layers. The hidden layer contains 8 neurons, while the output needs only one neuron and a total number of 65 weights are required. These patterns can be divided into two groups. Each group has an input of 5 bits, while the MSB is 0 with the first group and 1 with the second. The first group requires 4 neurons and 29 weights in the hidden layer, while the second needs 3 neurons and 22 weights. As a result of this, we may implement only 4 summing operations in the hidden layer (in spite of 8 neurons in case of non-MNNs) where as the MSB is used to select which group of weights must be connected to the neurons in the hidden layer. A similar procedure is done between hidden and output layer. Fig. 5 shows the structure of the first neuron in the hidden layer. A comparison between MNN and non-MNNs used to implement logic functions is shown in Table 5.

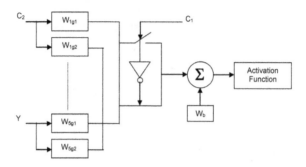

Figure 5. Realization of logic functions using MNNs (the first neuron in the hidden layer).

Type of Comparison	Realization using non MNNs	Realization using MNNs
No. of computations	O(121)	O(54)
Hardware requirements	9 neurons, 65 weights	5 neurons, 51 weights, 10 switches, 1 inverter

Table 5. A comparison between MNN and non MNNs used to implement 16 logic functions.

3. Implementation of 2-bits digital multiplier by using MNNs

In the previous section, to simplify the problem, we make division in input, here is an example for division in output. According to the truth table shown in Table 6, instead of treating the problem as mapping 4 bits in input to 4 bits in output, we may deal with each bit in output alone. Non MNNs can realize the 2-bits multiplier with a network of three layers with total number of 31 weights. The hidden layer contains 3 neurons, while the output one has 4 neurons. Using MNN we may simplify the problem as:

$$W = CA \tag{1}$$

$$\begin{aligned} X &= AD \otimes BC = AD(\bar{B} + \bar{C}) + BC(\bar{A} + \bar{D}) \\ &= (AD + BC)(\bar{A} + \bar{B} + \bar{C} + \bar{D}) \end{aligned} \tag{2}$$

$$Y = BD(\bar{A} + \bar{C}) = BD(\bar{A} + \bar{B} + \bar{C} + \bar{D}) \tag{3}$$

$$Z = ABCD \tag{4}$$

Equations 1, 2, 3 can be implemented using only one neuron. The third term in Equation 3 can be implemented using the output from Bit Z with a negative (inhibitory) weight. This eliminates the need to use two neurons to represent $\bar{A}$ and $\bar{D}$. Equation 2 resembles an XOR, but we must first obtain AD and BC. AD can be implemented using only one neuron. Another neuron is used to realize BC and at the same time oring (AD, BC) as well as anding the result with $(\overline{ABCD})$ as shown in Fig.6. A comparison between MNN and non-MNNs used to implement 2bits digital multiplier is listed in Table 7.

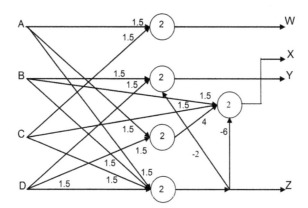

Figure 6. Realization of 2-bits digital multiplier using MNNs.

Input Patterns				Output Patterns			
D	C	B	A	Z	Y	X	W
0	0	0	0	0	0	0	0
0	0	0	1	0	0	0	0
0	0	1	0	0	0	0	0
0	0	1	1	0	0	0	0
0	1	0	0	0	0	0	0
0	1	0	1	0	0	0	1
0	1	1	0	0	0	1	0
0	1	1	1	0	1	1	0
1	0	0	0	0	0	0	0
1	0	0	1	0	0	1	0
1	0	1	0	0	1	0	0
1	0	1	1	0	1	1	0
1	1	0	0	0	0	0	0
1	1	0	1	0	0	1	1
1	1	1	0	0	1	1	0
1	1	1	1	1	0	0	1

Table 6. Truth table of 2-bit digital multiplier.

Type of Comparison	Realization using non MNNs	Realization using MNNs
No. of computations	O(55)	O(35)
Hardware requirements	7 neurons, 31 weights	5 neurons, 20 weights

Table 7. A comparison between MNN and non-MNNs used to implement 2-bits digital multiplier.

4. Hardware implementation of MNNs by using reconfigurable circuits

Advances in MOS VLSI have made it possible to integrate neural networks of large sizes on a single-chip [10,12]. Hardware realizations make it possible to execute the forward pass operation of neural networks at high speeds, thus making neural networks possible candidates for real-time applications. Other advantages of hardware realizations as compared to software implementations are the lower per unit cost and small size system.

Analog circuit techniques provide area-efficient implementations of the functions required in a neural network, namely, multiplication, summation, and the sigmoid transfer characteristic [13]. In this paper, we describe the design of a reconfigurable neural network in analog hardware and demonstrate experimentally how a reconfigurable artificial neural network approach is used in implementation of arithmetic unit that including full-adder, full-subtractor, 2-bit digital multiplier, and 2-bit digital divider.

One of the main reasons for using analog electronics to realize network hardware is that simple analog circuits (for example adders, sigmoid, and multipliers) can realize several of the operations in neural networks. Nowadays, there is a growing demand for large as well as fast neural processors to provide solutions for difficult problems. Designers may use either analog or digital technologies to implement neural network models. The analog approach boasts compactness and high speed. On the other hand, digital implementations offer flexibility and adaptability, but only at the expense of speed and silicon area consumption.

4.1. Implementation of artificial neuron

Implementation of analog neural networks means that using only analog computation [14,16,18]. Artificial neural network as the name indicates, is the interconnection of artificial neurons that tend to simulate the nervous system of human brain [15]. Neural networks are modeled as simple processors (neurons) that are connected together via weights. The weights can be positive (excitatory) or negative (inhibitory). Such weights can be realized by resistors as shown in Fig. 7.

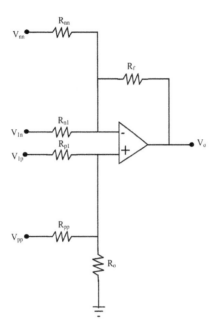

Figure 7. Implementation of positive and negative weights using only one opamp.

The computed weights may have positive or negative values. The corresponding resistors that represent these weights can be determined as follow [16]:

$$w_{in} = -R_f / R_{in} \qquad i = 1, 2, \ldots, n \tag{5}$$

$$\text{Wpp} = \frac{\left(1 + \sum_{i1}^{n} \text{Win}\right) \dfrac{\text{Ro}}{\text{Rpp}}}{\left(1 + \dfrac{\text{Ro}}{\text{R1p}} + \dfrac{\text{Ro}}{\text{R2p}} + \ldots\ldots\ldots + \dfrac{\text{Ro}}{\text{Rpp}}\right)} \tag{6}$$

The exact values of these resistors can be calculated as presented in [14,18]. The summing circuit accumulates all the input-weighted signals and then passes to the output through the transfer function [13]. The main problem with the electronic neural networks is the realization of resistors which are fixed and have many problems in hardware implementation [17]. Such resistors are not easily adjustable or controllable. As a consequence, they can be used neither for learning, nor can they be used for recall when another task needs to be solved. So the calculated resistors corresponding to the obtainable weights can be implemented by using CMOS transistors operating in continuous mode (triode region) as shown in Fig. 8. The equivalent resistance between terminal 1 and 2 is given by [19]:

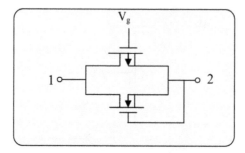

Figure 8. Two MOS transistor as a linear resistor.

$$R_{eq} = 1 / \left[K \left(V_g - 2V_{th} \right) \right] \tag{7}$$

4.2. Reconfigurability

The interconnection of synapses and neurons determines the topology of a neural network. Reconfigurability is defined as the ability to alter the topology of the neural network [19]. Using switches in the interconnections between synapses and neurons permits one to change the network topology as shown in Fig. 9. These switches are called "reconfiguration switches".

The concept of reconfigurability should not be confused with *weight programmability*. Weight programmability is defined as the ability to alter the values of the weights in each synapse. In Fig. 9, weight programmability involves setting the values of the weights w_1, w_2, w_3,....., w_n. Although reconfigurability can be achieved by setting weights of some synapses to zero value, this would be very inefficient in hardware.

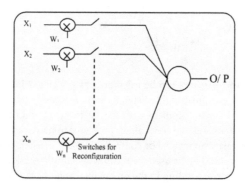

Figure 9. Neuron with reconfigurable switches.

Reconfigurability is desirable for several reasons [20]:

1. Providing a general problem-solving environment.
2. Correcting offsets.
3. Ease of testing.
4. Reconfiguration for isolating defects.

5. Design arithmetic and logic unit by using reconfigurable neural networks

In previous paper [20], a neural design for logic functions by using modular neural networks was presented. Here, a simple design for the arithmetic unit using reconfigurable neural networks is presented. The aim is to have a complete design for ALU by using the benefits of both modular and reconfigurable neural networks.

5.1. Implementation of full adder/full subtractor by using neural networks

Full-adder/full-subtractor problem is solved practically and a neural network is simulated and implemented using the back-propagation algorithm for the purpose of learning this network [10]. The network is learned to map the functions of full-adder and full-subtractor. The problem is to classify the patterns shown in Table 8 correctly.

I/P			Full-Adder		Full-Subtractor	
x	y	z				
			S	C	D	B
0	0	0	0	0	0	0
0	0	1	0	1	1	1
0	1	0	0	1	1	1
0	1	1	1	0	1	0
1	0	0	0	1	0	1
1	0	1	1	0	0	0
1	1	0	1	0	0	0
1	1	1	1	1	1	1

Table 8. Truth table of full-adder/full-subtractor

The computed values of weights and their corresponding values of resistors are described in Table 9. After completing the design of the network, simulations are carried out to test both the design and performance of this network by using H-spice. Experimental results confirm the proposed theoretical considerations. Fig. 10 shows the construction of full-adder/full-subtractor neural network. The network consists of three neurons and 12-connection weights.

I / P	Neuron (1)		Neuron (2)		Neuron (3)	
Weight	Resistance	Weight	Resistance	Weight	Resistance	
1	7.5	11.8 Ro	15	6.06 Ro	15	6.06 Ro
2	7.5	11.8 Ro	15	6.06 Ro	15	6.06 Ro
3	7.5	11.8 Ro	-10	0.1 Rf	-10	0.1 Rf
Bias	-10.0	0.1 Rf	-10	0.1 Rf	-10	0.1 Rf

Table 9. Computed weights and their corresponding resistances of full-adder/full-subtractor

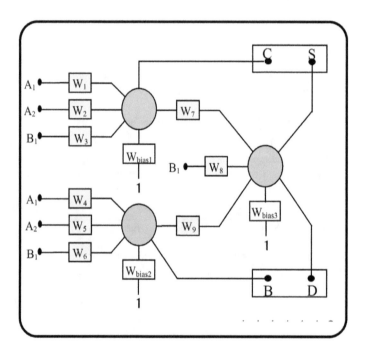

Figure 10. Full-adder/full-subtractor implementation.

5.2. Hardware implementation of 2-bit digital multiplier

2-bit digital multiplier can be realized easily using the traditional feed-forward artificial neural network [21]. As shown in Fig. 11, the implementation of 2-bit digital multiplier using the traditional architecture of a feed-forward artificial neural network requires 4-neurons, 20-synaptic weights in the input-hidden layer, and 4-neurons, 20-synaptic weights in the hidden-output layer. Hence, the total number of neurons is 8-neurons with 40-synaptic weights.

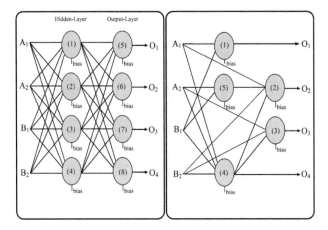

Figure 11. Bit digital multiplier using traditional feed-forward neural network

In the present work, a new design of 2-bit digital multiplier has been adopted. The new design requires only 5-neurons with 20-synaptic weights as shown in Fig. 12. The network receives two digital words, each word has 2-bit, and the output of the network gives the resulting multiplication. The network is trained by the training set shown in Table 10.

I/P				O/P			
B_2	B_1	A_2	A_1	O_4	O_3	O_2	O_1
0	0	0	0	0	0	0	0
0	0	0	1	0	0	0	0
0	0	1	0	0	0	0	0
0	0	1	1	0	0	0	0
0	1	0	0	0	0	0	0
0	1	0	1	0	0	0	1
0	1	1	0	0	0	1	0
0	1	1	1	0	0	1	1
1	0	0	0	0	0	0	0
1	0	0	1	0	0	1	0
1	0	1	0	0	1	0	0
1	0	1	1	0	1	1	0
1	1	0	0	0	0	0	0
1	1	0	1	0	0	1	1
1	1	1	0	0	1	1	0
1	1	1	1	1	0	0	1

Table 10. 2-bit digital multiplier training set

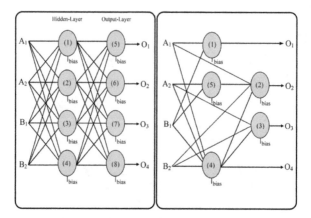

Figure 12. A novel design for 2-Bit multiplier using neural network

During the training phase, these input/output pairs are fed to the network and in each iteration; the weights are modified until reached to the optimal values. The optimal value of the weights and their corresponding resistance values are shown in Table 11. The proposed circuit has been realized by hardware means and the results have been tested using H-spice computer program. Both the actual and computer results are found to be very close to the correct results.

Neuron	I/P	W. Value	Resistor
	A_1	7.5	1200
(1)	B_1	7.5	1200
	Bias	-10.0	100
	A1	7.5	1450
	B2	7.5	1450
(2)	Bias	-10.0	100
	N4	-30.0	33
	N5	20.0	618
	A2	7.5	1200
(3)	B2	7.5	1200
	bias	-10.0	100
	N4	-10.0	100
	A1	3.0	1200
	A2	3.0	1200
(4)	B1	3.0	1200
	B2	3.0	1200
	bias	-10.0	100
	A2	7.5	1200
(5)	B1	7.5	1200
	Bias	-10.0	100

Table 11. Weight values and their corresponding resistance values for digital multiplier.

5.3. Hardware implementation of 2-bit digital divider

2-bit digital divider can be realized easily using the artificial neural network. As shown in Fig. 13, the implementation of 2-bit digital divider using neural network requires 4-neurons, 20-synaptic weights in the input-hidden layer, and 4-neurons, 15-synaptic weights in the hidden-output layer. Hence, the total number of neurons is 8-neurons with 35-synaptic weights. The network receives two digital words, each word has 2-bit, and the output of the network gives two digital words one for the resulting division and the other for the resulting remainder. The network is trained by the training set shown in Table 12

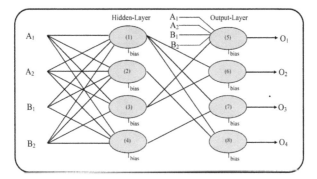

Figure 13. Bit digital divider using neural network.

I/P				O/P			
B_2	B_1	A_2	A_1	O_4	O_3	O_2	O_1
0	0	0	0	1	1	1	1
0	0	0	1	0	0	0	0
0	0	1	0	0	0	0	0
0	0	1	1	0	0	0	0
0	1	0	0	1	1	1	1
0	1	0	1	0	0	0	1
0	1	1	0	0	1	0	0
0	1	1	1	0	1	0	0
1	0	0	0	1	1	1	1
1	0	0	1	0	0	1	0
1	0	1	0	0	0	0	1
1	0	1	1	1	0	0	0
1	1	0	0	1	1	1	1
1	1	0	1	0	0	1	1
1	1	1	0	0	1	0	1
1	1	1	1	0	0	0	1

Table 12. 2-bit digital dividier training set

The values of the weights and their corresponding resistance values are shown in Table 13.

Neuron	I/P	W. Val.	Resistor
(1)	A1	-17.5	56
	A2	-17.5	56
	B1	5	2700
	B2	5	2700
	Bias	5	2700
(2)	A1	7.5	1200
	A2	7.5	1200
	B1	-10	100
	B2	7.5	1200
	Bias	-17.5	56
(3)	A1	7.5	1200
	A2	-10	100
	B2	7.5	1200
	Bias	-10	100
(4)	A1	-4.5	220
	A2	7.5	1200
	B1	7.5	1200
	B2	-4.5	220
	Bias	-10	100
(5)	A1	-20	50
	A2	-30	33
	B1	10	1200
	B2	25	500
	N3	-25	40
	Bias	17.5	700
(6)	N1	10	1000
	N3	10	1000
	Bias	-5	220
(7)	N1	10	1000
	N4	10	1000
	Bias	-5	220
(8)	N1	10	1000
	N2	10	1000
	Bias	-5	220

Table 13. Weight values and their corresponding resistance values for digital divider.

The results have been tested using H-spice computer program. Computer results are found to be very close to the correct results.

Arithmetic operations namely, addition, subtraction, multiplication, and division can be realized easily using a reconfigurable artificial neural network. The proposed network consists of only 8-neurons, 67-connection weights, and 32-reconfiguration switches. Fig. 14 shows the block diagram of the arithmetic operation using reconfigurable neural network. The network includes full-adder, full-subtractor, 2-bit digital multiplier, and 2-bit digital divider. The proposed circuit is realized by hardware means and the results are tested using H-spice computer program. Both the actual and computer results are found to be very close to the correct results.

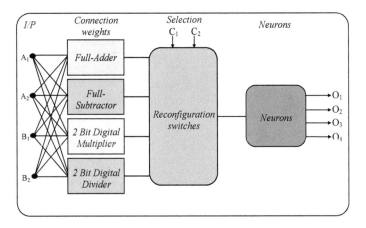

Figure 14. Block diagram of arithmetic unit using reconfigurable neural network.

The computed values of weights and their corresponding values of resistors are described in Tables 9,10,116. After completing the design of the network, simulations are carried out to test both the design and performance of this network by using H-spice. Experimental results confirm the proposed theoretical considerations as shown in Tables 14,15.

6. Conclusion

We have presented a new model of neural nets for classifying patterns that appeared expensive to be solved using conventional models of neural nets. This approach has been introduced to realize different types of logic problems. Also, it can be applied to manipulate non-binary data. We have shown that, compared to non MNNs, realization of problems using MNNs resulted in reduction of the number of computations, neurons and weights.

I/p			Neuron(1)		Neuron(2)		Neuron(3)	
X	Y	Z	Practical	Simulated	Practical	Simulated	Practical	Simulated
0	0	0	-2.79	-3.4157	-2.79	-3.4135	-2.79	-3.4135
0	0	1	-2.73	-2.5968	3.46	3.3741	3.46	3.3741
0	1	0	-2.73	-2.5968	3.46	3.2741	3.46	3.3741
0	1	1	3.46	3.3761	3.46	3.4366	-2.75	-3.3081
1	0	0	-2.73	-2.5968	-2.79	-3.4372	3.46	3.3741
1	0	1	3.46	3.3761	-2.75	-3.3081	-2.75	-3.3081
1	1	0	3.46	3.3761	-2.75	-3.3081	-2.75	-3.3081
1	1	1	3.46	3.4231	3.48	3.4120	3.48	3.4120

Table 14. Practical and Simulation results after the summing circuit of full-adder/full-subtractor

Neuron (1)		Neuron (2)		Neuron (3)		Neuron (4)		Neuron (5)	
Pract.	Sim.	Pract.	Sim.	Pract.	Sim.	Pract.	Sim.	Pract.	Sim.
-2.79	-3.415	-2.79	-3.409	-2.79	-3.413	-2.79	-3.447	-2.79	-3.415
-2.34	-2.068	-2.72	-2.498	-2.79	-3.314	-2.78	-3.438	-2.79	-3.415
-2.79	-3.415	-2.79	-3.409	-1.63	-1.355	-2.78	-3.438	-2.34	-2.068
-2.34	-2.068	-2.72	-2.498	-1.63	-1.355	-2.78	-3.423	-2.34	-2.068
-2.34	-2.068	-2.79	-3.409	-2.79	-3.413	-2.78	-3.438	-2.34	-2.068
3.46	3.390	-2.72	-2.498	-2.79	-3.413	-2.78	-3.423	-2.34	-2.068
-2.34	-2.068	3.45	3.397	-1.63	-1.355	-2.78	-3.423	3.46	3.390
3.46	3.390	3.45	3.424	-1.63	-1.355	-2.74	-3.384	3.46	3.390
-2.79	-3.415	-2.72	-2.498	-1.63	-1.355	-2.78	-3.438	-2.79	-3.415
-2.34	-2.068	3.45	3.373	-1.63	-1.355	-2.78	-3.423	-2.79	-3.415
-2.79	-3.415	-2.72	-2.498	3.45	3.399	-2.78	-3.423	-2.34	-2.068
-2.34	-2.068	3.45	3.373	3.45	3.399	-2.74	-3.384	-2.34	-2.068
-2.34	-2.068	-2.72	-2.498	-1.63	-1.355	-2.78	-3.423	-2.34	-2.068
3.46	3.390	3.45	3.373	-1.63	-1.355	-2.74	-3.384	-2.34	-2.068
-2.34	-2.068	3.45	3.373	3.45	3.399	-2.74	-3.384	3.46	3.390
3.46	3.390	-2.73	-3.398	-2.70	-2.710	1.86	2.519	3.46	3.390

Table 15. Practical and Simulation results after the summing circuit of 2-bit digital multiplier

Author details

Hazem M. El-Bakry

Faculty of Computer Science & Information Systems, Mansoura University, Egypt

References

[1] J, Murre, Learning and Categorization in Modular Neural Networks, Harvester Wheatcheaf. 1992.

[2] R. Jacobs, M. Jordan, A. Barto, Task Decomposition Through Competition in a Modular Connectionist Architecture: The what and where vision tasks, Neural Computation 3, pp. 79-87, 1991.

[3] G. Auda, M. Kamel, H. Raafat, Voting Schemes for cooperative neural network classifiers, IEEE Trans. on Neural Networks, ICNN95, Vol. 3, Perth, Australia, pp. 1240-1243, November, 1995.

[4] G. Auda, and M. Kamel, CMNN: Cooperative Modular Neural Networks for Pattern Recognition, Pattern Recognition Letters, Vol. 18, pp. 1391-1398, 1997.

[5] E. Alpaydin, , Multiple Networks for Function Learning, Int. Conf. on Neural Networks, Vol.1 CA, USA, pp. 9-14, 1993.

[6] A. Waibel, Modular Construction of Time Delay Neural Networks for Speach Recognition, Neural Computing 1, pp.39-46.

[7] D. E. Rumelhart, G. E. Hinton, and R. J. Williams, Learning representation by error backpropagation, Parallel distributed Processing: Explorations in the Microstructues of Cognition, Vol. 1, Cambridge, MA:MIT Press, pp. 318-362, 1986.

[8] K. Joe, Y. Mori, S. Miyake, Construction of a large scale neural network: Simulation of handwritten Japanese Character Recognition, on NCUBE Concurrency 2 (2), pp. 79-107.

[9] H. M. El-bakry, and M. A. Abo-elsoud, Automatic Personal Identification Using Neural Nets, The 24th international Conf. on Statistics computer Science, and its applications, Cairo, Egypt, 1999.

[10] Srinagesh Satyanarayna, Yannis P. Tsividis, and Hans Peter graf, "A Reconfigurable VLSI Neural Network," IEEE Journal of Solid State Circuits, vol. 27, no. 1, January 1992.

[11] E. R. Vittos, "Analog VLSI Implementation of Neural Networks," in proc. Int. Symp. Circuits Syst. (new Orleans, LA), 1990, pp. 2524-2527.

[12] H. P. graf and L. D. Jackel, "Analog Electronic Neural Network Circuits," IEEE Circuits Devices Mag., vol. 5, pp. 44-49, July 1989.

[13] H. M. EL-Bakry, M. A. Abo-Elsoud, and H. H. Soliman and H. A. El-Mikati " Design and Implementation of 2-bit Logic functions Using Artificial Neural Networks ," Proc. of the 6th International Conference on Microelectronics (ICM'96), Cairo, Egypt, 16-18 Dec. , 1996.

[14] Simon Haykin, "Neural Network : A comprehensive foundation", Macmillan college publishing company, 1994.

[15] Jack M. Zurada, "Introduction to Artificial Neural Systems," West Publishing Company, 1992.

[16] C. Mead, and M. Ismail, "Analog VLSI Implementation of Neural Systems," Kluwer Academic Publishers, USA, 1989

[17] H. M. EL-Bakry, M. A. Abo-Elsoud, and H. H. Soliman and H. A. El-Mikati " Implementation of 2-bit Logic functions Using Artificial Neural Networks ," Proc. of the 6th International Conference on Computer Theory and Applications, Alex., Egypt, 3-5 Sept. , 1996, pp. 283-288.

[18] I. S. Han and S. B. Park, "Voltage-Controlled Linear Resistor by Using two MOS Transistors and its Applications to RC Active Filter MOS Integration," Proceedings of the IEEE, Vol.72, No.11, Nov. 1984, pp. 1655-1657.

[19] Laurene Fausett, "Fundamentals of Neural Network : Architectures, Algorithms, and Applications," Prentice Hall International.

[20] H. M. El-bakry, "Complexity Reduction Using Modular Neural Networks," Proc. of IEEE IJCNN'03, Portland, Oregon, pp. 2202-2207, July, 20-24, 2003.

[21] H. M. El-Bakry, and N. Mastorakis "A Simple Design and Implementation of Reconfigurable Neural Networks Detection," Proc. of IEEE IJCNN'09, Atlanta, USA, June 14-19, 2009, pp. 744-750.

Chapter 11

Use of Artificial Neural Networks to Predict The Business Success or Failure of Start-Up Firms

Francisco Garcia Fernandez,
Ignacio Soret Los Santos, Javier Lopez Martinez,
Santiago Izquierdo Izquierdo and
Francisco Llamazares Redondo

Additional information is available at the end of the chapter

1. Introduction

There is a great interest to know if a new company will be able to survive or not. Investors use different tools to evaluate the survival capabilities of middle-aged companies but there is not any tool for start-up ones. Most of the tools are based on regression models and in quantitative variables. Nevertheless, qualitative variables which measure the company way of work and the manager skills can be considered as important as quantitative ones.

Develop a global regression model that includes quantitative and qualitative variables can be very complicated. In this case artificial neural networks can be a very useful tool to model the company survival capabilities. They have been large specially used in engineering processes modeling, but also in economy and business modeling, and there is no problem in mix quantitative and qualitative variables in the same model. This kind of nets are called mixed artificial neural networks.

2. Materials and methods

2.1. A snapshot of entrepreneurship in Spain in 2009

The Spanish entrepreneurship's basic indexes through 2009 have been affected by the economic crisis. After a moderate drop (8%) in 2008, the Total Entrepreneurial Activity index

(TEA) experienced a great drop (27.1%) in 2009, returning to 2004 levels ([1]de la Vega García, 2010) (Fig 1).

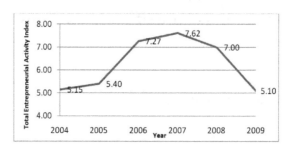

Figure 1. Executive Report. Global Entrepreneurship Monitor- Spain.

This rate implies that in our country there are 1,534,964 nascent businesses (between 0 and 3 months old). The owner-managers of a new business (more than 3 months but not more than 3.5 years) have also declined in 2009, returning to 2007 levels.

As in other comparable, innovation-driven, countries, the typical early stage entrepreneur in Spain is male (62.5% of all entrepreneurs), with a mean age of 36.6, and well educated (55.4% with a university degree). The female entrepreneurial initiatives have been declined in 2009 and the difference between female and male Total Entrepreneurial Activity index (TEA) rates is now bigger than in 2008. The gender difference in the TEA index has increased from two to almost three points. Now the female TEA index is 3.33% and the male TEA index is 6.29%.

Although most individuals are pulled into entrepreneurial activity because of opportunity recognition (80.1%), others are pushed into entrepreneurship because they have no other means of making a living, or because they fear becoming unemployed in the near future. These necessity entrepreneurs are 15.8% of the entrepreneurs in Spain.

In Spain, the distribution of early-stage entrepreneurial activity and established business owner/managers by industry sector is similar to that in other innovation-driven countries, where business services (i.e., tertiary activities that target other firms as main customers, such as finance, data analysis, insurance, real estate, etc.) prevail. In Spain, they accounted for 56.5% of early-stage activities and 46.1% of established businesses. Transforming businesses (manufacturing and construction), which are typical of efficiency-driven countries, were the second largest sector, accounted for 25.9% and 24.2% respectively. Consumer services (i.e., retail, restaurants, tourism) accounted for 12.8% and 17.3%, respectively. Extraction businesses (farming, forestry, fishing, mining), which are typical of factor-driven economies, accounted for 6.0% and 8.6%, respectively. The real estate activity in Spain was of great importance, and its decline explains the reduction in the business services sector in 2009.

The median amount invested by entrepreneurs in 2009 was around 30,000 Euros (less than the median amount of 50,000 Euros in 2008). Therefore the entrepreneurial initiative is less ambitious in general.

The factors that mostly constrain entrepreneurial activity are: first, financial support (e.g., availability of debt and equity), which was cited as a constraining factor by 62% of respondents. Second, government policies supporting entrepreneurship, which was cited as a constraining factor by 40% of respondents. Third, social and cultural norms, which was cited as a constraining factor by 32% of respondents.

More than one fifth of the entrepreneurial activity (21.5%) was developed in a familiar model. Therefore, the entrepreneurial initiatives, often driven by family members, received financial support or management assistance from some family members. Nevertheless, the influence of some knowledge, technology or research result developed in the University was bigger than expected. People decided to start businesses because they used some knowledge, technology or research result developed in the University (14.3% of the nascent businesses, and 10.3% of the owner-managers of a new business).

2.2. Questionnaire

It is clear that the company survival is greatly influenced by its financial capabilities, however, this numerical information is not always easy to obtain, and even when obtained, it is not always reliable.

Variable	Type	Range
Working Capital/Total Assets	Quantitative	R+
Retained Earnings/Total Assets	Quantitative	R+
Earnings Before Interest and Taxes/Total Assets	Quantitative	R+
Market Capitalization/Total Debts	Quantitative	R+
Sales/Total Assets	Quantitative	R+
Manager academic level	Qualitative	1-4
Company technological resources	Qualitative	1-4
Quality policies	Qualitative	1-5
Trademark	Qualitative	1-3
Employees education policy	Qualitative	1-2
Number of innovations areas	Qualitative	1-5
Marketing experience	Qualitative	1-3
Knowledge of the business area	Qualitative	1-3
Openness to experience	Qualitative	1-2

Table 1. Variables

There are some other qualitative factors that have influence in the company success, such as its technological capabilities, quality policies or academic level of its employees and manager.

In this study we will use both numerical and qualitative data to model the company survival (Table 1).

2.2.1. Financial data.

The most used ratios to predict the company success are the Altman ratios ([2]Lacher et al., 1995; [3]Atiya, 2001):

• Working Capital/Total Assets. Working Capital is defined as the difference between current assets and current liabilities. Current assets include cash, inventories, receivables and marketable securities. Current liabilities include accounts payable, short-terms provision and accrued expenses.

• Retained Earnings/Total Assets. This ratio is specially important because bankruptcy is higher for start-ups and young companies.

• Earnings Before Interest and Taxes/Total Assets. Since a company's existence is dependent on the earning power of its assets, this ratio is appropriate in failure prediction.

• Market Capitalization/Total Debts. This ratio weighs up the dimension of a company's competitive market place value.

• Sales/Total Assets. This ratio measures the firm's assets utilization.

2.2.2. Qualitative data.

The election on which qualitative data should be used is based on previous works as in references [4-6] Aragon Sánchez y Rubio Bañón (2002 y 2005) and Woods and Hampson (2005), where they establish several parameters to value the company positioning and its survival capabilities and the influence of manager personality in the company survival.

• Manager academic level, ranged from 1 to 4.

• PhD or Master (4).

• University degree (3).

• High school (2).

• Basic studies (1).

• Company technological resources, ranged from 1 to 4.

• The company uses self-made software programs (4).

• The company uses specific programs but it buys them (3).

• The company uses the same software than competitor (2).

• The company uses older software than competitors (1).

• Quality policies, ranged from 1 to 5.

• The company has quality policies based on ISO 9000 (5).

• The company controls either, production and client satisfaction (4).

• A production control is the only quality policy (2).

- Supplies control is the only quality control in the company (1).

- o The company has not any quality policy.

- Trademark, ranged from 1 to 3.

- The company trademark is better known than competitors' (3).

- The company trademark is as known than competitors' (2)

- The company trademark is less known than competitors' (3).

- Employees education policy, ranged from 1 to 2.

- The company is involved in its employees education (2).

- The company is not involved in its employees education (1).

- Number of innovations areas in the company, ranged from 1 to 5.

- Marketing experience, ranged from 1 to 3.

- The company has a great marketing experience in the field of its products and in others (3).

- The company has only marketing experience in his field of duty (2).

- The company has no marketing experience (1).

- Knowledge of the business area, ranged from 1 to 3.

- The manager knows perfectly the business area and has been working on several companies related whit it (3).

- The manager knows lightly the business area (2).

- The manager has no idea on the business area (1).

- Openness to experience, ranged from 1 to 2.

- The manager is a practical person who is not interested in abstract ideas, prefers works that is routine and has few artistic interest (2).

- The manager spends time reflecting on things, has an active imagination and likes to think up new ways of doing things, but may lack pragmatism (1).

Researchers will conduct these surveys with managers from 125 companies. The surveys will be conducted by the same team of researchers to ensure the consistency of questions involving qualitative variables.

2.3. Artificial neural networks

Predictive models based on artificial neural networks have been widely used in different knowledge areas, including economy and bankruptcy prediction ([2, 7-9]Lacher et al, 1995;

Jo et al, 1997; Yang et al, 1999; Hsiao et al, 2009) and forecast markets evolution ([10]Jalil and Misas, 2007).

Artificial neural networks are mathematical structures based on biological brains, which are capable of extract knowledge from a set of examples ([11] Perez and Martin, 2003). They are made up of a series of interconnected elements called neurons (Fig. 2), and knowledge is set in the connections between neurons ([12] Priore et al, 2002).

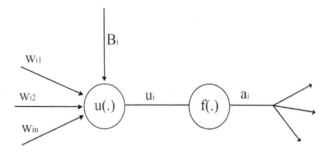

Figure 2. An artificial neuron. u(.): net function, f(.): transfer function, w_{ij}: connection weighs, B_i: Bias.

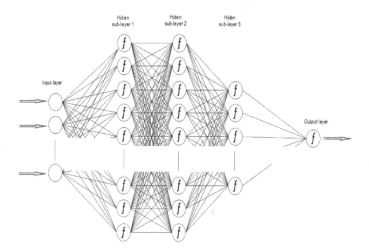

Figure 3. Artificial neuron network architecture.

Those neurons are organized in a series of layers (Fig. 3). The input layer receives the values from the example variables, the inner layer performs the mathematical operations to obtain the proper response which is shown by the output layer.

There is not a clear method to know how many hidden layers on how many neurons an artificial neural network must have, so the only method to perform the best net is by trial and error ([13]Lin and Tseng, 2000). In this work a special software will be develop, in order to find the optimum number of neurons and hidden layers.

There are lots of different types of artificial neural network structures, depending on the problem to solve or to model. In this work perceptron structure has been chosen. Perceptron is one of the most used artificial neural network and its capability of universal function aproximator ([14]Hornik, 1989) makes it suitable for modeling too many different kinds of variable relationships, specially when it is more important to obtain a reliable solution than to know how are the relations between the variables.

The hyperbolic tangent sigmoid function (Fig. 4) has been chosen as transfer function. This function is a variation of the hyperbolic tangent ([15] Chen, 1995) but the first one is quicker and improves the network efficiency ([16] Demuth et al, 2002).

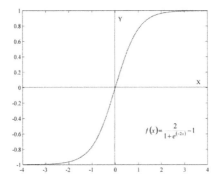

Figure 4. Tansig function. f(x): Neuron output, x: Neuron input.

As the transfer function output interval is (-1, 1) the input data were normalized before training the network by means of equation: (Ec.1) ([16-18]Krauss et al, 1997; Demuth et al, 2002, Peng et al, 2007).

$$X' = \frac{X - X_{min}}{X_{max} - X_{min}} \tag{1}$$

X': Value after normalization of vector X. X_{min} and X_{max}: Maximum and minimum values of vector X.

The network training will be carried out by means of supervised learning ([11, 19-21] Hagan et al., 1995; [20] Haykin, 1998; [11] Pérez & Martín, 2003; [21] Isasi & Galván, 2004). The whole data will be randomly divided into three groups with no repetition. The training set (60% of the data), test set (20% of the data) and validation set (20% of the data).

The resilient backpropagation training method will be used for training. This method is very adequate when sigmoid transfer functions are used ([16] Demuth et al, 2002).

To prevent overfitting, a very common problem during training, the training set error and the validation set error will be compared every 100 epochs. Training will be considered to be finished when training set error begins to decreases while validation set error increases.

As mentioned before, to find the optimum artificial neural network architecture an specific software will be develop. This software makes automatically different artificial neural network structures with different number of neurons and hidden layers. Finally the software will compare the results between all the nets developed and will choose the best one. (Fig. 5, 6)

```
Initilize_data
Preprocessing_data
// Sublayer loops
for h=1 to 15
for i=1 to h
Create_neural_network (net)
// Training loop
for k=1 to 500
Train(net)
Simulate(net)
Avoid_overfitting
end for //k
end for //i
end for //h
// Final
Get_best_net
Display_results
    ...
```

Figure 5. Program pseudocode.

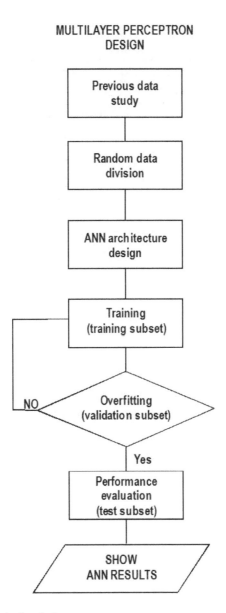

Figure 6. Neural network design flow chart.

The Matlab Artificial Neural Network Toolbox V.4. will be used for develop the artificial neural network.

3. Results and conclusions

This work is the initial steps of an ambitious project that pretend to evaluate the survival of start-up companies. Actually the work is on his third stage which is the data analysis by means of artificial neural network modeling method.

Once finished it is expected to have a very useful tool to predict the business success or failure of start-up firms.

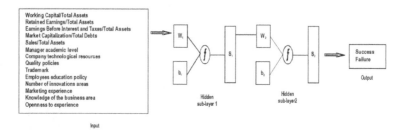

Figure 7. Most expected neural network architecture.

Acknowledgements

This study is part of the 07/10 ESIC Project "Redes neuronales y su aplicación al diagnóstico empresarial. Factores críticos de éxito de emprendimiento" supported by ESIC Business and Marketing School (Spain).

Author details

Francisco Garcia Fernandez[1*], Ignacio Soret Los Santos[2], Javier Lopez Martinez[3], Santiago Izquierdo Izquierdo[4] and Francisco Llamazares Redondo[2]

*Address all correspondence to: francisco.garcia@upm.es

1 Universidad Politecnica de Madrid, Spain

2 ESIC Business & Marketing School, Spain

3 Universidad San Pablo CEU, Spain

4 MTP Metodos y Tecnologia, Spain

References

[1] la Vega, e., & Garcia, Pastor. J. (2010). GEM Informe Ejecutivo 2009 España. Madrid: Instituto de Empresa Madrid Emprende. 2009. Paper presented at Memoria de Viveros de Empresa de la Comunidad de Madrid., Madrid: Madrid Emprende.

[2] Lacher, R. C., Coats, P. K., Sharma, S. C., & Fant, L. F. (1995). A neural network for classifying the financial health of a firm. *European Journal of Operational Research*, 85, 53-65.

[3] Atiya, A. F. (2001). Bankruptcy prediction for credit risk using neural networks: A survey and new results. *IEEE Transactions on Neural Networks*, 12, 929-935.

[4] Rubio, Bañón. A., & Aragón, Sánchez. A. (2002). Factores explicativos del éxito competitivo.Un estudio empírico en la pyme. *Cuadernos de Gestión*, 2(1), 49-63.

[5] Aragón, Sánchez. A., & Rubio, Bañón. A. (2005). Factores explicativos del éxito competitivo: el caso de las PYMES del estado de Veracruz. *Contaduría y Administración*, 216, 35-69.

[6] Woods, S. A., & Hampson, S. E. (2005). Measuring the Big Five with single items using a bipolar response scale. *European Journal of Personality*, 19, 373-390.

[7] Jo, H., Han, I., & Lee, H. (1997). Bankruptcy prediction using case-based reasoning, neural Networks and discriminant analysis. *Expert Systems With Applications*, 13(2), 97-108.

[8] Yang, Z. R., Platt, M. B., & Platt, H. D. (1999). Probabilistic neural networks in bankruptcy prediction. *Journal of Business Research*, 44, 67-74.

[9] Hsiao, S. H., & Whang, T. J. (2009). A study of financial insolvency prediction model for life insurers. *Expert Systems With Applications*, 36, 6100-6107.

[10] Jalil, M. A., & Misas, M. (2007). Evaluación de pronósticos del tipo de cambio utilizando redes neuronales y funciones de pérdida asimétricas. *Revista Colombiana de Estadística*, 30, 143-161.

[11] Pérez, M. L., & Martín, Q. (2003). Aplicaciones de las redes neuronales a la estadística. *Cuadernos de Estadística. La Muralla S.A. Madrid*.

[12] Priore, P., De La Fuente, D., Pino, R., & Puente, J. (2002). Utilización de las redes neuronales en la toma de decisiones. Aplicación a un problema de secuenciación. *Anales de Mecánica y Electricidad*, 79(6), 28-34.

[13] Lin, T. Y., & Tseng, C. H. (2000). Optimum design for artificial networks: an example in a bicycle derailleur system. *Engineering Applications of Artificial Intelligence*, 13, 3-14.

[14] Hornik, K. (1989). Multilayer Feedforward Networks are Universal Approximators. *Neural Networks*, 2, 359-366.

[15] Cheng, C. S. (1995). A multi-layer neural network model for detecting changes in the process mean. *Computers & Industrial Engineering*, 28, 51-61.

[16] Demuth, H., Beale, M., & Hagan, M. (2002). Neural Network Toolbox User's guide, version 4. Natick The Mathworks Inc. MA 01760, USA.

[17] Krauss, G., Kindangen, J. I., & Depecker, P. (1997). Using artificial neural network to predict interior velocity coefficients. *Building and environment*, 4, 295-281.

[18] Peng, G., Chen, X., Wu, W., & Jiang, X. (2007). Modeling of water sorption isotherm for corn starch. *Journal of Food Engineering*, 80, 562-567.

[19] Hagan, M. T., Demuth, H. B., & Beale, M. (1996). Neural Network Design. Boston:. PWS Pub. Co. USA.

[20] Haykin, S. (1999). Neural Networks: A Comprehensive Foundation. 2nd edition. Prentice Hall New Jersey, USA.

[21] Isasi, P., & Galván, I. M. (2004). Redes Neuronales Artificiales, un enfoque práctico. *Pearson Educación, S.A. Madrid.*

Chapter 12

Recurrent Neural Network Based Approach for Solving Groundwater Hydrology Problems

Ivan N. da Silva, José Ângelo Cagnon and
Nilton José Saggioro

Additional information is available at the end of the chapter

1. Introduction

Many communities obtain their drinking water from underground sources called aquifers. Official water suppliers or public incorporations drill wells into soil and rock aquifers looking for groundwater contained there in order to supply the population with drinking water. An aquifer can be defined as a geologic formation that will supply water to a well in enough quantities to make possible the production of water from this formation. The conventional estimation of the exploration flow involves many efforts to understand the relationship between the structural and physical parameters. These parameters depend on several factors, such as soil properties and hydrologic and geologic aspects [1].

The transportation of water to the reservoirs is usually done through submerse electrical motor pumps, being the electric power one of the main sources to the water production. Considering the increasing difficulty to obtain new electrical power sources, there is then the need to reduce both operational costs and global energy consumption. Thus, it is important to adopt appropriate operational actions to manage efficiently the use of electrical power in these groundwater hydrology problems. For this purpose, it is essential to determine a parameter that expresses the energetic behavior of whole water extraction set, which is here defined as *Global Energetic Efficiency Indicator* (*GEEI*). A methodology using artificial neural networks is here developed in order to take into account several experimental tests related to energy consumption in submerse motor pumps.

The *GEEI* of a depth is given in $Wh/m^3.m$. From a dimensional analysis, we can observe that the smaller numeric value of *GEEI* indicates the better energetic efficiency to the water extraction system from aquifers.

For such scope, this chapter is organized as follows. In Section 2, a brief summary about water exploration processes are presented. In Section 3, some aspects related to mathematical models applied to water exploration process are described. In Section 4 is formulated the expressions for defining the *GEEI*. The neural approach used to determine the *GEEI* is introduced in Section 5, while the procedures for estimation of aquifer dynamic behavior using neural networks are presented in Section 6. Finally, in Section 7, the key issues raised in the chapter are summarized and conclusions are drawn.

2. Water Exploration Process

An aquifer is a saturated geologic unit with enough permeability to transmit economical quantities of water to wells [10]. The aquifers are usually shaped by unconsolidated sands and crushed rocks. The sedimentary rocks, such as arenite and limestone, and those volcanic and fractured crystalline rocks can also be classified as aquifers.

After the drilling process of groundwater wells, the test known as *Step Drawdown Test* is carried out. This test consists of measuring the aquifer depth in relation to continue withdrawal of water and with crescent flow on the time. This depth relationship is defined as *Dynamic Level* of the aquifer and the aquifer level at the initial instant, i.e., that instant when the pump is turned on, is defined as *Static Level*. This test gives the maximum water flow that can be pumped from the aquifer taking into account its respective dynamic level. Another characteristic given by this test is the determination of *Drawdown Discharge Curves*, which represent the dynamic level in relation to exploration flow [2]. These curves are usually expressed by a mathematical function and their results have presented low precision.

Since aquifer behavior changes in relation to operation time, the *Drawdown Discharge Curves* can represent the aquifer dynamics only in that particular moment. These changes occur by many factors, such as the following: i) aquifer recharge capability; ii) interference of neighboring wells or changes in its exploration conditions; iii) modification of the static level when the pump is turned on; iv) operation cycle of pump; and v) rest time available to the well. Thus, the mapping of these groundwater hydrology problems by conventional identification techniques has become very difficult when all above considerations are taken into account. Besides the aquifer behavior, other components of the exploration system interfere on the global energetic efficiency of the system.

On the other hand, the motor-pump set mounted inside the well, submersed on the water that comes from the aquifer, receives the whole electric power supplied to the system. From an eduction piping, which also supports physically the motor pump, the water is transported to the ground surface and from there, through an adduction piping, it is transported to the reservoir, which is normally located at an upper position in relation to the well. To transport water in this hydraulic system, it is necessary several accessories (valves, pipes, curves, etc.) for its implementation. Figure 1 shows the typical components involved with a water extraction system by means of deep wells.

The resistance to the water flow, due to the state of the pipe walls, is continuous along all the tubing, and will be taken as uniform in every place where the diameter of the pipe to be constant.

This resistance makes the motor pump to supply an additional pressure (or a load) in order to water can reach the reservoir. Thus, the effect created by this resistance is also called "load loss along the pipe". Similar to the tubing, other elements of the system cause a resistance to the fluid flow, and therefore, load losses. These losses can be considered local, located, accidental or singular, due to the fact that they come from particular points or parts of the tubing.

Regarding the hydraulic circuit, it is observed that the load loss (distributed and located) is an important parameter, and that it varies with the type and the state of the material.

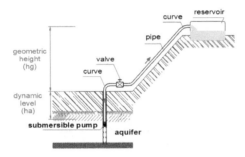

Figure 1. Components of the pumping system.

Therefore, old tubing, with aggregated incrustation along the operational time, shows a load loss different of that present in new tubing. A valve turned off twice introduces a bigger load loss than that when it is totally open. A variation on the extraction flow also creates changes on the load loss. These are some observations, among several other points, that could be done.

Another important factor concerning the global energetic efficiency of the system is the geometrical difference of level. However, this parameter does not show any variation after the total implantation of the system. Concerning this, two statements can be done: i) when mathematical models were used to study the lowering of the piezometric surface, these models should frequently be evaluated in certain periods of time; ii) the exploration flow of the aquifer assumes a fundamental role in the study of the hydraulic circuit and it should be carefully analyzed.

In order to overcome these problems, this work considers the use of parameters, which are easily obtained in practice, to represent the capitation system, and the use of artificial neural networks to determine the exploration flow. From these parameters, it is possible to determine the *GEEI* of the system.

3. Mathematical Models Applied to Water Exploration Process

One of the most used mathematical models to simulate aquifer dynamic behavior is the Theis' model [1,9]. This model is very simple and it is used to transitory flow. In this model, the following hypotheses are considered: i) the aquifer is confined by impermeable formations, ii) the aquifer structure is homogeneous and isotropic in relation to its hydro-geological parameters, iii) the aquifer thickness is considered constant with infinite horizontal extent, and iv) the wells penetrate the entire aquifer and their pumping rates are also considered constant in relation to time.

The model proposed by Theis can be represented by the following equations:

$$\frac{\partial^2 s}{\partial r^2} + \frac{1}{r} \cdot \frac{\partial s}{\partial r} = \frac{S}{T} \cdot \frac{\partial s}{\partial t} \tag{1}$$

$$s(r,0) = 0 \tag{2}$$

$$s(\infty, t) = 0 \tag{3}$$

$$\lim_{r \to 0}[r(\frac{\partial s}{\partial r})] = -\frac{Q}{2 \cdot \pi \cdot T} \tag{4}$$

where:

s is the aquifer drawdown;

Q is the exploration flow;

T is the transmissivity coefficient;

r is the horizontal distance between the well and the observation place.

Applying the Laplace's transform on these equations, we have:

$$\frac{d^2 s^-}{dr^2} + \frac{1}{r} \cdot \frac{ds^-}{dr} = \frac{S}{T} \cdot w \cdot s^- \tag{5}$$

$$s^-(r,w) = A \cdot K_0 \cdot (r \cdot \sqrt{(S/T)} \cdot w) \tag{6}$$

$$\lim_{r \to 0}[r(\frac{ds^-}{dr})] = -\frac{Q}{2 \cdot \pi \cdot T \cdot w} \tag{7}$$

where:

w is the Laplace's parameter;

S is the storage coefficient.

Thus, the aquifer drawdown in the Laplace's space is given by:

$$\bar{s}(r,w) = \frac{q}{2 \cdot \cdot T} \cdot \frac{K_0 \cdot (r \cdot \sqrt{(S/T) \cdot w})}{w} \qquad (8)$$

This equation in the real space is as follows:

$$h - h_0(r,t) = s(r,t) = \frac{Q}{2 \cdot \cdot T} \cdot L^{-1} \left[\frac{K_0 \cdot (r \cdot \sqrt{(S/T) \cdot w})}{w} \right] \qquad (9)$$

The Theis' solution is then defined by:

$$s = \frac{q}{4 \cdot \cdot T} \int\limits_{u}^{\infty} \frac{e^{-y}}{y} dy = \frac{Q}{4 \cdot \cdot T} \cdot W(u) \qquad (10)$$

where:

$$u = \frac{r^2 \cdot S}{4 \cdot T \cdot t} \qquad (11)$$

Finally, from Equation (10), we have:

$$W(u) = 2 \cdot L^{-1} \left[\frac{K_0 \cdot (r \cdot \sqrt{(S/T) \cdot w})}{w} \right]. \qquad (12)$$

where:

L^{-1} is the Laplace's inverse operator.

K_0 is the hydraulic conductivity.

From analysis of the Theis' model, it is observed that to model a particular aquifer is indispensable a high technical knowledge on this aquifer, which is mapped under some hypotheses, such as confined aquifer, homogeneous, isotropic, constant thickness, etc. Moreover, other aquifer parameters (transmissivity coefficient, storage coefficient and hydraulic conductivity) to be explored must be also defined. Thus, the mathematical models require expert knowledge of concepts and tools of hydrogeology.

It is also indispensable to consider that the aquifer of a specific region shows continuous changes in its exploration conditions. The changes are normally motivated by the companies that operate the exploration systems, by drilling of new wells or changes of the exploration conditions, or still, motivated by drilling of illegal wells. These changes have certainly required immediate adjustment on the Theis' model. Another fact is that the aquifer dynamic level modifies in relation to exploration flow, operation time, static level, and obviously with those intrinsic characteristics of the aquifer under exploration. In addition, neighboring wells will also be able to cause interference on the aquifer.

Therefore, although to be possible the estimation of aquifer behavior using mathematical models, such as those presented in [11]-[16], they present low precision because it is more difficult to consider all parameters related to the aquifer dynamics. For these situations, intelligent approaches [17]-[20] have also been used to obtain a good performance.

4. Defining the Global Energetic Efficiency Indicator

As presented in [3], "Energetic Efficiency" is a generalized concept that refers to set of actions to be done, or then, the description of reached results, which become possible the reduction of demand by electrical energy. The energetic efficiency indicators are established through relationships and variables that can be used in order to monitor the variations and deviations on the energetic efficiency of the systems. The descriptive indicators are those that characterize the energetic situation without looking for a justification for its variations or deviations.

The theoretical concept for the proposed Global Energetic Efficiency Indicator will be presented using classical equations that show the relationship between the absorbed power from the electric system and the other parameters involved with the process.

As presented in [3], the power of a motor-pump set is given by:

$$P_{mp} = \frac{\gamma \cdot Q \, H_T}{75 \cdot \eta_{mp}} \tag{13}$$

where:

P_{mp} is the power of the motor-pump set (CV);

γ is the specific weight of the water (1000 kgf/m³);

Q is the water flow (m³/s);

H_T is the total manometric height (m);

η_{mp} is the efficiency of the motor-pump set ($\eta_{motor} \cdot \eta_{pump}$).

Substituting the following values {1 CV $\cong$ 736 Watts;1 m³/s = 1/3600 m³/h; γ= 1000 kgf/m³ } in equation (13), we have:

$$P_{mp} = \frac{2.726 \cdot Q \cdot H_T}{mp} \tag{14}$$

The total manometric height (H_T) in elevator sets to water extraction from underground aquifers is given by:

$$H_T = H_a + H_g + \Delta h \, f_t \tag{15}$$

where:

H_T is the total manometric height (m);
H_a is the dynamic level of the aquifer in the well (m);
H_g is the geometric difference in level between the well surface and the reservoir (m);
Δhf_t is total load loss in the hydraulic circuit (m).

From analyses on the variables in (15), it is observed that only the variable corresponding to the geometric difference in level (H_g) can be considered constant, while other two will change along the operation time of the well.

The dynamic level (H_a) will change (to lower) since the beginning of the pumping until the moment of stabilization. This observation is verified in short period of time, as for instance, a month. Besides this variation, which can present a cyclic behavior, it is possible that other types of variation, due to interferences from other neighboring wells, can take place as well as alterations in the aquifer characteristics.

The total load loss will also vary during the pumping, and it is dependent on hydraulic circuit characteristics (diameter, piping length, hydraulic accessories, curves, valves, etc.).

These characteristics can be considered constant, since they usually do not change after installed. However, the total load loss is also dependent on other characteristic of the hydraulic circuit, which frequently changes along the useful life of the well. These variable characteristics are given by: i) roughness of the piping system, ii) water flow, and iii) operational problems, such as semi-closed valves, leakage, etc.

Observing again Figure 1, it is verified that the necessary energy to transport the water from the aquifer to the reservoir, overcoming all the inherent load losses, it is supplied by the electric system to the motor-pump set. Thus, using these considerations and substituting (15) in (14), we have:

$$P_{el} = \frac{2.726 \cdot Q \cdot (H_a + H_g + \Delta h \, f_t)}{\eta_{mp}} \tag{16}$$

where:

P_{el} is the electric power absorbed from electric system (W);

Q is the water flow (m³/h);

H_a is the dynamic level of the aquifer in the well (m);

H_g is the geometric difference of level between the well surface and the reservoir (m);

Δhf_t is the total load loss in the hydraulic circuit (m);

η_{mp} is the efficiency of the motor-pump set ($\eta_{motor} \cdot \eta_{pump}$).

From (16) and considering that an energetic efficiency indicator should be a generic descriptive indicator, the *Global Energetic Efficiency Indicator* (*GEEI*) is here proposed by the following equation:

$$GEEI = \frac{P_{el}}{Q \cdot (H_a + H_g + \Delta h\, f_t)} \qquad (17)$$

Observing equation (17), it is verified that the *GEEI* will depend on electric power, water flow, dynamic level, geometric difference of level, and total load loss of the hydraulic circuit.

The efficiency of the motor-pump set does not take part in (17) because its behavior will be reflected inversely by the *GEEI*. Thus, when the efficiency of the motor-pump set is high, the *GEEI* will be low. Therefore, the best *GEEI* will be those presenting the smallest numeric values.

Another reason to exclude the efficiency of the motor-pump set in (17) is the difficulty to obtain this value in practice. Since it is a fictitious value, it is impossible to make a direct measurement and its value is obtained through relationships between other quantities. After the beginning of the pumping, it is occurred the lowering of water level inside the well. Then, the manometric height changes and as result the water flow also changes. The efficiency of a motor-pump set will also change along its useful life due to the equipment wearing, piping incrustations, leakages in the hydraulic system, obstructions of filters inside the well, closed or semi-closed valves, etc.

Therefore, converting all variables in (17) to meters, the most generic form of the *GEEI* is given by:

$$GEEI = \frac{P_{el}}{Q.H_T} \qquad (18)$$

The *GEEI* defined in (18) can be used to analyze the well behavior along the time.

5. Neural Approach Used to Determine the Global Energetic Efficiency Indicator

Among all necessary parameters to determine the proposed *GEEI*, the determination of the exploration flow is the most difficult to obtain in practice. The use of flow meters, as the electromagnetic ones, is very expensive. The use of rudimentary tests has provided imprecise results.

To overcome this practical problem, it is proposed here the use of artificial neural networks to determine the exploration flow from other parameters that have been measured before determining the *GEEI*.

Artificial Neural Networks (ANN) are dynamic systems that explore parallel and adaptive processing architectures. They consist of several simple processor elements with high degree of connectivity between them [4]. Each one of these elements is associated with a set of parameters, known as network weights, that allows the mapping of a set of known values (network inputs) to a set of associated values (network outputs).

The process of weight adjustment to suitable values (network training) is carried out through successive presentation of a set of training data. The objective of the training is the minimization between the output (response) generated by the network and the respective desired output. After training process, the network will be able to estimate values for the input set, which were not included in the training data.

In this work, an ANN will be used as a functional approximator, since the exploration flow of the well is a dependent variable of those ones that will be used as input variables. The functional approximation consists of mapping the relationship between the several variables that describe the behavior of a real system [5].

The ability of neural artificial networks to mapping complex nonlinear functions makes them an attractive tool to identify and to estimate models representing the dynamic behavior of engineering processes. This feature is particularly important when the relationship between several variables involved with the process is nonlinear and/or not very well defined, making its modeling difficult by conventional techniques.

A multilayer perceptron (MLP), as that shown in Figure 2, trained by the backpropagation algorithm, was used as a practical tool to determine the water flow from the measured parameters.

The input variables applied to the proposed neural network were the following:

• Level of water in meters (H_a) inside the well at the instant t.

• Manometric height in meters of water column (H_m) at the instant t.

• Electric power in Watts (P_{el}) absorbed from the electric system at the instant t.

The unique output variable was the exploration flow of the aquifer (Q), which is expressed in cubic meters per hour. It is important to observe that for each set of input values at a certain instant t, the neural network will return a result for the flow at that same instant t.

The determination of GEEI will be done by using in equation (18) the flow values obtained from the neural network and other parameters that come from experimental measurements.

To training of the neural network, all these variables (inputs and output) were measured and provided to the network. After training, the network was able to estimate the respective output variable. The values of the input variables and the respective output for a certain pumping period, which were used in the network training, are given by a set composed by 40 training patterns (or training vectors).

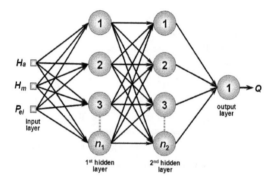

Figure 2. Multilayer perceptron used to determine the water flow.

These patterns were applied to a neural network of MLP type (Multilayer Perceptron) with two hidden layers, and its training was done using the *backpropagation* algorithm based on the Levenberg-Marquardt's method [6]. A description of the main steps of this algorithm is presented in the Appendix.

The network topology that was used is similar to that presented in Figure 2. The number of hidden layers and the number of neurons in each layer were determined from results obtained in [7,8]. The network is here composed by two hidden layers and the following parameters were used in the training process:

• Number of neurons of the 1st hidden layer: 15 neurons.

• Number of neurons of the 2nd hidden layer: 10 neurons.

• Training algorithm: Levenberg-Maquart.

• Number of training epochs: 5000 epochs.

At the end training process, the mean squared error obtained was 7.9×10^{-5}, which is a value considered acceptable for this application [7].

After training process, values of input variables were applied to the network and the respective values of flow were obtained in its output. These values were then compared with the measured ones in order to evaluate the obtained precision.

Table I shows some values of flow that were given by the artificial neural network (Q_{ANN}) and those measured by experimental tests (Q_{ET}).

H_a(m)	H_m(m)	P_{el}(W)	Q_{ANN}(m³/h)	Q_{ET}(m³/h)
25.10	8.25	26,256	74.99	75.00
31.69	**40.50**	**26,155**	**53.00**	**62.00**
31.92	48.00	25,987	56.00	56.00
31.12	48.00	25,953	55.00	55.00
32.50	**48.00**	**25,970**	**54.08**	**54.00**
32.74	48.00	25,970	54.77	54.50
33.05	48.00	25,937	54.15	54.00
33.26	**48.00**	**25,954**	**58.54**	**54.00**
33.59	48.00	25,869	53.01	53.00
33.83	48.00	25,886	53.49	53.50
34.15	**48.00**	**25,887**	**53.50**	**53.00**
34.41	48.00	25,886	53.48	53.50
34.71	48.00	25,785	53.25	53.30
34.95	**48.00**	**25,870**	**53.14**	**53.00**
35.00	48.00	25,801	53.14	53.00

Table 1. Comparison of results.

In this table, the values in bold were not presented to the neural network during the training.

When the patterns used in the training are presented again, it is noticed that the difference between the results is very small, reaching the maximum value of 0.35% of the measured value. When new patterns are used, the highest error reaches the value of 14.5%. It is also observed that the error value to new patterns decreases when they represent an operational stability situation of the motor-pump set, i.e., they are far away from the transitory period of pumping.

At this point, we should observe that it would be desirable a greater number of training patterns for the neural network, especially if it could be obtained from a wider variation of the range of values.

The proposed *GEEI* was determined by equation (18) and the measured values used were the electric power, the dynamic level, the geometric difference of level, the pressure of output in the well, and the water flow obtained from the neural network.

Figure 3 shows the behavior of *GEEI* during the analyzed pumping period.

The numeric values that have generated the graphic in Figure 3 are presented in Table 2.

Operation Time (min)	$GEEI_{(t)}$ (Wh/m³.m)	Operation Time (min)	$GEEI_{(t)}$ (Wh/m³.m)
0	7.420*	40	5.054
1	4.456*	45	5.139
2	5.738*	50	5.134
3	5.245*	55	5.115
4	4.896*	60	5.073
5	4.951*	75	5.066
6	4.689*	90	5.060
7	5.078*	105	5.042
8	4.840*	120	5.037
9	5.027*	135	5.042
10	5.090*	155	5.026
11	5.100*	185	5.032
12	5.092*	215	5.030
14	5.066*	245	5.040
16	5.044*	275	5.034
18	5.015*	305	5.027
20	5.006*	335	5.017
22	5.017	365	5.025
24	5.022	395	5.030
26	5.032	425	5.031
28	5.049	455	5.020
30	5.062	485	5.015
35	4.663		

* GEEI in transitory period (from 0 to 20 min of pumping).

Table 2. *GEEI* calculated using the artificial neural network.

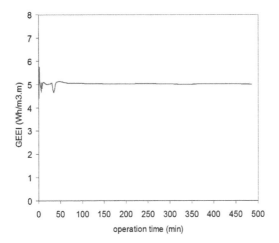

Figure 3. Behavior of the *GEEI* in relation to time.

6. Estimation of Aquifer Dynamic Behavior Using Neural Networks

In this section, artificial neural networks are now used to map the relationship between the variables associated with the identification process of aquifer dynamic behavior.

The general architecture of the neural system used in this application is shown in Figure 4, where two neural networks of type MLP, MLP-1 and MLP-2, constituted respectively by one and two hidden layers, compose this architecture.

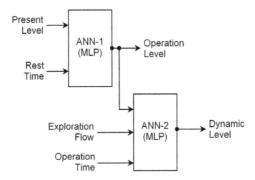

Figure 4. General architecture of the ANN used for estimation of aquifer dynamic behavior.

The first network (ANN-1) has 10 neurons in the hidden layer and it is responsible by the computation of the aquifer operation level. The training data for ANN-1 were directly obtained from experimental measurements. It is important to note that this network has taken into account the present level and rest time of the aquifer.

The second network (ANN-2) is responsible by the computation of the aquifer dynamic level and it is composed by 2 hidden layers with both having 10 neurons. For this network, the training data were also obtained from experimental measurements. As observed in Figure 4, the ANN-1 output is provided as an input parameter to the ANN-2. Therefore, the computation of the aquifer dynamic level takes into account the aquifer operation level, the exploration flow and operation time.

After training process of the neural networks, they were used for estimation of the aquifer dynamic level. The simulation results obtained by the networks are presented in Table 3 and Table 4.

Present Level (meters)	Rest Time (hours)	Operation Level (ANN-1)	Operation Level (Exact)	Relative Error (%)
115.55	4	103.59	104.03	0.43 %
125.86	9	104.08	104.03	0.05 %
141.26	9	105.69	104.03	1.58 %
137.41	8	102.95	104.03	1.05 %

Table 3. Simulation results (ANN-1).

Table 3 presents the simulation results obtained by the ANN-1 for a particular well. The operation levels computed by the network taking into account the present level and rest time of the aquifer were compared with those results obtained by measurements. In this table, the 'Relative Error' column provides the relative error between the values estimated by the network and those obtained by measurements.

Operation Flow (m³/h)	Operation Time (hours)	Dynamic Level (ANN-2)	Dynamic Level (Exact)	Relative Error (%)
145	14	115.50	115.55	0.04 %
160	2	116.10	116.14	0.03 %
170	6	118.20	117.59	0.52 %
220	21	141.30	141.26	0.03 %

Table 4. Simulation results (ANN-2).

The simulation results obtained by the ANN-2 are provided in Table 4. The dynamic level of the aquifer is estimated by the network in relation to operation level (computed by the ANN-1), exploration flow and operation time. These results are also compared with those obtained by measurements. In Table 4, the 'Relative Error' column gives the relative error between the values computed by the network and those from measurements.

These results show the efficiency of the neural approach used for estimation of aquifer dynamic behavior. The values estimated by the network are accurate to within 1.5% of the exact values for ANN-1 and 0.5 for ANN-2. From analysis of the results presented in Table 3 and 4, it is verified that the relative error between values provided by the network and those obtained by experimental measurements is very small. For ANN-1, the greatest relative error is 1.58 % (Table 3) and for ANN-2 is 0.52% (Table 4).

7. Conclusion

The management of systems that explore underground aquifers includes the analysis of two basic components: the water, which comes from the aquifer; and the electric energy, which is necessary to the transportation of the water to the consumption point or reservoir. Thus, the development of an efficiency indicator that shows the energetic behavior of a certain capitation system is of great importance to efficient management of the energy consumption, or still, to convert the obtained results in actions that become possible a reduction of energy consumption.

The obtained *GEEI* will indicate the global energetic behavior of the water capitation system from aquifers and will be an indicator of occurrences of abnormalities, such as tubing breaks or obstructions.

The application of the proposed methodology uses parameters that have easily been obtained in the water exploration system. The *GEEI* calculus can also be done by operators or to be implemented by means of computational system.

In addition, a novel methodology for estimation of aquifer dynamic behavior using artificial neural networks was also presented in this chapter. The estimation process is carried out by two feedforward neural networks. Simulation results confirm that proposed approach can be efficiently used in these types of problem. From results, it is possible to simulate several situations in order to define appropriate management plans and policies to the aquifer.

The main advantages in using this neural network approach are the following: i) velocity: the estimation of dynamic levels are instantly computed and it is appropriated for application in real time, ii) economy and simplicity: reduction of operational costs and measurement devices, and iii) precision: the values estimated by the proposed approach are as good as those obtained by physical measurements.

8. Appendix

The mathematic model that describes the behavior of the artificial neuron is expressed by the following equation:

$$u = \sum_{i=1}^{n} w_i \cdot x_i + b \tag{19}$$

$$y = g(u) \tag{20}$$

where n is the number of inputs of the neuron; x_i is the i-th input of the neuron; w_i is the weight associated with the i-th input; b is the threshold associated with the neuron; u is the activation potential; $g(\ )$ is the activation function of the neuron; y is the output of the neuron.

Basically, an artificial neuron works as follows:

(a) Signals are presented to the inputs.
(b) Each signal is multiplied by a weight that represents its influence in that unit.
(c) A weighted sum of the signals is made, resulting in a level of activity.
(d) If this level of activity exceeds a certain threshold, the unit produces an output.

To approximate any continuous nonlinear function a neural network with only a hidden layer can be used. However, to approximate non-continuous functions in its domain it is necessary to increase the amount of hidden layers. Therefore, the networks are of great importance in mapping nonlinear processes and in identifying the relationship between the variables of these systems, which are generally difficult to obtain by conventional techniques.

The network weights (w_j) associated with the j-th output neuron are adjusted by computing the error signal linked to the k-th iteration or k-th input vector (training example). This error signal is provided by:

$$e_j(k) = d_j(k) - y_j(k) \tag{21}$$

where $d_j(k)$ is the desired response to the j-th output neuron.

Adding all squared errors produced by the output neurons of the network with respect to k-th iteration, we have:

$$E(k) = \frac{1}{2} \sum_{j=1}^{p} e_j^2(k) \tag{22}$$

where p is the number of output neurons.

For an optimum weight configuration, $E(k)$ is minimized with respect to the synaptic weight w_{ji}. The weights associated with the output layer of the network are therefore updated using the following relationship:

$$w_{ji}(k+1) \leftarrow w_{ji}(k) - \eta \frac{\partial E(k)}{\partial w_{ji}(k)} \qquad (23)$$

where w_{ji} is the weight connecting the j-th neuron of the output layer to the i-th neuron of the previous layer, and η is a constant that determines the learning rate of the backpropagation algorithm.

The adjustment of weights belonging to the hidden layers of the network is carried out in an analogous way. The necessary basic steps for adjusting the weights associated with the hidden neurons can be found in [4].

Since the backpropagation learning algorithm was first popularized, there has been considerable research into methods to accelerate the convergence of the algorithm.

While backpropagation is a steepest descent algorithm, the Marquardt-Levenberg algorithm is similar to the quasi-Newton method, which was designed to approach second-order training speed without having to compute the Hessian matrix.

When the performance function has the form of a sum of squared errors like that presented in (22), then the Hessian matrix can be approximated as

$$\boldsymbol{H} = \boldsymbol{J}^T \cdot \boldsymbol{J} \qquad (24)$$

and the gradient can be computed as

$$\boldsymbol{g} = \boldsymbol{J}^T \cdot \boldsymbol{e} \qquad (25)$$

where e is a vector of network errors, and J is the Jacobean matrix that contains first derivatives of the network errors with respect to the weights and biases.

The Levenberg-Marquardt algorithm uses this approximation to the Hessian matrix in the following Newton-like update:

$$w(k+1) \leftarrow w(k) - (\boldsymbol{J}^T \cdot \boldsymbol{J} + \mu \cdot \boldsymbol{I})^{-1} \cdot \boldsymbol{J}^T \cdot \boldsymbol{e} \qquad (26)$$

When the scalar μ is zero, this is Newton's method, using the approximate Hessian matrix. When μ is large, this produces a gradient descent with a small step size. Newton's method is faster and more accurate near to an error minimum, so the aim is to shift toward Newton's method as quickly as possible.

Thus, μ is decreased after each successful step (reduction in performance function) and is increased only when a tentative step would increase the performance function. In this way, the performance function is always reduced at each iteration of the algorithm [6].

This algorithm appears to be the fastest method for training moderate-sized feedforward neural networks (up to several hundred weights).

Author details

Ivan N. da Silva[1*], José Ângelo Cagnon[2] and Nilton José Saggioro[3]

*Address all correspondence to: insilva@sc.usp.br

1 University of São Paulo (USP), São Carlos, SP, Brazil

2 São Paulo State University (UNESP), Bauru, SP , Brazil

3 University of São Paulo (USP), Bauru, SP, Brazil

References

[1] Domenico, P. A. (2011). Concepts and Models in Groundwater Hydrology. New York: McGraw-Hill.

[2] Domenico, P. A., & Schwartz, F. W. (1990). Physical and Chemical Hydrogeology. New York: John Wiley and Sons.

[3] Saggioro, N. J. (2001). Development of Methodology for Determination of Global Energy Efficiency Indicator to Deep Wells. Master's degree dissertation (in Portuguese). São Paulo State University.

[4] Haykin, S. (2008). Neural Networks and Learning Machines. New York: Prentice-Hall, 3rd edition.

[5] Anthony, M., & Barlett, P. L. (2009). Neural Network Learning: Theoretical Foundations. Cambridge: Cambridge University Press.

[6] Hagan, M. T., & Menhaj, M. B. (1994). Training Feedforward Networks with the Marquardt Algorithm. *IEEE Transactions on Neural Networks*, 5(6), 989-993.

[7] Silva, I. N., Saggioro, N. J., & Cagnon, J. A. (2000). Using neural networks for estimation of aquifer dynamical behavior. *In: proceedings of the International Joint conference on Neural Networks, IJCNN2000*, 24-27 July 2000, Como, Italy.

[8] Cagnon, J. A., Saggioro, N. J., & Silva, I. N. (2000). Application of neural networks for analysis of the groundwater aquifer behavior. *In: Proceedings of the IEEE Industry Applications Conference, INDUSCON2000*, 06-09 November, Porto Alegre, Brazil.

[9] Driscoll, F. G. (1986). Groundwater and Wells. Minneapolis: Johnson Division.

[10] Allen, D. M., Schuurman, N., & Zhang, Q. (2007). Using Fuzzy Logic for Modeling Aquifer Architecture. *Journal of Geographical Systems* [9], 289-310.

[11] Delhomme, J. P. (1989). Spatial Variability and Uncertainty in Groundwater Flow Parameters: A Geostatistical Approach. *Water Resources Research*, 15(2), 269-280.

[12] Koike, K., Sakamoto, H., & Ohmi, M. (2001). Detection and Hydrologic Modeling of Aquifers in Unconsolidated Alluvial Plains though Combination of Borehole Data Sets: A Case Study of the Arao Area, Southwest Japan. *Engineering Geology*, 62(4), 301-317.

[13] Scibek, J., & Allen, D. M. (2006). Modeled Impacts of Predicted Climate Change on Recharge and Groundwater Levels. *Water Resources Research* [42], 18, doi: 10.1029/2005WR004742.

[14] Fu, S., & Xue, Y. (2011). Identifying aquifer parameters based on the algorithm of simple pure shape. *In: Proceedings of the International Symposium on Water Resource and Environmental Protection, ISWREP2011*, 20-22 May, Xi'an, China.

[15] Jinyan, G., Yudong, L., Yuan, M., Mingchao, H., Yan, L., & Hongjuan, L. (2011). A mathematic time dependent boundary model for flow to a well in an unconfined aquifer. *In: Proceedings of the International Symposium on Water Resource and Environmental Protection, ISWREP2011*, 20-22 May 2011, Xi'an, China.

[16] Hongfei, Z., & Jianqing, G. (2010). A mathematic time dependent boundary model for flow to a well in an unconfined aquifer. *In: Proceedings of the 5th International Conference on Computer Sciences and Convergence Information Technology, ICCIT2010*, 30 November to 02 December 2010, Seoul, Korea.

[17] Cameron, E., & Peloso, G. F. (2001). An Application of Fuzzy Logic to the Assessment of Aquifers' Pollution Potential. *Environmental Geology*, 40(11-12), 1305-1315.

[18] Gemitzi, A., Petalas, C., Tsihrintzis, V. A., & Pisinaras, V. (2006). Assessment of Groundwater Vulnerability to Pollution: A Combination of GIS, Fuzzy Logic and Decision Making Techniques. *Environmental Geology*, 49(5), 653-673.

[19] Hong, Y. S., Rosen, M. R., & Reeves, R. R. (2002). Dynamic Fuzzy Modeling of Storm Water Infiltration in Urban Fractured Aquifers. *Journal of Hydrologic Engineering*, 7(5), 380-391.

[20] He, X., & Liu, J. J. (2009). Aquifer parameter identification with ant colony optimization algorithm. *In: Proceedings of the International Workshop on Intelligent Systems and Applications, ISA2009*, 23-24 May, Wuhan, China.

Permissions

The contributors of this book come from diverse backgrounds, making this book a truly international effort. This book will bring forth new frontiers with its revolutionizing research information and detailed analysis of the nascent developments around the world.

We would like to thank Kenji Suzuki, Ph.D., for lending his expertise to make the book truly unique. He has played a crucial role in the development of this book. Without his invaluable contribution this book wouldn't have been possible. He has made vital efforts to compile up to date information on the varied aspects of this subject to make this book a valuable addition to the collection of many professionals and students.

This book was conceptualized with the vision of imparting up-to-date information and advanced data in this field. To ensure the same, a matchless editorial board was set up. Every individual on the board went through rigorous rounds of assessment to prove their worth. After which they invested a large part of their time researching and compiling the most relevant data for our readers. Conferences and sessions were held from time to time between the editorial board and the contributing authors to present the data in the most comprehensible form. The editorial team has worked tirelessly to provide valuable and valid information to help people across the globe.

Every chapter published in this book has been scrutinized by our experts. Their significance has been extensively debated. The topics covered herein carry significant findings which will fuel the growth of the discipline. They may even be implemented as practical applications or may be referred to as a beginning point for another development. Chapters in this book were first published by InTech; hereby published with permission under the Creative Commons Attribution License or equivalent.

The editorial board has been involved in producing this book since its inception. They have spent rigorous hours researching and exploring the diverse topics which have resulted in the successful publishing of this book. They have passed on their knowledge of decades through this book. To expedite this challenging task, the publisher supported the team at every step. A small team of assistant editors was also appointed to further simplify the editing procedure and attain best results for the readers.

Our editorial team has been hand-picked from every corner of the world. Their multi-ethnicity adds dynamic inputs to the discussions which result in innovative outcomes. These outcomes are then further discussed with the researchers and contributors who give their valuable feedback and opinion regarding the same. The feedback is then collaborated with the researches and they are edited in a comprehensive manner to aid the understanding of the subject.

Apart from the editorial board, the designing team has also invested a significant amount of their time in understanding the subject and creating the most relevant covers. They scrutinized every image to scout for the most suitable representation of the subject and create an appropriate cover for the book.

The publishing team has been involved in this book since its early stages. They were actively engaged in every process, be it collecting the data, connecting with the contributors or procuring relevant information. The team has been an ardent support to the editorial, designing and production team. Their endless efforts to recruit the best for this project, has resulted in the accomplishment of this book. They are a veteran in the field of academics and their pool of knowledge is as vast as their experience in printing. Their expertise and guidance has proved useful at every step. Their uncompromising quality standards have made this book an exceptional effort. Their encouragement from time to time has been an inspiration for everyone.

The publisher and the editorial board hope that this book will prove to be a valuable piece of knowledge for researchers, students, practitioners and scholars across the globe.

List of Contributors

João Luís Garcia Rosa
Bioinspired Computing Laboratory (BioCom), Department of Computer Science, University of São Paulo at São Carlos, Brazil

Ma. del Rosario Martínez-Blanco and Héctor René Vega-Carrillo
Estudios Nucleares, Universidad Autónoma de Zacatecas, Unidades Académicas, México

José Manuel Cervantes Viramontes and José Manuel Ortiz-Rodríguez
Ingeniería Eléctrica, Universidad Autónoma de Zacatecas, Unidades Académicas, México

Siti Mariyam Shamsuddin, Ashraf Osman Ibrahim and Citra Ramadhena
Soft Computing Research Group, Faculty of Computer Science and Information Systems, Universiti Teknologi Malaysia, Malaysia

Shingo Noguchi and Osana Yuko
Tokyo University of Technology, Japan

Thiago M. Geronimo, Carlos E. D. Cruz, Fernando de Souza Campos, Paulo R. Aguiar and Eduardo C. Bianchi
Universidade Estadual Paulista "Júlio de Mesquita Filho" (UNESP), Bauru campus, Brazil

Giovanni Caocci and Giorgio La Nasa
Division of Hematology and Hematopoietic Stem Cell Transplantation, Department of Internal Medical Sciences, University of Cagliari, Cagliari, Italy

Roberto Baccoli
Technical Physics Division, Faculty of Engineering, Department of Engineering of the Territory, University of Cagliari, Cagliari, Italy

Roberto Littera, Sandro Orrù and Carlo Carcassi
Medical Genetics, Department of Internal Medical Sciences, University of Cagliari, Cagliari, Italy

Amr Radi
Department of Physics, Faculty of Sciences, Ain Shams University, Abbassia, Cairo, Egypt
Center of Theoretical Physics at the British University in Egypt (BUE), Egypt

Samy K. Hindawi
Department of Physics, Faculty of Sciences, Ain Shams University, Abbassia, Cairo, Egypt

Lucie Gráfová, Jan Mareš and Aleš Procházka
Department of Computing and Control Engineering, Institute of Chemical Technology, Prague, Czech Republic

Pavel Konopásek
Department of Nephrology, First Faculty of Medicine and General Faculty Hospital, Prague, Czech Republic

Vinícius Gonçalves Maltarollo
Centro de Ciências Naturais e Humanas – UFABC – Santo André – SP

Káthia Maria Honório
Centro de Ciências Naturais e Humanas – UFABC – Santo André – SP Escola de Artes, Ciências e Humanidades – USP – São Paulo – SP

Albérico Borges Ferreira da Silva
Departamento de Química e Física Molecular – Instituto de Química de São Carlos – USP – São Carlos – SP

Hazem M. El-Bakry
Faculty of Computer Science & Information Systems, Mansoura University, Egypt

Francisco García Fernandez
Universidad Politecnica de Madrid, Spain

Ignacio Soret Los Santos and Francisco Llamazares Redondo
ESIC Business & Marketing School, Spain

Javier Lopez Martinez
Universidad San Pablo CEU, Spain

Santiago Izquierdo Izquierdo
MTP Metodos y Tecnologia, Spain

Ivan N. da Silva
University of São Paulo (USP), São Carlos, SP, Brazil

José Ângelo Cagnon
São Paulo State University (UNESP), Bauru, SP, Brazil

Nilton José Saggioro
University of São Paulo (USP), Bauru, SP, Brazil